THE JOY OF OUR Salvation

Other volumes in the BYU–Relief Society Women's Conference series

THE JOY OF OUR *Salvation*

TALKS FROM THE 2004 BYU
WOMEN'S CONFERENCE

DESERET
BOOK

SALT LAKE CITY, UTAH

Library of Congress Cataloging-in-Publication Data

Women's Conference (2004 : Brigham Young University)
   The joy of our salvation : talks from the 2004 BYU Women's Conference.
      p.   cm.
   Includes bibliographical references and index.
   ISBN 1-59038-434-2 (hardbound : alk. paper)
   1. Mormon women—Religious aspects—Congresses.   I. Title.
   BX8641.W73 2005
   289.3'32'082—dc22   2005000752

Printed in the United States of America   72076
Publishers Printing, Salt Lake City, UT

10   9   8   7   6   5   4   3   2   1

Contents

JOY IN ADVERSITY

JOY IN PRAYER AND LEARNING

JOY IN OUR FAMILIES

JOY IN GOD'S PURPOSES

JOY IN VIRTUE AND SERVICE

"With Joy Shall Ye Draw Water Out of the Wells of Salvation"

Sandra Rogers

I grew up in arid, alkaline northern Arizona. All my great-grandparents were sent there by Brigham Young. It wasn't an easy assignment. If they weren't being blown away by stinging, dust-bringing, sand-flinging winds, they were waging war for water. A barrel of water from the river had to sit several days while the clay settled to the bottom in order to produce a gallon of drinkable water. White clothing, bedding, and kitchen linen turned reddish brown when washed in river water. The fledgling community built a dam to harness the water for their fields and gardens. It washed away the first summer. Eight additional dams were constructed and lost before modern technology allowed the next generation to drill wells to provide water.[1]

Even with wells for culinary water, our community spent, it seemed to me, every summer fasting and praying for rain. One of the most powerful spiritual events of my teenage years was the cloudburst we received one Sunday while completing a ward fast for rain. I have also worked in tropical climates where the heat and humidity suck you so dry you become weak and disoriented, not to mention sticky, oily, and grimy. I've washed my petite frame in less than a gallon of water and rejoiced to have it. I come from a long line of people who know what it means

Sandra Rogers is international vice president at Brigham Young University and teaches Gospel Doctrine in her ward.

to be without water and who know the relief and happiness that water brings—whether it is a cup or a bucket, a raindrop or a shower.

Here in the western United States we continue to experience drought conditions. For some of us the drought means an inconvenient adjustment to our landscape plans and recreational agendas. For others, the drought brings the very real stress of loss of livelihood.

I sense, though, there are times when I—and maybe you as well— suffer from a more serious drought. It's the drought of hope and good cheer, an unquenched thirst for meaning and purpose in life. But in the arid and sometimes spirit-withering circumstances of mortality, with its attendant losses, regrets, sorrows, sins, and tests, we have been offered the "good news" which is "as cold waters to a thirsty soul" (Proverbs 25:25).

That good news is the gospel of Jesus Christ. Like the woman of Samaria at Jacob's well, we are promised "living water" that shall be "a well of water springing up into everlasting life" (John 4:10, 14). Isaiah proclaimed: "Behold, God is my salvation; I will trust, and not be afraid: for the Lord JEHOVAH is my strength and my song; he also is become my salvation. Therefore with joy shall ye draw water out of the wells of salvation" (Isaiah 12:2–3).

Joseph Smith wrote: "Now, what do we hear in the gospel which we have received? A voice of gladness! A voice of mercy from heaven; . . . a voice of gladness for the living and the dead; glad tidings of great joy. . . . Let the mountains shout for joy, and all ye valleys cry aloud; and all ye seas and dry lands tell the wonders of your Eternal King!" (D&C 128:19, 23).

When you hear those verses, don't you just want to shout hallelujah! And this isn't the first time. We know who we really are, spirit daughters of God the Father and covenant daughters of Jesus Christ because we were baptized. We know our origins. We were there when the Father explained the plan to us: that he was granting us the privilege of mortality, to grow and learn and become like Him, to eventually inherit everything He has; and we "shouted for joy" (see Job 38:7). We were also there when our elder brother, Jesus Christ, stepped forward to take the critical role of Savior and Redeemer. What joy we must have felt in His humble offering. We chose to follow Him, joyfully I think, through the war in heaven.

With great interest we watched the events in the Garden of Eden. I think we rejoiced that Adam and Eve fell that we might be and that we might have joy. Adam blessed God, "for because of my transgression my eyes are opened, and in this life I shall have joy" (Moses 5:10). When Eve "heard all these things and was glad," she said, "Were it not for our transgression we never should have had seed, and never should have known good and evil, and the joy of our redemption, and the eternal life which God giveth unto all the obedient" (Moses 5:11).

I also like to imagine that, despite my incredibly below-average singing voice, I was with the heavenly hosts who sang "good tidings of great joy" (Luke 2:10) above a humble stable in Bethlehem. I want to think we were there when the hosts of heaven wept as the Savior suffered in Gethsemane and died on the cross for us. In our grief, and aware of the depth of the grief of the Father, I believe we also felt sustaining peace and joy when our dear Lord said, "It is finished" (John 19:30), and we knew the ransom had been paid, that we could be redeemed, and that Christ had won the victory over death and hell. I also like to think we might have had another joyous moment when the risen Christ and our Eternal Father in Heaven appeared to the boy prophet, Joseph Smith, beginning the restoration of the glorious gospel.

What incredible joy—to know who we are, to know there is a purpose in life, to know there is a Redeemer. We have God's promise that the faithful "shall enter into the joy of [the] Lord, and shall inherit eternal life" (D&C 51:19) and that a "fulness of joy" awaits those who are resurrected to a celestial glory (see D&C 76:50–70; 93:33).

Because mortality is a time for tests, a time for preparation, a time to prepare to meet God, and because the veil has been drawn over our memory of the many joyous moments we experienced in pre-earth life, I suspect that many of us are like Nephi. We have a background in the gospel and give the right answers in Sunday School and Relief Society. But we still have rotten days with our families or our work. We are sometimes criticized. We work as hard as we can and still aren't appreciated. Our loved ones make poor decisions and blame us for their discomfort. Things don't always work out the way we had hoped. Frustration with others and with our own mistakes causes momentary lapses in our otherwise calm, poised, and cheerful outlook.

After an angry confrontation with Laman and Lemuel, and while still grieving the death of his father, Nephi sought solace in the scrip-tures. "Notwithstanding the great goodness of the Lord" he wrote, "[I feel] wretched [and] sorrow[ful and] my soul grieveth because of mine iniquities. I am encompassed about, because of the temptations and the sins which do so easily beset me. And when I desire to rejoice, my heart groaneth because of my sins" (2 Nephi 4:17–19).

I've been there! You've been there. And, like Nephi, in our dark, uncomfortable, and challenging moments, we can "know in whom [we] have trusted" (2 Nephi 4:19). We too can say, "if the Lord in his conde-scension unto the children of men hath visited men in so much mercy, why should [our] heart[s] weep and [our] soul[s] linger in the valley of sorrow? . . . Yea, why should [we] give way to temptations, that the evil one have place in [our] heart[s] to destroy [our] peace and afflict [our] soul[s]? Awake. . . . Rejoice, O [our] heart[s]. . . . Yea, [our] soul[s] will rejoice in thee, [our] God" (2 Nephi 4:26–28, 30).

With the reassurance of the Lord, who is our salvation, like wilted plants in dry ground, our souls will spring back to vitality with water, drawn with joy from the wells of salvation. We read the scriptures and we pray and we write in our journals so that we can remember the Lord's tender mercies in the bleak times and be refreshed with His living water. No wonder Alma says to his little flock, "if ye have felt to sing the song of redeeming love, I would ask, can ye feel so now?" (Alma 5:26).

I was raised in a home where my father treated his sons and his daughter equally. I never felt I was less important to him. Despite this positive childhood and adolescence, I had a period when I worried about the position of women in the Church, wondering about my own place and value. I eventually decided to take this concern to the Lord. I pleaded to know what my value was to the Lord and to the Church, being a woman first of all and, worse yet, a single one. I just needed to know how the Lord felt about me. The answer I received was very direct, simple, and powerful. It was, "Sandra, I love my daughters as much as I love my sons. My daughters are as important to the kingdom as are my sons. I value my daughters as much as I value my sons."

Since then I continue to have experiences that tempt me to tug this old doubt out of the closet again. Yet, because I have felt to sing, as it were, the song of redeeming love once, it is easier to center myself and joyfully sing it again.

I suggest that when we feel true joy, bits of truth and pieces of heaven are being revealed to us. The joy we have in mortality comes when we are briefly united with heaven while still here on earth. Elder Dallin H. Oaks explained that "joy is more than happiness. Joy is the ultimate sensation of well-being. It comes from being complete and in harmony with our Creator and his eternal laws."[2]

True joy is brought to life in us through Him who is the light and life of the world. It comes when the Holy Ghost bears witness to our souls of a divine truth—a truth that provides comfort, strength, insight, encouragement, and perhaps an occasional reproof—to fit our unique needs. And it comes through obedience to Christ's doctrine and principles. "And moreover, I would desire that ye should consider on the blessed and happy state of those that keep the commandments of God. For behold, they are blessed in all things, both temporal and spiritual; and if they hold out faithful to the end they are received into heaven, that thereby they may dwell with God in a state of never-ending happiness. O remember, remember that these things are true; for the Lord God hath spoken it" (Mosiah 2:41).

One of the challenges of mortality is to know what true joy is and, because of the importance of opposition in all things, to understand what real misery is (see 2 Nephi 2:11). We don't need to be confused about this. Alma the Younger knew the difference (see Alma 36:17–21). When his mind caught hold upon the thought of the coming of Jesus Christ to atone for the sins of the world, his soul was filled with joy. Nothing had been as bitter as his misery, and nothing was sweeter than his joy.

We know that Satan seeks the misery of all mankind because he wants all men to be as miserable as he is (see 2 Nephi 2:18). We also know that the Lord's plan is that we might have joy. Misery or joy—it doesn't seem like a hard choice when it's put in simple terms. But, going it alone, without the living water, we could be enticed by Satan's cunning counterfeits. He wants us to be like a desperate woman in the desert, using our last gasp of energy to chase a shimmering, tempting mirage, when life-giving water from a humble well is within our reach.

Satan wants us to believe that pleasure is joy; that momentary thrills are joyous. He wants us to think that the world's honors, fashions, music, comforts, achievements, and glories bring lasting joy. In truth, very few of them last longer than a single season. In the absence of true joy, many are left with nothing more than escalating bungee-jumping, mistaking an adrenalin rush for peace and joy.

Satan wants us to be confused. Like a circus magician, he hopes that we will never discover the smoke and mirrors and know the truth about his fraud. He hopes we will never learn that joy in mortality comes from experiences that connect us to heaven, when the Spirit has enlightened our minds and filled our souls with joy (see D&C 11:13).

Think of your most joyous moments. The birth of a child—better yet, the birth of a grandchild. The moment a certain passage of scripture leaps into your heart and gives you insight and comfort. The calming influence of a priesthood blessing before a difficult assignment. The day you feel forgiven. The day you forgive someone else. The moments when a relationship is mended and trust is restored. The day you can finally "move on" from a hard situation. When you find great-great Uncle Harry on the census record. The day the Holy Ghost comforts you in the loss of a loved one with the sure knowledge of a reunion in heaven. When your son opens his mission call, and the day he returns to report with honor. The reassuring balm of the Spirit when you know you have done all you could even as your loved ones exercised their agency. The day a child comes back into the light. The spring a daughter chooses a modest prom dress. A grand moment like the closing session of Women's Conference two years ago when thousands of women spontaneously stood in quiet testimony to sing "How Firm a Foundation." The "sweet hour of prayer . . . that calls me from a world of care" and "in seasons of distress and grief" provides solace and relief.[3] The grandeur of nature that compels you to acknowledge the power of the Creator and the magnificence of His creations. The quiet moments when the Spirit whispers peace to your heart even when things are not going particularly well and your pillows are wet with painful tears. When you realize you did your visiting teaching because you love the sisters you visit. When your feeble attempts in assignments and callings are made whole by a kind and gracious God. All of these joyful moments, and many more, are brought to us because of the abiding truths of the gospel of Jesus Christ.

Mortality can also bring us the thrill of winning a hard-fought basketball game, buying the set of books we've always wanted, the pleasure of Baskin-Robbins chocolate almond ice cream, the satisfaction of accomplishing a goal and of improving a talent, seeing a truly "feel-good" movie, placing second out of two contestants in a women's over-forty 5K race, seeing an exquisite painting, listening to beautiful music, and many other wonderful things. We should continue to enjoy these things and realize that many of them bless our lives and our spirits. They are things to please the eye and gladden the heart (see D&C 59:17–19) as we stay focused on meeting the measure of our creation and receiving a fulness of joy.

The living water Christ provides also gives us a perspective about mortality that can help us feel joy even when we may be experiencing less than joyful feelings. I have learned that joy can be present in my soul, even when I think my heart is breaking. Joy can be in hearts and minds even when things around us seem to be falling apart. In fact, it is the well of living water springing up from an abiding testimony of Jesus Christ that refreshes and soothes our figuratively fevered brows as we face mortality head on. It keeps us steady and constant, fed with the sustaining joy of faith, even when life is hard. It is what will help us not simply endure, but endure well (see D&C 121:8). I loved Sister Hinckley's comment about President Hinckley's missionary service. She said, "I was very thrilled [with my husband's mission] because I desperately wanted him to go on a mission, but I will never forget the feeling of loneliness and emptiness that I felt when the train pulled out of the station and he was gone."[4] She could feel joy in his service and still feel loneliness in the parting.

I have tested this principle in countless ways. I testify that we can feel joy as we draw water from the wells of salvation even when we are worried, wounded, grieving, or frustrated. Worry, pain, grief, and frustration wither the soul with bitterness unless the living water from Christ's well is poured back into our hearts.

There was a time during my missionary service when I wondered if I was doing any good. I have now forgotten the context of this experience; all I have left are a few lines from my missionary journal dated June 24, 1975:

I cried out—impatient, hurt
Where is the me inside that I must find?
For the wise man said "we cannot be that which we wish
*   without knowing that which we are."*
My soul's plea, struggling, hope
What is the gift that I can give to him?
For the prophet said, "if ye would serve him all the days of
*   thy life still thou wouldst be an unprofitable servant."*
Who am I? Thoughts? Words? Deeds?
For the mirror gives no answers—neither do comparisons
For the poet said, "To thine own self be true and then thou
*   canst not be false to any man."*
I seek, yes, desire to know
The seed I have inside—for from it will my eternity grow,
And the mission president said, "your mission sets the sails
*   of your ship of life."*
Give me then, I pray, insight into myself, and faith in Him
*   whose child I am,*
For the Master said, "Come unto me, all ye who are weary
*   and heavy laden, and I will give you rest."*

The joy promised from the wells of salvation is not just the joy at the end of the road, but it is the joy to sustain us on the walk. Peter said, "That the trial of your faith, being much more precious than of gold that perisheth, though it be tried with fire, might be found unto praise and honour and glory at the appearing of Jesus Christ: Whom having not seen, ye love; in whom, though now ye see him not, yet believing, ye rejoice with joy unspeakable and full of glory: Receiving the end of your faith, even the salvation of your souls" (1 Peter 1:7–9). Is it any wonder that the early Saints sang, "Come, come, ye Saints, no toil nor labor fear; / But with joy wend your way."[5]

The biggest obstacle to joy, I've learned, is not my circumstances, but my choices. Joy is not accidental. It isn't given to lucky winners like a lottery prize. We choose it. We choose it when we choose to be obedient to the principles upon which joy is predicated (see D&C 130:20–21). Perhaps one of the saddest scriptures is found in Doctrine and Covenants 88:32. The Lord describes those who will receive a telestial glory and then says, "And they who remain shall also be quickened; nevertheless, they shall return again to their own place, to enjoy that which they are willing to receive, because they were not willing to enjoy that which they might have received."

What are some of the things we can do to choose to joyously draw water from the well of living water? We can begin by working to develop a deeper love and abiding trust in the Savior. If we have doubts, then start by making an attempt to believe. As Alma explained, "yea, even if ye can no more than desire to believe, let this desire work in you, even until ye believe in a manner that ye can give place for a portion" of the truth (Alma 32:27). As we nourish the tender plant, it will put down roots and grow and bring forth fruit.

Through this process we will gain a better understanding of truth and find happiness in following truth. We more earnestly follow Christ's invitation to "call upon me while I am near—draw near unto me and I will draw near unto you; seek me diligently and ye shall find me; ask, and ye shall receive; knock, and it shall be opened unto you" (D&C 88:62–63).

As this happens we may become aware of habits, actions, or thoughts that are keeping us from feeling close to the Savior and having the influence of the Holy Ghost in our lives. If so, we can follow the example of one of the Book of Mormon's great converts, the father of King Lamoni, who exclaimed, "If thou art God, wilt thou make thyself known unto me, and I will give away all my sins to know thee" (Alma 22:18).

As we begin to conquer habits and shortcomings through our faith in Christ, we may find that we become more aware of our weaknesses. Don't let this discourage you. Funny as it may seem, we can rejoice that our weaknesses are coming to the surface. It means we are making progress. As we acknowledge our weaknesses before the Savior and work with His help, we will find that they can become strengths (see Ether 12:27). As we feel His mercy and grace helping us to put off the natural man, our love for Him will grow. When we love Him, we will want to do all we can to build the Kingdom of God, to magnify our callings, and to strengthen those around us.

I played the piano for Primary for some time. I never thought about magnifying my calling. It was a snap. I didn't have to practice and I enjoyed the children. I had fun in Primary. Then came the sacrament meeting talk on magnifying our callings. For several days after that talk I had the impression that I should pray about magnifying my calling. I resisted, thinking, "I'm doing fine, I don't even have to practice. How can I get any better than this?" But, when the impression wouldn't go away, I finally prayed about magnifying my calling as the Primary pianist. The thought came that I should use only the songs that were familiar to the children as prelude and postlude music. So I stopped playing all the songs that I thought were so fun and unusual and started playing songs the children knew. The children started humming the hymns they knew and seemed to be a little more reverent. I learned from that simple experience that every calling can be magnified if we aren't too proud to ask for the Lord's help.

As we experience the Lord's mercy and serve His children well, we will become grateful and humble. Joyously drawing water from the wells of salvation causes us to view the world with meekness and thanksgiving. When we are grateful we are far less critical, far less bitter, and much less likely to take offense.

While I was on my mission in the Philippines I was in an extremely poor area. Most of the sisters didn't have electricity, much less a refrigerator or a car. I recall a Relief Society meeting where the homemaking lesson was on "how to shop for groceries." The lesson, prepared for the Saints in a more developed part of the world, gave so many helpful hints. In fact, I still use some of them. But I was chagrined when the sister teaching the lesson told the sisters to be sure to buy their frozen and refrigerated items last so that these items wouldn't melt or go bad in the car on the way home from the store. I thought, "I'll bet these sisters think the Relief Society is so dumb for preparing a lesson that is so out of line with their reality. They don't have refrigerators, they don't buy frozen things, and they sure don't have a car to take them home in. Don't the folks in Salt Lake realize everybody doesn't live in America?"

Just when those critical thoughts were at their peak, the sister teaching the lesson said, "Sisters, I know we don't have cars or refrigerators. But, I bear my testimony that this lesson is an example of how much the Lord loves us. He loves us enough to give us this important message so that when we do have refrigerators and cars we will know what to do. Our neighbors who don't have Relief Society won't have this wonderful truth. Doesn't this prove to us that God is always mindful of us?"

To the critical and out-of-tune missionary, the lesson was an example of dumb Americans being offensive. To a faithful, grateful, and joy-filled Filipino Latter-day Saint, the lesson was a manifestation of God's love.

As our feelings of gratitude grow, our desire to be like Him, to be truly charitable with all its attendant virtues (see 1 Corinthians 13), also grows. We start to concentrate on the things that really matter while letting go of the things that don't. We find ourselves living closer to the Spirit and being able to respond to its promptings.

One morning when I was in junior high school, my brother complained of a severe headache. In that gentle way that only older sisters have, I accused him of just wanting to get out of going to school. My mother gave in and let him stay home. I marched off to school but found myself with a headache, too, and returned home. I don't know how long it was, but soon my two brothers and I were deathly ill. My mother had no idea what was wrong and she didn't feel well herself. She put us together in her bed and soon we were all unconscious.

My grandfather was on his way to a work assignment and his route took him through the town where we lived. He received the impression that he should come and see us. He acknowledged the impression but said to himself, "I'll stop by after I finish my work." The impression came more emphatically, "Go now." My grandfather didn't need to be told a third time. When he arrived at the door he was surprised that no one answered his knock. Why would the Spirit compel him to visit us when we weren't home? He knocked again. Just as he was turning to leave, he looked through the window in the door and saw my mother stumble into the living room and pass out.

As he walked through the door, his first thought was to call my aunt. When my aunt heard the phone ring she immediately felt impressed to say, "Open the windows and the doors." This chain of spiritual impressions saved our lives. In a short time we would have been dead from carbon monoxide poisoning.

What joy there was in our family that my grandfather and my aunt had been sensitive to the Holy Ghost and that our lives had been spared. When there are dangers lurking in a perilous world, we must do everything we can to have the Spirit's guidance, for we, as mothers, daughters, sisters, and aunts, "have precious souls to save."[6]

We can teach our children to know Him, love Him, and trust Him, because they see us getting to know Him, love Him, and trust Him—being joyous while we are doing it. We can choose to focus on the positive. We can sustain our leaders instead of constantly seeking to steady the ark. We can do our duty and support and encourage others in doing theirs. We can see that another's successes in no way minimize our own. We can focus on possibilities rather than limitations. We can worship in the temple. We can pray and study the scriptures. We can read our patriarchal blessings and take counsel from them.

In general conference, President Hinckley said: "There is still so much of conflict in the world. There is terrible poverty, disease, and hatred. Man is still brutal in his unhumanity to man. Yet there is this glorious dawn. The 'Sun of righteousness' has come 'with healing in his wings' (Malachi 4:2). God and His Beloved Son have revealed Themselves. We know Them. We worship Them 'in spirit and in truth' (John 4:24). We love Them. We honor Them and seek to do Their will. . . .

" . . . Somehow, through all of the darkness, there has been a faint but beautiful light. And now with added luster it shines upon the world. It carries with it God's plan of happiness for His children. It carries with it the great and unfathomable wonders of the Atonement of the Redeemer."[7]

My African friends used to bear their testimonies about being convicted to the gospel. They meant living so that their actions "convicted" or proved them to be followers of Christ. President Hinckley once quoted Wallace Stegner, who wrote the story of the Mormon Trail. Mr. Stegner said: "That I do not accept the faith that possessed [the Mormons] does not mean I doubt their frequent devotion and heroism in its service, especially their women. Their women were incredible."[8]

Let us choose to be incredible: incredibly convicted to the gospel, incredibly trusting that Christ can heal our thirsty souls, incredibly faithful and devoted to the cause of truth, incredibly grateful for our Redeemer's love, incredibly joyous as we draw water from the wells of salvation.

NOTES

1. See Adele B. Westover and J. Morris Richards, eds., *Unflinching Courage* (n. p.).
2. Dallin H. Oaks, "Joy and Mercy," *Ensign*, November 1991, 73.
3. William W. Walford, "Sweet Hour of Prayer," *Hymns of The Church of Jesus Christ of Latter-day Saints* (Salt Lake City: The Church of Jesus Christ of Latter-day Saints, 1985), no. 142.
4. Quoted in "Wisdom and Wit of Sister Hinckley," *Church News*, April 10, 2004, 3.
5. William Clayton, "Come, Come, Ye Saints," *Hymns*, no. 30.
6. Eliza R. Snow, "In Our Lovely Deseret," *Hymns*, no. 307.
7. Gordon B. Hinckley, "The Dawning of a Brighter Day," *Ensign*, May 2004, 83.
8. Wallace Stegner, quoted in *Teachings of Gordon B. Hinckley* (Salt Lake City: Deseret Book, 1997), 698.

"If Thou Art Merry, Praise the Lord"

Mary Ellen Edmunds

Whiplash

One winter's morning during a snowstorm, I took my mother to have some blood tests done. It was "white-knuckle" driving on snowy, icy roads. We were headed home and going around a corner very slowly. The car hit black ice and, as if in slow motion, we headed for the curb. THUNK! I quickly asked Mom, "Are you OK?"

"Yes."

We continued cautiously, slowly.

Then I said in an oh-so-sarcastic kind of way, "So I suppose you're going to sue me for whiplash." Instantly she jumped in, moaning and holding her neck. "Oh . . . ohhhhhh . . . oh, my neck hurts. . . . Oh, I can't move my head. . . . Oh dear, I have to call . . ." and she tried to say the name of one of the lawyers who advertise on TV. ("One call . . . that's all!") It was so spontaneous and so hilarious that we both laughed until we were screaming.

We eventually came up for air, but Mom kept the fun going for days, calling me, moaning and whining about her whiplash the minute I'd answer.

Mary Ellen Edmunds is a Happifier At Large who has just met with a government official about Social Security and Medicare. Please send condolences c/o Deseret Book. She receives joy from 30 nieces and nephews and close to that many "greats."

I'm so grateful for what I have learned from my parents about being cheerful, lighthearted, and—yes—sometimes silly.

The Prophet Joseph Smith taught that "happiness is the object and design of our existence."[1]

That's why our Heavenly Father's plan is so often called the great plan of happiness. Happiness is part of our nature, as it is part of God's nature. As Alma taught his son Corianton: "And now, my son, all men that are in a state of nature, or I would say, in a carnal state, . . . are without God in the world, and they have gone contrary to the nature of God; therefore, they are in a state contrary to the nature of happiness" (Alma 41:11).

We are born with a naturally sunny, optimistic, cheerful disposition. Feeling joy and happiness doesn't mean we're always laughing our heads off, although laughter *is* very therapeutic! President James E. Faust has said: "Don't forget to laugh at the silly things that happen. Humor . . . is a powerful force for good when used with discretion. Its physical expression, laughter, is highly therapeutic."[2] He's right! When we laugh hard, our heart rate speeds up, the circulatory and immune systems are stimulated, and more endorphins are produced. (And then they go perform at Sea World.)

In Proverbs we read, "A merry heart doeth good like a medicine" (17:22). I was told that Picabo Street, the great Olympic skier, wants to become a nurse and work in the ICU so she can answer the phone with "Picabo, ICU." Isn't it like a dose of good medicine when we laugh together? It feels unifying!

Abraham Lincoln once said, "With the fearful strain that is on me night and day, if I did not laugh I should die."[3] I heard that if you want or need to laugh and you don't—if you suppress laughter—it goes to your hips and spreads out.

Sister Hinckley had (and I'm sure still has) a delightful sense of humor. She said: "The only way to get through life is to laugh your way through it. You either have to laugh or cry. I prefer to laugh. Crying gives me a headache."[4] How we miss her.

A good sense of humor can help us in many ways in life. President Gordon B. Hinckley once said: "We've got to have a little humor in our lives. You had better take seriously that which should be taken seriously but, at the same time, we can bring in a touch of humor now and again. If the time ever comes when we can't smile at ourselves, it will be a sad time."[5]

Several years ago my friend Helen told me that in her little town of Vernon, Utah, where there were way too many crickets, they included some cricket recipes in their ward newsletter! I have a special appreciation for those who can laugh even in the midst of challenges.

Someone who tells jokes all the time—to whom everything is funny—does *not* have a sense of humor. And if we hurt someone's feelings, it's not funny. The essence of good humor is love! Thomas Carlyle wrote, " 'True humour springs not more from the head than from the heart; it is not contempt, its essence is love.' "[6]

For a few years at the Missionary Training Center, I supervised those learning American Sign Language. One day the supervisor brought her group to my office door to announce they'd been asked to sing for the MTC Christmas program. I could tell something funny was about to happen by the look on her face.

"Do you want to know what they've chosen to sing?"

"Of course I do!"

"Our two numbers are 'Do You Hear What I Hear?' and 'I Heard Him Come.' " The missionaries, several of whom were deaf, laughed and clapped. So did I!

LIGHTHEARTEDNESS VS. LIGHTMINDEDNESS

I want to return to President Faust's comment about humor being "a powerful force for good when used with discretion."[7] I've done a lot of thinking about the difference between lightheartedness and light-mindedness. I think lightmindedness is thoughtless—literally, without thought. It is empty, meaningless, and wasteful. Often there is hypocrisy and scorn associated with lightminded laughter. It is irreverent and unholy. It separates us from the Spirit. It's the things we talk and laugh about that don't encourage, cheer, or edify.

Lightheartedness is goodness—joyful goodness. It includes all that blesses and happifies us and others. It's being of good cheer while focusing on the things that matter. It's a virtue.

Truman G. Madsen tells a story about Heber C. Kimball: "He is praying with his family and in the midst of the prayer says, 'Father, bless Brother So-and-So.' Then he bursts into a loud laugh. I can imagine the heads of his children popping up and their eyes opening. There is a slight pause, and then he says, 'Lord, it makes me laugh to pray about some people,' and he goes on with his prayer. (See Whitney, *Heber C. Kimball,* 427.) I leave you to say whether that is lightmindedness or profound intimacy with the Lord. He knows. We have a funny bone. He gave it to us."[8]

President Harold B. Lee wrote: "I have never believed that in order to be righteous one must be sad-faced and solemn. People approved of the Lord have always been those who have laughed and danced and sung as well as worshipped, but at all times within proper bounds and not to excess."[9]

I took note when Elder Ballard, in a visit to the MTC in September 1985, told the missionaries that "lightmindedness offends," and he said, "You can tell!" Then he added, "If we said you couldn't have a sense of humor, all the Brethren would be in jeopardy."[10]

President Boyd K. Packer wrote: "A good sense of humor is a characteristic of a well-balanced person. It has always been apparent that the prophets were men with very alert and pleasing senses of humor."[11] I remember a time in the Tabernacle years ago on a Sunday morning during general conference when it was *hot.* Everyone was fanning themselves with whatever they could find. President Hinckley got up and said something like, "It's hot in here. We know you're hot. But you're not as hot as you're going to be if you don't repent!" The laughter was instant and joyful.

We really are happy people. We can't help it! We know too much! We are like the Nephites—"we [live] after the manner of happiness" (2 Nephi 5:27). And we work at having happy hearts without being lightminded.

We certainly recognize the importance of reverence for all that is sacred. President Boyd K. Packer said: "There are some things just too sacred to discuss. . . . It is not that they are secret, but they are sacred; . . . to be harbored and to be protected and regarded with the deepest of reverence."[12] We are reverent about our Heavenly Father and His holy Son, Jesus Christ, including being reverent with Their names. Jesus's name is the only name under heaven that can save us! (see Acts 4:12; 2 Nephi 25:20).

President David O. McKay said: "The greatest manifestation of spirituality is reverence. . . . Reverence is profound respect mingled with love."[13]

HAPPINESS AND ADVERSITY

Happiness does not mean an absence of adversity. Why would our baptismal covenant include bearing one another's burdens if no one had any burdens? Why would we covenant to mourn with those who mourn and comfort those who stand in need of comfort if no one ever mourned and no one ever needed comforting? (see Mosiah 18:8–9).

Elder Jack H. Goaslind has said: "I am convinced if we are to have happiness in our hearts, we must learn how to preserve it, in our hearts, in the midst of trouble and trial. We can control our attitude toward adversity. Some people are defeated and embittered by it, while others triumph over it and cultivate godlike attributes in the midst of it."[14]

Probably each of us can think of someone who has been refined and who has become more godlike through trials. Elder Goaslind uses the word *cultivate*. It indicates work, doesn't it? We work to develop godlike attributes. President Hinckley has invited us to "cultivate an attitude of happiness. Cultivate a spirit of optimism."[15]

Life may not always be exactly what we had in mind, but we're not alone. Have you noticed that sometimes you draw closer to your Heavenly Father when you are deeply in need? That's been my experience. And He comes. He is always willing to come. Listen again to what happened to the people of Alma when they were being persecuted by the former priests of Noah: "Lift up your heads and be of good comfort. . . . And I will . . . ease the burdens . . . upon your shoulders, that even you cannot feel them upon your backs, even while you are in bondage; and this will I do that ye may stand as witnesses for me hereafter, and that ye may know of a surety that I, the Lord God, do visit my people in their afflictions" (Mosiah 24:13–14).

Many of you can also be witnesses for Him hereafter, testifying that He also visited you in your afflictions.

Elder James E. Talmage said: "[Happiness] springs from the deeper fountains of the soul, and is not infrequently accompanied by tears. Have you never been so happy that you have had to weep? I have."[16] We have too, haven't we?

Psalm 30 teaches, "Weeping may endure for a night, but joy cometh in the morning" (v. 5). The Doctrine and Covenants adds, "If thou art sorrowful, call on the Lord thy God with supplication, that your souls may be joyful" (136:29).

Happiness Is a Result of Righteousness

In 2 Nephi 2:13, Lehi is teaching his son Jacob about opposition: "And if ye shall say there is no law, ye shall also say there is no sin. If ye shall say there is no sin, ye shall also say there is no righteousness. And if there be no righteousness there be no happiness. And if there be no righteousness nor happiness there be no punishment nor misery. And if these things are not there is no God."

There *is* a God, there *is* righteousness, and there *is* happiness.

President Gordon B. Hinckley said, "Happiness comes of righteousness." He went on to teach that wickedness, sin, selfishness, and greed never bring happiness. And then he said, "Happiness lies in living the principles of the gospel of Jesus Christ."[17]

It's true that "wickedness never was happiness" (Alma 41:10). And so righteousness never was misery—adversity, deep water, and fiery trials for sure, but not misery. We can choose to cultivate either happiness or misery. Elder Goaslind has said, "Our joy in God's kingdom will be a natural extension of the happiness we cultivate in this life."[18]

A woman shared with me a very interesting experience she had during her stake conference. She said her stake president invited all those who were happy to raise their hands. To them he said, "Congratulations! You are candidates for the celestial kingdom. The rest of you need to repent!" Then he added, "I'm convinced that in the celestial kingdom there will only be happy people!"

Moroni illustrates this principle in Mormon 9:14: "And then cometh the judgment of the Holy One upon them; and then cometh the time that he that is filthy shall be filthy still; and he that is righteous shall be righteous still; and he that is happy shall be happy still; and he that is unhappy shall be unhappy still."

We will be "raised to happiness according to [our] desires of happiness" (Alma 41:5) and according to the degree to which we have cultivated happiness right here, right now.

An Attitude of Happiness and a Spirit of Optimism

Joy is a gift of the Spirit (see Galatians 5:22). Elder Marion G. Romney said, "The key to happiness [or joy] is to get the Spirit and keep it."[19] Heber C. Kimball said: "I am perfectly satisfied that my Father and my God is a cheerful, pleasant, lively, and good-natured Being. Why? Because I am cheerful, pleasant, lively, and good-natured when I have His Spirit."[20] Has that been your experience? As you have felt the Spirit, have you also felt joy? Joy brings the Spirit, and the Spirit brings joy.

Brigham Young asked: "Where is happiness, real happiness? Nowhere but in God. By possessing the spirit of our holy religion, we are happy in the morning, we are happy at noon, [and] we are happy in the evening. . . . Every Latter-day Saint, who has experienced the love of God in his heart, . . . realizes that he is filled with joy . . . happiness, and consolation."[21]

Think of someone you enjoy being around, and think about *why.* Through the many years I've asked others this question, I can't think of a single time when someone has said, "Oh, I like to be around Fifi—she is such a downer! What a pessimist! She's so negative! I can't be around her more than two minutes without feeling just awful!" Cheerful, optimistic people are pleasant to be around. This certainly includes President Hinckley, who has helped so many of us smile and laugh in a happy way. I feel that his optimism and good cheer come in large measure because of his goodness, his righteousness, and his absolute obedience.

Brigham Young said, "It does make the Devil mad . . . that he cannot afflict this people so as to make them have a sad countenance."[22] Another time, he noted, "There is not a man or woman on this earth, whose peace is made with God, and who are associated with holy beings, and seeking after holy principles, but their countenances are lit up with a lamp of divine cheerfulness."[23] This is taught in Proverbs—"A merry heart maketh a cheerful countenance" (15:13)—and by President Hinckley, who said, "Let the light of the gospel shine in your faces wherever you go and in whatever you do."[24]

PASSING ALONG JOY AND HAPPINESS TO CHILDREN

More than 100 years ago, President George Q. Cannon said: "My experience has proved that there is greater happiness, purer joy and more delight to be obtained in serving God and being active in His work than can be obtained in any other direction. . . .

" . . . We illustrate the great truth that a people can be a profoundly religious people and at the same time be a very happy people. I do not believe there is any happier people on the earth than the Latter-day Saints. . . . There must be the fountain of [happiness] within us; and wherever we go and have that spirit within us, we shall be happy. . . . We should cultivate this, and teach it to our children."[25]

President Gordon B. Hinckley has encouraged us: "Enjoy your membership in the Church. . . . Enjoy your activity. . . . Be happy in that which you do. Cultivate a spirit of gladness in your homes."[26] I'm so thankful for the spirit my parents cultivated in our home. I thank both of them for the difference it has made in my life to have them share and nurture a sense of humor, a spirit of optimism, and a cheerful disposition. Another time I can share more about my father, but for now I have a few more things to say about my mother, who is close to ninety years old.

One of Mom's most wonderful qualities is her ability to laugh at herself. Eleven years ago she suffered a major stroke. This affected her in many ways, including her speech, reading, and writing. Just four months after the stroke, she gave a talk at Women's Conference. One of the things she said in her halting way was not to wait to have a stroke—that you could probably enjoy it more if you had it when you were younger. She felt she had waited too long.

One time in her hospital room, my brother Frank and I were watching as she went to the mirror to brush her teeth. She picked up the tube of toothpaste and stood looking at it. Then, very carefully, she put a little dab on her finger. We kept watching, not wanting to interrupt and trying not to laugh. She looked in the mirror and down at her finger, and then she began to rub the toothpaste on her nose. That did it. We started laughing, and she laughed harder than we did. Frank commented that she wouldn't be getting any cavities on her nose!

My mother went with me to a women's conference during the annual senior games in St. George, and as we shuffled into the motel— Mom leaning on her walker and me dragging our luggage—we noticed all the shipshape senior athletes. I said to her, "Hey, Mom. They think we're here for the senior games! They're wondering what our sport is!" That cracked us up!

I've spent some challenging times in places far away from my family and from basic conveniences. One thing that has made all the difference is to receive letters and packages from home. Once when I was in Hong Kong, Mom sent me a nose-and-glasses combination. How did she know I'd love that? She's my mother, that's how. I'd wear it around, including on the busses, and watch for the fun and smiles all around me. When I was in Indonesia, she'd send boxes filled with lovely things she'd found in her basement or at Deseret Industries or received from neighbors wanting to get rid of stuff—from rat traps to aprons, from old drapes to kazoos. While I was in Africa she sent me a Tupperware catalogue, saying that she thought it'd be nice for the sisters out in the bush to have a Tupperware party. We *can* pass along joy and good cheer—and a good sense of humor—to our children and others.

President James E. Faust commented: "For many years as I have blessed newborn children, including my own, I have blessed them with a sense of humor. I do this with the hope that it will help guard them against being too rigid, that they will have balance in their lives, and that situations and problems and difficulties will not be overdrawn."[27]

A mother who was diagnosed with cancer told of being isolated in a bare room for many long days behind closed lead-lined doors, feeling like a prisoner convicted of a crime she didn't commit. Then she tells of her oldest daughter coming to visit: "She sat down behind the lead screen that separated us and proceeded to take off her boots and socks. She slipped her socks on her hands and pretended they were puppets and spoke through them. I laughed for the first time in months. That simple act brightened my outlook instantly."[28]

"Count your many blessings; Name them one by one"[29]—you never know when one might be missing! Gratitude leads to joy and happiness, just as joy and happiness lead to gratitude and contentment. President Lorenzo Snow said, "It is . . . the duty of every Latter-day Saint to cultivate a spirit of gratitude."[30]

HEAVENLY FATHER WANTS US TO BE HAPPY

Our Heavenly Father and the Savior want us to experience joy, happiness, and good cheer. President Gordon B. Hinckley has said, "I am satisfied that our Father in Heaven likes to see His children happy—not miserable, but happy."[31] A *Church News* article states: "Some unfortunate souls think that joy is a luxury, one of life's frills they cannot afford or do not deserve. But . . . it is God who decided that joy is the very purpose for our existence."[32] His plan really *is* the great plan of happiness!

Elder Matthew Cowley commented: "I like to get fun out of this business—good, wholesome, righteous fun—get a kick out of it. When I obey the principles of this gospel, I am the happiest man on earth. When I don't, then I am depressed, then I have a right to worry about myself; but, when I am trying to do the best I know, then I tell you, I am having the time of my life."[33]

Elder Neal A. Maxwell said: "Ultimate hope and daily grumpiness are not reconcilable. It is ungraceful, unjustified, and unbecoming of us as committed Church members to be constantly grumpy or of woeful countenance."[34]

President Hinckley has several quotes on this topic in the collection of his teachings: "It is very important to be happy in this work. We have a lot of gloomy people in the Church because they do not understand, I guess, that this is the gospel of happiness. It is something to be happy about, to get excited about."[35] "I hope you enjoy this work. I really do. Notwithstanding all the problems, this is a work of happiness. This is the good news! This is a work of joy! I hope you can laugh and smile and be happy and rejoice before the Lord."[36] "Your happiness lies in following the gospel of Jesus Christ. . . . Happiness lies in faithfulness and in righteousness."[37] That's it! That's the key! Our happiness lies in following the gospel of Jesus Christ—in having faith in Him, believing Him, coming unto Him, and becoming more like Him.

May our deep and tender feelings about the Savior bring us comfort, peace, hope, joy, gratitude, contentment, optimism, a countenance of divine cheerfulness, and genuine happiness. He is the one who invites us to "be of good cheer, and do not fear, for I the Lord am with you, and will stand by you" (D&C 68:6).

He will. He does. I know it.

NOTES

1. Joseph Smith, *Teachings of the Prophet Joseph Smith,* sel. Joseph Fielding Smith (Salt Lake City: Deseret Book, 1976), 255.

2. James E. Faust, "Learning for Eternity," *Brigham Young University 1997–98 Speeches* (Provo: Brigham Young University, 1998), 78.

3. Abraham Lincoln, quoted in James E. Faust, "The Need for Balance in Our Lives," *Ensign,* March 2000, 4.

4. Marjorie Pay Hinckley, *Glimpses into the Life and Heart of Marjorie Pay Hinckley,* ed. Virginia H. Pearce (Salt Lake City: Deseret Book, 1999), 107.

5. Gordon B. Hinckley, *Teachings of Gordon B. Hinckley* (Salt Lake City: Deseret Book, 1997), 432.

6. Thomas Carlyle, quoted in Faust, "The Need for Balance in Our Lives," 4.

7. Faust, "Learning for Eternity," 78.

8. Truman G. Madsen, *The Radiant Life,* in *Five Classics by Truman G. Madsen* (Salt Lake City: Deseret Book, 2001), 295.

9. Harold B. Lee, *Decisions for Successful Living* (Salt Lake City: Deseret Book, 1973), 154.

10. From author's personal notes.

11. Boyd K. Packer, *Teach Ye Diligently* (Salt Lake City: Deseret Book, 1975), 210.

12. Boyd K. Packer, "'The Spirit Beareth Record,'" *Ensign,* June 1971, 87.

13. David O. McKay, "Meditation, Communion, Reverence in Our Houses of Worship," *Instructor*, October 1966, 371.

14. Jack H. Goaslind, "Happiness," *Ensign*, May 1986, 54.

15. Gordon B. Hinckley, "If Thou Art Faithful," *Ensign*, November 1984, 92.

16. James E. Talmage, "A Greeting to the Missionaries," *Improvement Era*, December 1913, 173.

17. Gordon B. Hinckley, "Fast-paced schedule for the prophet," *Church News*, April 20, 1996, 3.

18. Goaslind, "Happiness," 53.

19. Marion G. Romney, in Conference Report, October 1961, 61.

20. Heber C. Kimball, in *Journal of Discourses*, 4:222.

21. Brigham Young, *Discourses of Brigham Young*, comp. John A. Widtsoe (Salt Lake City: Deseret Book, 1954), 236.

22. Young, *Discourses of Brigham Young*, 236.

23. Young, quoted in Truman G. Madsen, "'The Joy of the Lord Is Your Strength' (Nehemiah 8:10)," *Brigham Young University 2000–2001 Speeches* (Provo: Brigham Young University, 2001), 145.

24. Gordon B. Hinckley, "Live the Gospel," *Ensign*, November 1984, 86.

25. George Q. Cannon, *Collected Discourses Delivered by President Wilford Woodruff, His Two Counselors, the Twelve Apostles, and Others*, comp. and ed. Brian H. Stuy (n.p.: B. H. S. Publishing, 1992), 5:394–95.

26. Hinckley, "Live the Gospel," 86.

27. Faust, "The Need for Balance in Our Lives," 4.

28. Emily Farmer, "'What Do I Say to Someone Who Is Dying?'" *Ensign*, April 1990, 73.

29. Johnson Oatman, Jr., "Count Your Blessings," *Hymns of The Church of Jesus Christ of Latter-day Saints* (Salt Lake City: The Church of Jesus Christ of Latter-day Saints, 1985), no. 241.

30. Lorenzo Snow, *Teachings of Lorenzo Snow*, ed. Clyde J. Williams (Salt Lake City: Bookcraft, 1984), 61.

31. Hinckley, *Teachings of Gordon B. Hinckley*, 256.

32. "Choosing joy," *Church News*, February 6, 1993, 16.

33. Matthew Cowley, *Matthew Cowley Speaks* (Salt Lake City: Deseret Book, 1954), 133.

34. Neal A. Maxwell, in *The Neal A. Maxwell Quote Book*, ed. Cory H. Maxwell (Salt Lake City: Bookcraft, 1997), 164.

35. Hinckley, *Teachings of Gordon B. Hinckley*, 256.

36. Hinckley, *Teachings of Gordon B. Hinckley*, 255.

37. Hinckley, *Teachings of Gordon B. Hinckley*, 256.

the cat was mad. But we were also out of what my son calls "human food," so the cat had to get in line. I mistakenly dropped a tax-refund check in the trash, which had gone to the street for the next day's collection, so the neighbors got to watch me rummage through my own garbage like a vagrant bag lady. Then, at the worst moment, the right front tire on my car was flat to the rim.

Sometime during all this, I made some soup for a family in our neighborhood. It was now after 10 at night, but I decided this was the only time I could deliver my pot of compassionate service. I convinced my husband that he should help me take it to a family where the father was very ill. I knew someone would still be up. So I held the soup in my lap while my husband drove the car, with the tire now repaired by AAA. (You think I am going to say that I spilled the soup, don't you? Well, I didn't! There has to be some joy in the story.) I tiptoed to the porch and nudged my shoulder against the front door and knocked gently. I cautioned my husband to be quiet, thinking that a quiet interruption in the middle of the night somehow was more like charity.

From inside I thought I heard the doorbell ring and chided my husband, "I told you, don't ring the doorbell!" Then I heard it again. "Stop it," I said. He just looked at me with a blank face. I thought I could hear the doorbell ringing again and again. Finally, the granddaughter came to the door. "Hi," I whispered. "Sorry we are so late; we won't come in. We just wanted to let you know that we are thinking about you. I hope we didn't disturb you."

"Thank you," she said patiently, as she nudged me away in what I thought was going to be a hug. As she pushed, she said, "You are leaning on the doorbell!" It was the end of a perfect day according to my personal mission statement, "No good deed goes unpunished—there's no joy in Mudville."

I also know of the days when washes of grief or despair nearly drown you; when it is all you can do to wake up and breathe one more time. I have had days like that. Following a turbulent marriage and the loss of my son, we had months and years of days filled with pain and stress and hassles.

Are you willing to pull your own handcart, but some days it feels like everyone else has climbed into it? The whole burden is yours, with everyone depending on you to pull and no one to share? You wonder, "Where is the joy in this life?"

On those days, whether bleak with despair or just full of last straws like leaning on the neighbor's doorbell, "there is no joy in Mudville." Do you feel like Casey at the bat, when the whole town waits with bated breath? It's the last inning; the score is 4 to 2; two men are on base; and two strikes are already against you. Everything depends on you, and, like Casey, you are poised to swing one more time to hit the ball with a crack. But instead the ball passes, and you swing with futility at the wind. Ernest Thayer's poem ends:

> *Oh! somewhere in this favored land the sun is shining bright;*
> *The band is playing somewhere, and somewhere hearts are light.*
> *And somewhere men are laughing, and somewhere children shout;*
> *But there is no joy in Mudville—mighty Casey has Struck Out.*[1]

Do you feel like you have "struck out"? Are there days when you feel like joy is a doctrine that pertains only to the hereafter? How do we sustain a joyful life? How does one live every day joyfully and keep any semblance of sanity? I have discovered a few principles of finding joy.

JOY IS AN ACT OF COURAGE

First, to live joyfully you must be brave. True joy is not for the faint-hearted. You must decide to be happy. Joy is an act of courage. Joy will not abide until you make a conscious decision to treasure it. Ten years ago, one evening in March, I was in the ward kitchen putting pink mints on glass plates for my niece's wedding reception. The organdy lace wedding apron was barely holding my soul together. I was quietly just hanging on spiritually and emotionally. It was a time in my life of little joy. My mother and her sister were talking together nearby. I heard my aunt ask my mother, "How is Elaine?" Mom responded, "I believe she has made a decision to be happy. She has a garden and flowers in her yard. She sews and writes, and she works hard. She keeps a clean house and plays beautiful music. Her children are doing well. I think she has decided to be brave and to be happy."

I wept a few tears as I eavesdropped on my mother's conversation. I was lonely, tired, and grief stricken. I didn't know if I had made a conscious decision to be happy. But hearing my mother's hopeful description of me, I wanted it to be true. So I did decide to be happy. I decided that night to find joy in every day. It has been difficult. But I was brave. I am not so brave every day, but I do try to remember that joy is a decision that requires courage.

In the book of Moses, we learn that after being driven out of the Garden of Eden, Adam and Eve made the decision upon entering this lone and dreary world to have joy. They had lived in a kind of paradise, having no needs, no hassles, no evil. But they learned that in order to have joy, they must know pain. More than that, they learned that to know joy in the face of pain requires courage. They wanted that experience for themselves and for us, their posterity. We read that "Adam blessed God and was filled, and began to prophesy concerning all the families of the earth," blessing the name of God as he said, "in this life I shall have joy" (Moses 5:10). "And Eve, his wife, heard all these things and was glad" (Moses 5:11). When Adam and Eve realized the cost of obedience, of enduring sorrow to meet God again, they decided that they would have joy. They made a decision. They were brave. When we learned of the divine plan of salvation before we came to earth, "when the morning stars sang together," we joined "the sons of God," and we too "shouted for joy" (Job 38:7).

TO HAVE JOY YOU MUST BE GRATEFUL

After you find the courage to make a decision for joy, the next step is to be grateful. Gratitude is the gateway to joy. How presumptuous we are to question the trials of our lives. We are blessed to be born with the greatest daily comforts of any time or place in history. We are blessed to be here on this day to share in the feast of the word of God. This very morning my eyes caught the photograph of my healthy grandson. I walked past my nostalgic lilacs now in full bloom and watered my pots of new geraniums and daisies. I am surrounded by people that I love. Surely I have reason enough for gratitude to open my heart to joy!

On 1 January 2002, I began a daily gratitude journal. (OK, I admit I got the idea from Oprah!) Every day I wrote five things for which I was grateful. I did not miss a day until Easter morning in April. On that morning I was called to be the ward Relief Society president. I believe that the act of being grateful, of thinking every day of five specific things for which I was thankful, helped me to be open to invite the Spirit, to freely love, and to accept the calling with joy.

I found that my gratitude journal filled nearly every day with little things, mostly with daily joys of my family. I began to ponder the memories of small moments of joys past. The more I meditated on things for which I was grateful, the more my heart became flooded with moments of joy—funny things my children had said, my Mom making goulash, my husband's pride at finding tickets to the sold-out opera, spreading with a kiss my ward's sisters quilt on a dear friend who was dying. From a daily focus on gratitude sprang a daily dose of joy.

Joy Requires Forgiveness

Even in the face of such daily joys, some of us suffer chronic sorrow or anger toward others who have hurt us. Joy requires forgiveness. Has your life been changed by pain of an event, loss, or action of your own or another? Is there a moment or a decision that you regret, that you want to take back and start again? Go to the Lord, forgive yourself, and let it go. Has someone hurt you? Take it to the Lord, find help to heal, forgive, and let it go.

Forgiving is not forgetting. The memory of the pain will always linger. It is because you remember that you must forgive, in order to allow joy into your life. Forgiving is not excusing or tolerating wrong or sin or living with hurtful behavior. Hold the person appropriately accountable, take appropriate action—then forgive. Do it for yourself. Give it to the Lord, find faith in the Atonement, and let it go. To forgive is not easy. It extracts all the strength you have. It requires practice over and over. But there is healing comfort in forgiving, and it frees the soul to welcome joy.

Joy Comes from Service

It is not enough simply to forgive others. Joy requires that we take the next step to serve others. I feel like I am on 24-hour call to serve others at the moment. I am a wife, mother, grandmother, ward Relief Society president, nurse, and dean. My friend Martha recently sent me a note that asked, "If it's true that we are here to help others, then what exactly are the *others* here for?" The "others" in my life expect me to be wise, helpful, organized, professional, and to have all the answers. May I share a secret? I don't have a clue! You know how it is. I make it up as I go!

My sister introduced me to *The Daffodil Principle*, by Jaroldeen Asplund Edwards. It is an enchanting story of a woman who planted 50,000 daffodil bulbs on a hillside over thirty-five years. She says she did it "one at a time. One woman. Two hands, two feet, and very little brain" until she filled five acres of a San Bernardino mountainside. Every spring it is a gift of joy, given one bulb at a time.[2]

I know that you know, only too well, that when you take the time to serve another in time of need, when you unexpectedly wave and smile to the jerk who cut you off in traffic, when you surprise your daughter by cleaning her room, when you make those carbohydrate-rich potatoes for the funeral, you nearly always feel a little burst of joy, a sense that God is in His heaven and all is nearly right with the world.

Joy Requires Your Presence

In order to know joy, you have to *be* there. Joy requires presence. My friends know that if I were not too stingy to buy personalized vanity license plates for my car, I would choose my favorite word. The word is *vivace*. *Vivace* is an Italian word used in music. It *sounds* like music. It means life, lively, quickening. It sounds alive. It reminds me to wake up, to be acute and sensitive, alert, alive. It means vitality, *la joie de vivre*, vibrance, vigor. It reminds me to touch the palpable gift and reality of life.

Joy often lights in little fairy twinkles. I call them angel gifts. They are fleeting moments of sparkling enlightenment, like gentle kisses of meaning when everything comes together. They are little heavenly glimpses of eternal joy. Joy can happen quickly, so you have to pay attention.

If you are not present in your life today, you will miss the joy as it happens. We cannot change the hurts of the past, but we can let go of the grudges and reflect today on past joys. We won't recognize joy in the future if we don't practice noticing it today.

I once heard Annie Dillard say, "Grace happens anyway; the least we can do is be there." The least we can do is be there in our own lives. It is not enough to simply take breath. We must *live* every moment of life. We must find the joy that is there to be had anyway. This life today is part of our eternal life and a time to practice knowing eternal joy.

The Message of the Atonement Is a Message of Joy

The message of the Atonement is a message of joy. Our Savior knows our suffering. He took upon Himself our suffering that we might have joy. Joy is life. To have joy is to live life fully. The meaning of the Resurrection in our own daily lives is that He lives! He lives, and because He lives, we live. This truth brings meaning, purpose, and joy to our lives. It gives us a reason to get up every morning (even in times of despair), to laugh with abandon, to embrace life. The good news of the gospel is for each of us to live. To live is to know joy in our own personal lives, every day, every now.

We don't live only after we die. We don't find joy only in the hereafter. We live today because of His gift of the Atonement. To live anew, repent, and begin again are gifts from our Savior. We can live again every day. Some days are exhilarating; some days are exhausting. Some days are full of pain and others are full of grace. I get up every day and say aloud, "Okay, I am going to try this just one more time . . ."

The Atonement allows us every day to try one more time. For a while after the death of my son, this principle did not matter to me. It didn't matter if I died. I might have wished it. All I knew was his absence. The void without him was all there was. I had no sense of where he was or if he was. All I knew was that he was gone.

But the greatest gift of the Atonement is that it is real and there for us regardless of the state of our testimony. Whether we believe it or not, it is true. The Savior lives. His Atonement allows us to try again, to repent, to have hope, and to live. He suffered, died, and rose again for us, regardless of where we are in our belief or doubt about that reality. Sorrows and losses will come. We will sin and regret and need to try again. We will be hurt and need to forgive again. We will grieve and need to find joy again. We must help each other to remember the gift of life, that "men [and women] *are*, that they might have joy" (2 Nephi 2:25; emphasis added). Our very existence today is to know joy.

That night with the wedding mints, hearing my mother's conversation, I made a decision. Perhaps it was not a decision but a gift. But I decided that since I cannot die, then I must live. If I must live, then I am going to live fully, embrace life, and engage in each moment. I have little patience for those who are not engaged. I have little patience for those who see some hassles of daily life as matters of life or death (unless, of course, they are my own hassles). I have little patience for those who don't understand my favorite word: *vivace*.

The Savior lives, and because He lives, we live. It is this life, one day at a time now to forever, in which we find joy. We learn that with Martha on the path to the house of her brother Lazarus as she grieved his death, when the Savior said, "I am the resurrection, and *the life*" (John 11:25; emphasis added). We learn it with the disciples on the road to Emmaus (see Luke 24:13–32), with Paul on the road to Damascus (see Acts 9:3–5), and with Mary Magdalene at the empty sepulcher (see John 20:11–17). How many times need He tell us?

The truth, the sacred truth, and our gift of joy is that He lives. Because of the Atonement, we can repent of sin and give up our fears and all of those mortal burdens that diminish our life. Because He lives, we must live every day of our eternal life. That includes today. We must live to bear vibrant testimony. We must live in joy. If we who know the truth of salvation and the truth of the mission of Christ, if we are not the very model of joy in this often thankless world, who is left to show the world what is joy? If we do not have joy, who will?

Let's move out of Mudville. Let's practice the joy described so many times in the Psalms: to "be glad and sing for joy" (Psalm 67:4), to "make a joyful noise unto the Lord" (Psalm 100:1; see Psalm 81:1; 98:6), to "make a joyful noise to the rock of our salvation" (Psalm 95:1). With Isaiah, let us say, "With joy shall [we] draw water out of the wells of salvation" (Isaiah 12:3), and "I will greatly rejoice in the Lord, my soul shall be joyful in my God; for he hath clothed me with the garments of salvation, he hath covered me with the robe of righteousness, . . . as a bride adorneth herself with her jewels" (Isaiah 61:10).

In the Book of Mormon, King Benjamin blessed his people with a promise and assurance we may receive today: "For the Lord hath heard thy prayers, and hath judged of thy righteousness, and hath sent me to declare unto thee that thou mayest rejoice; and that thou mayest declare unto thy people, that they may also be filled with joy" (Mosiah 3:4).

I take this as permission and assurance from God Himself that in this life I may have joy, that joy is a divine principle whose eternal implications may be beyond our understanding but are significant to God Himself. Let us find the courage, gratitude, forgiveness, service, and presence to honor our divine gifts of joy. "In this life [let us] have joy" (Moses 5:10).

NOTES

1. Ernest Lawrence Thayer, *Casey at the Bat* (New York: Atheneum Books for Young Readers, 1994).
2. Jaroldeen Asplund Edwards, *The Daffodil Principle* (Salt Lake City: Shadow Mountain, 2004), 23.

"Oh, Say But I'm Glad"

Shauna V. Brown

Oh, say but I'm glad, I'm glad
Oh, say but I'm glad
Jesus has come and my cup's over run
Oh, say but I'm glad

Wonderful, marvelous things He brings
Into a heart that's sad;
Through darkest tunnel the soul just sings
Oh, say but I'm glad.[1]

I can't tell you how many times I have heard my sweetheart, Rick, sing that born-again Christian melody that he learned prior to joining the Church. It has vibrated, invigorated, and resonated through the walls of our home, especially the shower.

There have been many spontaneous outbursts of that simple sweet melody—a lilting song that brings a generous smile—realizing that our cup is overrun with immeasurable blessings and promises from God. It's a sweet message that each of us can rejoice in.

Shauna Van Wagenen Brown graduated from Brigham Young University in Speech and Dramatic Arts. She continues to craft her skills as a songwriter, playwright, author, actress, and pioneer enthusiast. Her favorite hobbies are those centered around her family and building sunshine memories. She and her husband, Rick, are the parents of six children. She is currently serving in her ward Relief Society presidency.

"Oh, Say but I'm Glad, I'm Glad. . . . Jesus Has Come!"

We all need to rejoice, as Joseph Smith shares in the Doctrine and Covenants 128:23:

"Let the mountains shout for joy, and all ye valleys cry aloud; and all ye seas and dry lands tell the wonders of your Eternal King! And ye rivers, and brooks, and rills, flow down with gladness. Let the woods and all the trees of the field praise the Lord; and ye solid rocks weep for joy! And let the sun, moon, and the morning stars sing together, and let all the sons [and daughters] of God shout for joy! And let the eternal creations declare his name forever and ever!"

Are we doing all that we can do to join in and proclaim our happiness for Christ? He came into this world for us. He paid a glorious price to call us His.

Elder Bruce R. McConkie joined in with his affirmation and counsel: "I think the Latter-day Saints have a great obligation pressing in upon them to rejoice in the Lord, to praise him for his goodness and grace, to ponder his eternal truths in their hearts, and to set their hearts on righteousness."[2]

I interviewed some of my friends, acquaintances, and family as to how they came to be such positive people. Many were shocked to think that I considered them to be positive-attitude possessors. As I collected data to substantiate my findings, they interestingly each believed it was because of the gratitude they felt for the Savior and for the blessings that God has given them.

When was the last time you wrote down a list of all your blessings?

Do we feel an obligation pressing upon us to rejoice in the marvelous truth and light that the Savior has brought into our lives?

Do we pause often, ponder, and focus on the beautiful eternal messages He has prepared and presented for us?

Or are we so distracted with life and the running of life that we seldom even think about shouting to the world our joyous beliefs?

My favorite song as a young Primary child was "Jesus Wants Me for a Sunbeam." I believed it! I wanted to "beam" for him each day. I wanted to shine! I wanted to be the perfect sunbeam.

Each Sunday my goal was to return home with a glorious star stuck to the middle of my forehead, evidence for all to see that I had achieved it! I was a sunbeam with a star. It was my simple measure at that time that I was doing His will; I was shining and I was becoming a bright light.

Sadly, I haven't seen many little children with shiny sticky stars secured to foreheads lately. I guess it's a thing of the past. However, I think we each need to fill our pockets full of stars ready to stick to other people's foreheads when we see them shine, lift others, or hear them rejoicing in the Lord and ultimately loving one another. No one would want to be seen without a star. Heavens, it could become a fashion statement, a new trend.

And with each of us having that singular goal—to shine for Him each day, in every way trying to please Him—well, just imagine the possibilities.

Elder Neal A. Maxwell enlightened us about being stars: "Just as there is divine design in the universe, so each of us has been placed in our own orbits in this life to love, to serve, to help light the world."[3]

So growing up in my own orbit I determined that I love sunshine and rainbows with promises, singing meadowlarks, stink bugs, and God's endless gardens of beauty planted just for my enjoyment and adventure.

I realize now that I have been given a sweet spiritual gift of POSITIVITY! Positivity is the blending of a positive attitude with the firm realization of the divinity within oneself. Positivity! Don't you like it? I coined it: Positivity!

Our prophet, Gordon B. Hinckley, has encouraged us each to discover and develop it. He said, "We are children of God, . . . who have . . . a touch of divinity within us."[4]

So you and I are on an adventure, or pursuit, to find the qualities that will bring joy and excellence into our lives by discovering those traits that are inherent possibilities within.

The Prophet Joseph Smith said, "Happiness is the object and design of our existence; and will be the end thereof."[5]

Happiness—"and My Cup's Over Run"

So when we ask, What is our responsibility in feeling joy? we are told, "men are, that they might have joy" (2 Nephi 2:25), with a cup running over—Not rarely, not once a month, not just on Christmas morning, but continually.

When I married my sweetheart, we determined early that the Holy Ghost was the most valuable source needed in creating an environment where the Spirit could touch and influence our little flock. Our design was to find true happiness.

So I'm sure it won't surprise you to hear we called our family The Brown's Sunshine Factory. With the added blessing of six little rays of light bestowed within our walls, we learned that we constantly need to seek the source of the true and everlasting light.

Thus, together we set forth the plan to live, to love, to laugh often, to shine, to build, to serve and become a ready instrument in the hands of the Lord.

We continue to believe and realize that His light and life needs to be the center of our home, sunshine factory, and personal hearts.

"Wonderful, Marvelous Things He Brings— into a Heart That's Sad"

Oh, there have been days—blue cloud days I call them—when storm clouds have depleted the production of sunshine and light within our little factory. I admit, I have felt discouraged, endured anxiety attacks, felt alone, and depression has pounded at our doors. There have been burnouts, blowups, and mental meltdowns. We have left our sunshine posts and positions. We have closed early—temporarily shut down. We have allowed the pelting rain to take center stage. We admittedly have been hindered by negative thoughts and distracted by stormy actions and sudden surges of stress. Energy failures, broken hearts, and gray cloud attitudes have caused unnecessary and abrupt sunshine shortages.

We ultimately found we were experiencing a divine energy deficiency. Whatever the reason, we had temporarily lost the constant, certain, and absolute supreme source of light. Our divine power supply had been mistakenly turned off.

Humbled, we have gathered on bended knee and pushed the levers closer to God. Spontaneous divine connections have brought almost immediate light and clarity.

Yes, we all know that storm clouds gather. Adversity is around many corners; challenges are a planned part of our existence. But the way we choose to face them, to have a sense of positivity, is set within the mind.

My wonderful mother often said that our challenges and trials are "compliments from God." I must let you know she was given many intense and varied compliments.

Thinking of challenges as compliments naturally gives one a different perspective. How do you accept a compliment?

Our joy, our daily appreciation for all the marvelous things He brings into our lives, should turn our drenched hearts closer to His.

So let's answer the question, What is our responsibility in feeling joy—especially when we are in the middle of a crisis, an energy shortage, or a dark downpour?

Just like the brother of Jared, who asked the Lord to touch the stones so they would give light, we too can ask the Lord to touch us—to bring light, positivity, into our souls.

Years ago my little three-year-old Brooke found a pair of scissors. You all will identify quickly. Right in the middle of her forehead she clipped a perfect swath. "Oh!" I exclaimed in terror. Then instinctively I saw a brighter side. I said, "Look, Brooke's got a kissing square!" And from then on kisses were bestowed there until her hair grew back.

Gray skies are going to clear up. Put on a happy face. Pop the umbrella and wait upon the Lord for direction and impressions. We need to seek answers with positivity. We need to accept compliments with a smile.

God is the author of our hearts and knows well a happy ending. We have been written upon His palms and plans. Our responsibility is to look well to Him in every thought and prayer.

Our Savior, and our Father in Heaven, understands and values each one of our journeys. As surely as They love the little sparrows—and know when they fall—solutions to our challenges and circumstances are being formed. It is our challenge to humble our hearts and then to heed the inspired direction.

President David O. McKay, years ago, said, "Happiness is found only along that well beaten track, narrow as it is, though straight, which leads to life eternal."[6]

Well beaten track. He didn't say smooth. He said narrow and straight and well beaten.

"Through Darkest Tunnel the Soul Just Sings"

My grandmother Josephine Johnson wrote in her life's history, "We have loved life, had just enough rain to make life sparkle when the clouds had passed."

I love that thought and I love to see life sparkle, don't you? I love the smell just after a fresh rain.

President Gordon B. Hinckley gives us a forecast as he encourages us all to "stop seeking out the storms and enjoy more fully the sunlight."[7]

One day years ago, I remember it well, I was experiencing a thunderstorm of sorts: Lots of *little* children with *big* messes, throwing-up babies, dirty dishes in the sink, laundry mounting into a mountain, unorganized matter and things that did matter, phone calls, dreams of another nap time, the endless ringing of the doorbell by neighborhood children, lost shoes and missing baby blankets, gum in hair, and "spilled something" on the floor. I thought I was organized, but WOW! I was finally at the end of my rope. I usually tie a knot and hold on. But that day I curled up and hid in the velvet wingback chair and screamed loudly, "I quit, I'm sick of all this!" I pouted and cried until someone heard me. It was my oldest, six-year-old Heather. Quietly inspecting her desperate, storm-shaken, windblown mess of a mother, she boldly informed me, "Mother, you can't quit! You run it around here!" Climbing on my lap, she gave me a long hug and planted a gooey peanut butter kiss on my cheek. And that inspired a song, called "Peanut Butter Kisses." Now I don't write songs when the sink doesn't drain or the tire goes flat. But I have learned, come rain or come shine, God is very much aware of each of us. Having a positive attitude can and will make a difference in our storms. It is important to switch on our divine power supply.

"Wherefore, be of good cheer, and do not fear, for I the Lord am with you, and will stand by you" (D&C 68:6).

Remember the sacred feeling you felt after passing through a soul-stretching trial, when you realized He was ever close?

I have learned that there is a glorious, brilliant lining to the clouds that cover and darken our paths at times. We can, you and I, turn stumbling blocks into stepping-stones. Gulp the tart-tasting lemonade. Look ourselves squarely in the mirror and smile more. Put on those rose-colored glasses and see the difference. Place a bandage on a boo-boo and kiss it all better. We can change negative thoughts for positive ones—negativity to positivity!

I have long been impressed by the teaching of Dr. Karl G. Maeser. Speaking to the students at the BYU Academy years ago he said, "'Not only will you be held accountable for the things you do, but you will be held responsible for the very thoughts you think.'"[8]

Most people who surround themselves with thoughts of God have little time to wander dark pathways or surround themselves with people who are a draining influence on their spirit. It takes a lot of energy to change a negative behavior or attitude. But believe me, it can be done.

I am attracted to positivity believers.

So how do we access or develop positivity? Let me take you on a walk with a few of my good friends and worthy examples.

Mary Alice was everyone's best friend. She made you feel that way. You loved being around her. The mother of ten children, she found herself divorced and the sole support for them all. A storm? *Yes.* Her dreams and desires—washed away—but she took out the umbrella of faith and sheltered all from the penetrating impact. When cancer came knocking upon her door, we all sorrowed with the thought of losing her. Her lessons became our lessons; her patience taught us patience. Her love of the Lord was constant within her words, actions, and prayers. Her smiles, her upbeat attitude, and her sweet love taught us of positivity.

We thought our visits would cheer her, but she was the light that lifted us. She accepted God's compliments with grace and appreciation.

Joyce was blind when I met her, suffering from the effects of diabetes. She always had a smile, even when she couldn't see yours. She recognized your voice, and by a simple touch of her hand she made you feel important. Because of the effects of diabetes, Joyce couldn't bear children and so they adopted. With bells attached to his little shoes, she followed. Life may have been filled with darkness, but it was evident that in her heart, mind, and soul she was brilliant and illuminating.

Carol Jean, a widow with seven children, understood life was filled with tests, pop quizzes, and essays written into journals. Overwhelmed, lonely, she pushed forward. Prayers were asked and prayers were answered as she felt divine tutoring. Where one could have felt sorry for her, you found you couldn't. She always wore a happy grin. "It will all work out!" she cheerfully rendered. Carol Jean understood the meaning of "Thy will be done."

I just met Dora, eighty-five years young and blind in one eye, hearing gone, widowed, walking with the aid of a cane, and a great grand smile. I was immediately drawn to her. She reminded me of my mother, who has passed way. She has beautiful white hair. Dora, every inch of her, possessed positivity. I drew closer. She was warm and welcoming. As we spoke I realized she had accepted many a compliment with grace, gratitude, and a sunny disposition. "Hearing aids, I have to have them to hear my grandbabies!" "I use this cane because I had a stroke." "I wear a wig 'cause I lost my hair." "My sweetheart died in my arms. Wasn't that kind of the Lord to take him that way?" Oh, she was wonderful. Her love and appreciation for a loving Father in Heaven flowed in our every conversation.

These women have developed and then shared the gift of a positive attitude. They have come to know the Master and feel of their divine purpose and direction.

Perhaps they didn't hear this quote by Lorenzo Snow, but they lived it: "Look around you and find somebody that is in a worse plight than yourself; go to him and find out what the trouble is, then try to remove it with the wisdom which the Lord bestows upon you; and the first thing you know, your gloom is gone, you feel light, the Spirit of the Lord is upon you, and everything seems illuminated."[9]

"Oh, Say but I'm Glad, I'm Glad"

Yes, I'm glad, we're glad, but we cannot assume that those living around us are enjoying the same sunny day we are, even those who live within the walls of our homes.

So if we desire to have a positive attitude, we need to surround ourselves with positives. I believe the saying is true: "If you sit in a barbershop long enough, you will likely get your hair cut."

Positive people, positive desires, positive thoughts should surround every one of us! Here are some ideas you might like to try:

Carry a journal and collect thoughts, impressions, and stories that touch and stimulate your mind.

Play music that resonates light and beauty.

Sing more. Sing at every traffic light.

Smile at yourself, first thing in the morning.

Collect happy thoughts, cartoons, even some movies: *I Love Lucy*, Shirley Temple, *Anne of Green Gables*, *Pollyanna*, *Little House on the Prairie*—to name just a few of my favorites.

Learn to laugh more.

Walk in the sunshine, or

On a rainy day carry a big red umbrella and splash in the puddles just because you can.

Glory in the beauties of the Lord.

Pray to have the spirit of peace around you.

Read scriptures; circle the words *joy*, *light*, and *happiness* in yellow.

Forgive quickly.

Ask God what you can do this morning to be on His errand.

Plant a flower.

Write a poem.

Serve gladly.

Write a thank-you note once a week.

Smile; smile again just to get in the habit.

Do you know that studies show that the power of a smile or a laugh can boost the immune system? Let the healing begin!

Make a sunshine phone call, just because.

Remember birthdays.

Light a yummy-smelling candle.

Clean a drawer; de-junk a negative feeling or thought.

Give out four genuine compliments every day.

Count your blessings and write them down in a "thank-you journal."

Do not ask for anything in your prayers (for one week)—just express gratitude.

Ban sarcasm from your vocabulary—just use sincere building words.

Fill a pocketful of stars and get sticking!

But if we are sincerely looking for the ultimate way in which to develop a positive enduring attitude—POSITIVITY—we must first ponder the words of Elder Neal A. Maxwell: "Please submit your will to God. It is the only gift you've got to give. And the sooner it is placed on the altar, the better it will be for all."[10]

The sooner the better, for all—as we come to an understanding that our will is meant to be His will. And if we are seeking to be like Him, we will be positive and we will radiate His light and be filled with the Holy Ghost. As Parley P. Pratt shares, this will bring "joy to the heart, light to the eyes, music to the ears, and life to the whole being."[11]

Oh, say but I'm glad, I'm glad and thankful and grateful for positivity!

We will count blessings, shine and serve, reach out and touch others who can't comprehend or feel the warmth yet. We can share our testimony that God is standing near. We can face the storms realizing the sun (Son) continues to shine. God's plan is perfect.

So let's stand in the sunshine. Get your divine power supply plugged in today. Let's get our sunshine factories pumping the light. Go forth and be of good cheer! Ask for the blessing of a positive attitude. Learn to accept God's compliments.

"In ev'ry way try to please him, . . . A sunbeam, a sunbeam, [let's] be [His] sunbeam"—today![12]

NOTES

1. James P. Sullivan, "O Say But I'm Glad," in Ken Bible, *Master Chorus Book I* (n.p.: Lillenas Publishing Company, 1987).
2. Bruce R. McConkie, "'Think on These Things,'" *Ensign*, January 1974, 47.
3. Neal A. Maxwell, quoted in Lee Davidson, "News of the Church," *Ensign*, March 2003, 76.
4. Gordon B. Hinckley, *Teachings of Gordon B. Hinckley* (Salt Lake City: Deseret Book, 1997), 117.
5. Joseph Smith, *Teachings of the Prophet Joseph Smith*, sel. Joseph Fielding Smith (Salt Lake City: Deseret Book, 1976), 255.
6. David O. McKay, in Conference Report, October 1919, 180.
7. Gordon B. Hinckley, "The Continuing Pursuit of Truth," *Ensign*, April 1986, 2.
8. Karl G. Maeser, quoted by George Albert Smith, in *Sharing the Gospel with Others* (Salt Lake City: Deseret Book, 1948), 63.
9. Lorenzo Snow, in Conference Report, April 1899, 2–3.
10. Neal A. Maxwell, "Sharing Insights from My Life," January 12, 1999, BYU Devotional (Provo, Utah: Brigham Young University, 1999), 117.
11. Parley P. Pratt, *Key to the Science of Theology* (Salt Lake City: Deseret Book, 1978), 61.
12. Nellie Talbot, "Jesus Wants Me for a Sunbeam," *Children's Songbook* (Salt Lake City: The Church of Jesus Christ of Latter-day Saints, 1989), 60–61.

"BE OF GOOD CHEER; I HAVE OVERCOME THE WORLD"

Camille Fronk

To the paralytic man lying helpless on a bed, Jesus proclaimed, "Be of good cheer" (Matthew 9:2). To the frightened Apostles battling the tempestuous sea, Jesus appeared on the water, declaring, "Be of good cheer" (Matthew 14:27). To Nephi the son of Nephi, who was subject to an arbitrary law threatening his life and the lives of other righteous Nephites if the signs prophesied by Samuel the Lamanite didn't occur, the Lord said, "Lift up your head and be of good cheer" (3 Nephi 1:13). As Joseph Smith met with ten elders about to be sent out, two by two, to missions fraught with trouble and danger, the Lord announced, "Be of good cheer" (D&C 61:36). In each instance the people had every reason to be anxious, fearful, and hopeless, yet the Lord directed them toward a reason to rejoice.

How does the Lord's admonition of cheer sound when it is applied to you and me in our world today? When economic uncertainties, terrorist threats, and corruption provide top stories for the evening news, where does the good news of the gospel intervene? When we experience personal loss in so many ways and on so many days, what is left to be cheerful about?

Camille Fronk is an associate professor of Ancient Scripture at Brigham Young University and has a Ph.D. in Sociology of the Middle East. She is the wife of Paul F. Olson, a Provo ophthalmologist. She serves as a Relief Society teacher in her Provo ward.

The Key to Cheerfulness

We find the key to understanding this seeming contradiction in the context of the Last Supper. Speaking to the Apostles in His final moments before Gethsemane, Jesus said, "In the world ye shall have tribulation: but be of good cheer; I have overcome the world" (John 16:33).

"How was it possible for the Twelve to be of good cheer?" Elder Neal A. Maxwell asked. "The unimaginable agony of Gethsemane was about to descend upon Jesus; Judas' betrayal was imminent. Then would come Jesus' arrest and arraignment; the scattering of the Twelve like sheep; the awful scourging of the Savior; the unjust trial; the mob's shrill cry for Barabbas instead of Jesus; and then the awful crucifixion on Calvary. What was there to be cheerful about? Just what Jesus said: He had overcome the world! The atonement was about to be a reality. The resurrection of all mankind was assured. Death was to be done away with—Satan had failed to stop the atonement."[1]

I wish to focus on the role of Christ's enabling power in our ability to feel cheer amid mortal gloom and doom. Misfortune and hardship lose their tragedy when viewed through the lens of the Atonement. The process could be explained this way: The more we know the Savior, the longer becomes our view. The more we see His truths, the more we feel His joy. But it is one thing to know that's the right answer in a Sunday School class and quite another to experience firsthand a cheerful outlook when current circumstances are far from what we hoped. If we would develop faith to apply the Atonement in this manner and not merely talk about it, awareness of imaginary finite boundaries inadvertently placed on the Savior's infinite sacrifice can be meaningful. Consider two false assumptions that, if pursued, will block our appreciation and access to the Lord's divine assistance.

False Assumption 1—We Can Avoid Tribulation

First is the false assumption that, if we are good enough, we can avoid having bad things happen to us and those we love. If we can just keep all of the commandments and pay an honest tithing and have daily prayer and scripture study, we can appease God, earn His good pleasure, and thereby assure ourselves of His protection from heartache, accident, or tragedy. When such thinking drives us, we "want victory without battle," Elder Maxwell observed, "and expect campaign ribbons merely for watching."[2] So trials will surely come, including when we are trying to do everything right. Elder Richard G. Scott warned, "Just when all seems to be going right, challenges often come in multiple doses applied simultaneously." He explains that a "reason for adversity is to accomplish the Lord's own purposes in our life that we may receive the refinement that comes from testing."[3]

If we hold the belief that God will shield us from tribulation because of our obedience, and then adversity strikes, we may be tempted to accuse God of not hearing our prayers or, worse, of not honoring His promises. Obedience to God is not insurance against pain and sadness. Some unpleasant things just come with this telestial turf. Challenges have always been included in God's great plan to test our faith, to stimulate in us growth, humility, and compassion. Heartache and struggle were divinely designed to stretch us to where we have nowhere else to turn but to God.

The ground was cursed for Adam's sake, and Eve was promised that her sorrow (or hardships) would be multiplied (see Genesis 3:16–17). The Apostle Paul acknowledged, "There was given to me a thorn in the flesh, . . . to buffet me, lest I should be exalted above measure" (2 Corinthians 12:7). The Lord required Sariah to send her sons back into harm's way before she found her own conviction of God's will for her family (see 1 Nephi 5:1–8). Christ's mission was never intended to prevent hearts from breaking but to heal broken hearts; He came to wipe away our tears, not to ensure that we would never weep (see Revelation 7:17). He clearly promised, "In the world ye shall have tribulation" (John 16:33).

False Assumption 2—We Can Trust in Our Own Efforts

A second false assumption when we face tribulation can be just as destructive to our faith in Christ. We may conclude that hardships come because we haven't done enough good in the world.

We may believe that lifelong cheerfulness is achieved through our own management and efforts. After all, we are bright, capable, and resourceful women. When considering tribulation and the Lord's Atonement through this angle, we can look at the scripture that says, "It is by grace that we are saved, after all we can do" (2 Nephi 25:23), and deduce that we must first prove our worth through our obedience and our righteousness before the Lord's sacrifice will cover us or His grace enable us. Trusting in our own efforts rather than humbly acknowledging God is reflected in the term *self-righteousness*.

When we look through the lens of our righteousness and take comfort in our good efforts, the idea of depending wholly on Christ (see 2 Nephi 31:19; Moroni 6:4) seems a bit risky. Listen to a series of domino-like sentiments that such a perspective can produce: What if I depend on God, but He doesn't answer me when I need His immediate help? With all the serious problems in the universe, why would He have time or interest in my personal crisis? Then again, if I organize my life carefully and think smart, I could resist temptation and not have to lean upon on the Lord for help at all. What is more, I will then not be one of those who contributed to His suffering in Gethsemane. If I just use my skills and brain, I can actually help the Lord rather than drawing on His strength. After all, so many people around here are in worse circumstances than I.

Unwittingly, when we reason this way, we sound eerily similar to Korihor's humanistic preaching in the Book of Mormon that "every man fared in this life according to the management of the creature; therefore every man prospered according to his genius, and that every man conquered according to his strength" (Alma 30:17), thereby arguing that his listeners had no need for Christ and His Atonement. "And thus [Korihor] did preach unto them, leading away the hearts of many, . . . yea, leading away many women, and also men, to commit whoredoms" (Alma 30:18).

Being fearful and unsettled by the unexpected, our faith in Christ fades into "gratify[ing] our pride" by "our vain ambition" (D&C 121:37). Such thinking easily leads to justifying wrongdoing because we are in control; we know better than others, so sin is not a problem for us. Our efforts focus on personal success to show that we don't need anyone else. If we can just get control over our world—our addictions in all their varieties, our eating disorders and obsession with thinness, our insistence that our house always be immaculate, our fascination with outward evidence of education and success—then we can finally be cheerful. The scriptural listing of women before men in the reaction to Korihor's teachings is curious wording. I don't know all that such wording could imply, but we can at least conclude that women were not exempt and maybe even particularly attracted to Korihor's "management of the creature" philosophy.

Christ declared, "In the world ye shall have tribulation: but be of good cheer; *I* have overcome the world" (John 16:33; emphasis added). He didn't say *you* must overcome the world or that He overcame the world just for the weak ones who weren't smart enough or strong enough to do it on their own. The Savior said, "*I* have overcome the world."

Christ Has Overcome the World

Prophets in every era have testified that Christ's grace is sufficient. *Sufficient* means "enough" or "as much as is needed." Prophets also remind us of our own nothingness and indebtedness to Christ, that we are less than the dust of the earth, that without Him we are unprofitable servants (see Mosiah 2:21–25), and that "no flesh . . . can dwell in the presence of God, save it be through the merits, and mercy, and grace of the Holy Messiah. . . . He shall make intercession for all the children of men; and they that believe in him shall be saved" (2 Nephi 2:8–9).

The Apostle Paul learned that lesson. Arguably the best prepared missionary this world has known, Paul was brilliant in languages, highly educated in the Jewish religion, and well versed in the Greco-Roman culture and philosophy of his day. Drawing on his rich education and superior intellect, he attempted to teach the intellectuals of Athens about Christ as their "unknown God" (see Acts 17:23), quoting their poets and using their philosophy. While Paul's knowledge and presentation may have been impressive to his philosophical audience, his erudite approach in Athens produced a disappointing harvest.

From Athens, Paul traveled to Corinth, where he found tremendous success. Later, in an epistle to the Corinthian Saints, Paul explained his missionary approach among them—possibly a rethinking of his experience in Athens:

"And I, brethren, when I came to you, came not with excellency of speech or of wisdom, declaring unto you the testimony of God.

"For I determined not to know any thing among you, save Jesus Christ, and him crucified.

"And I was with you in weakness, and in fear, and in much trembling.

"And my speech and my preaching was not with enticing words of man's wisdom, but in demonstration of the Spirit and of power" (1 Corinthians 2:1–4).

Trusting that the Lord will support us in our trials and give us what to say and do in the moment that we need it can be frightening when we have become accustomed to relying on our own familiar skills. Why was Paul willing to set aside his educational prowess when it would clearly be impressive to investigators of his religion? He explained: "That your faith should not stand in the wisdom of men, but in the power of God" (1 Corinthians 2:5).

The LDS Bible Dictionary describes grace as a "divine means of help or strength, given through the bounteous mercy and love of Jesus Christ. . . . Through faith in the atonement of Jesus Christ and repentance of their sins, [individuals] receive strength and assistance to do good works that they otherwise would not be able to maintain if left to their own means."[4]

The Atonement not only blesses us after we obey but is actually the power that sustains us while we do the deed. Likewise, Joseph Smith learned that "according to the grace of our Lord" (D&C 20:4), he was given "commandments which inspired him; and . . . power from on high" (20:7–8). Because of Christ's magnanimous grace, He gives us commandments, not to curtail and restrict, but to inspire and strengthen us to understand and accomplish all that He invites.

When we look through the clarifying lens showing that Christ has already overcome the world, the scripture "It is by grace that we are saved, after all we can do" (2 Nephi 25:23) looks very different. What is "all we can do"? A group of converted Lamanites, the Anti-Nephi-Lehies, recognized the answer. Their leader wisely taught, "It has been all that we could do . . . to repent of all our sins . . . and to get God to take them away from our hearts" (Alma 24:11). These humble Saints desired to please God far more than to receive their kinsmen's acceptance. They manifested their sincere repentance by burying their weapons of war and making a covenant with God.

We can do likewise. We can admit that we have sinned and need the Lord's redemption. We can confess His power and goodness and our constant need for His sustaining and strengthening influence. We can bury our weapons of war—tools we are prone to use to survive without Him that only serve to fortify our pride and self-righteousness. And we can make and keep our covenants with Him.

I watched a young student make that connection this semester. After studying the remarkable epistles of the Apostle Paul, she commented to the class:

"Paul taught that the grace of Christ will make up for everything that we lack, if we will have faith in Him. During this semester, I was called to teach Gospel Doctrine in my ward. This was the scariest calling for me because I am just not one to stand in front of a class, especially for 45 minutes. But as I prepared for my first lesson, I remembered what Paul said about the grace of Christ. So I prepared everything that I could and then intensely prayed that the grace of Christ would make up for all I lacked. What happened was amazing. It was amazing because it wasn't me. The Spirit was so strong and the lesson was powerful because the grace of Christ made up the difference between my preparation and what needed to be taught by the Spirit. His grace is a powerful gift. It is nothing that we earn."

BE OF GOOD CHEER

Cheerfulness in the scriptural context connotes a divinely assured optimism, "a deep trust in God's unfolding purposes,"[5] a grounded conviction that God will always keep His promises. When Christ proclaims,

"Be of good cheer," He is not requesting a naive, Pollyanna-like response to life's cruel twists and turns. Nor is He promising a pain-free life of constant bliss. Trial is no respecter of persons. Tragedy and hardship do not discriminate. Our world sees opposition among rich and poor, men and women, the righteous as well as the wicked. And while increasing dishonesty and vanity in our society are self-evident, the Savior specifically prayed that God would not take us "out of the world" (John 17:15). "In this world your joy is not full," He taught us, "but in me your joy is full" (D&C 101:36). How else do we learn that true satisfaction is found only by turning away from the world and coming to Christ?

Only after fearing the loss of her sons and realizing that her prophet-husband's testimony of Christ was not enough to sustain her own, Sariah found the Lord herself and declared,

"Now I know of a surety that the Lord hath commanded my husband to flee into the wilderness; yea, and I also know of a surety that the Lord hath protected my sons, and delivered them out of the hands of Laban, and given them power whereby they could accomplish the thing which the Lord hath commanded them" (1 Nephi 5:8).

She discovered that Christ's grace was sufficient. And when the sons returned to their father's tent, Nephi reported, "Our father . . . was filled with joy, and also my mother, Sariah, was exceedingly glad" (1 Nephi 5:1). Naturally such gladness and cheer came because her sons had returned safely. But such joy is also evident in her witness that the Lord's power enabled her sons to do good works that they otherwise would not have been able to do if left to their own means.

After suffering physical and emotional persecution throughout years of missionary labors, Paul landed in a Roman prison and then declared:

"I have learned, in whatsoever state I am, therewith to be content.

"I know both how to be abased, and I know how to abound: every where and in all things I am instructed both to be full and to be hungry, both to abound and to suffer need.

"I can do all things through Christ which strengtheneth me" (Philippians 4:11–13).

What does this mean for each of us here today? I can start by acknowledging that I have had tribulation from which no one else could deliver me but the Lord. Circumstances I would never happily choose have sent me to my knees and turned me to God. And, further, I anticipate additional trials down the road, because God loves me.

While the Lord clearly promises, "In the world ye shall have tribulation" (John 16:33), life's challenges are rarely the same for you as they are for me. I can also acknowledge that you have challenges that I will likely never experience, challenges and crosses that will be just as stretching for your soul as mine are for me. I can resist the temptation to assume the role of the Master Physician by announcing to you in your despair, "Be of good cheer" or "I understand just how you feel," being aware that it is from His voice that you and I both need to receive this message if we will be healed. He is the only one who truly understands our sorrow. Only He has felt our personal pain.

But I can also come to know the Lord and choose to bear witness of His supernal gift every time I have opportunity to speak or teach. I can realize that I will do more to help another person find the Lord by admitting my utter dependence on Christ in my actions and informal conversations than by parading a seemingly perfect outward appearance, which all too frequently communicates that I no longer need Him. We should be competing against sin, not trying to determine who needs the Savior less. When we acknowledge that we each face difficulties, that the Savior overcame the world, that He has lifted and strengthened and given vision to each of us in very personal ways, we will realize that we are never alone. We will feel a peace within even though the crisis without still rages. We will be filled with hope and even cheer.

CONCLUSION

The words of one of our sacrament hymns reflect great reason to lift our heads and rejoice:

> *No creature is so lowly,*
> *No sinner so depraved,*
> *But feels thy presence holy,*
> *And thru thy love is saved.*

> *Tho craven friends betray thee,*
> *They feel thy love's embrace;*
> *The very foes who slay thee*
> *Have access to thy grace.*
>
> *Thy sacrifice transcended*
> *The mortal law's demand;*
> *Thy mercy is extended*
> *To ev'ry time and land.*
> *No more can Satan harm us,*
> *Tho long the fight may be,*
> *Nor fear of death alarm us;*
> *We live, O Lord, thru thee.*[6]

Jesus Christ has indeed overcome the world! As darkness has no power when light appears, so the world cannot overcome or comprehend the Light of the World (see John 1:5). He is the victor, come to earth "with healing in his wings" (3 Nephi 25:2) for both ourselves and those who disappoint us. He will not forsake us. He leads us along even when we don't know all the answers. Like Sariah and the Apostle Paul, who found His matchless love in their distress, we too can know the Savior's grace in our profound need.

As the mother hen covers her chicks with her wings, so the Redeemer will surround us with His comprehensive power if we will come to Him (see Matthew 23:37). There is room under those wings for all of us, for He declares, "Wherefore, be of good cheer, and do not fear, for I the Lord am with you, and will stand by you; and ye shall bear record of me, even Jesus Christ, that I am the Son of the living God, that I was, that I am, and that I am to come" (D&C 68:6).

True, we live in a time of war, a day of conflicts and terrors not only among nations but within our own hearts. But He who is the balm of Gilead (see Jeremiah 8:22) is the captain of all creation; only in Him is peace and serenity found. Amid all our mortal gloom and doom, Jesus Christ has overcome the world. Come, let us rejoice.

NOTES

1. Neal A. Maxwell, *"But a Few Days,"* Address to Church Educational System religious educators, September 10, 1982 (Salt Lake City: The Church of Jesus Christ of Latter-day Saints, 1982), 4.

2. Neal A. Maxwell, *Men and Women of Christ* (Salt Lake City: Bookcraft, 1991), 2.

3. Richard G. Scott, "Trust in the Lord," *Ensign*, November 1995, 16.

4. LDS Bible Dictionary, s.v. "Grace," 697.

5. Maxwell, *"But a Few Days,"* 4.

6. Karen Lynn Davidson, "O Savior, Thou Who Wearest a Crown," *Hymns of The Church of Jesus Christ of Latter-day Saints* (Salt Lake City: The Church of Jesus Christ of Latter-day Saints, 1985), no. 197, vv. 2–3.

"MY SOUL DELIGHTETH IN PLAINNESS"

Claudia J. Dansie

Nephi said, "My soul delighteth in plainness unto my people, that they may learn" (2 Nephi 25:4). He later explains that "after this manner doth the Lord God work among the children of men" (2 Nephi 31:3). The Lord truly does work according to plainness. *Plain* means pure, clear, uncomplicated, honest, simple, and without ornamentation.[1] Sometimes in the worldly scope of things *plain* has picked up a derogatory sense, meaning ordinary, not pretty, or old-fashioned, but it does not carry this sense in the eternal scope of our Heavenly Father. It is His way. In Genesis 25:27 Jacob of old is called a "plain man"; according to the accompanying footnote in the Church's 1979 edition of the Bible, *plain* here means whole, complete, perfect, and simple.

The gospel of Jesus Christ is plain in the same way as was Jacob. Its principles and commandments are taught in powerful, plain, simple, honest ways by the Lord and His prophets. As we look closely at the scriptures, we see that directives are given in three main areas: living with plainness, teaching with plainness, and speaking with plainness. By

Claudia Johnson Dansie, called "Lolly" by her family, is married to Boyd Dansie; they have three children. She graduated from Brigham Young University in education and has taught in both elementary and junior high schools. She has served in many callings in the Church and is currently a Gospel Doctrine teacher. She has also been a member of the BYU Women's Conference committee for three years.

following these principles, we can become more whole, complete, and perfect.

LIVING WITH PLAINNESS

We are told in the scriptures that we can live with more plainness, simplifying our lives. We can live with fewer material wants, freeing up our resources for something better, for something more lasting. The Lord Himself advises us in the Sermon on the Mount:

"Lay not up for yourselves treasures upon earth, where moth and rust doth corrupt, and where thieves break through and steal:

"But lay up for yourselves treasures in heaven, . . .

"For where your treasure is, there will your heart be also" (Matthew 6:19–21).

It is beneficial for all of us to examine periodically where we spend our time and money and realize that this denotes the state of our hearts. As we adapt to simplicity, we feel more joy and gratitude. We appreciate more fully what we already have. Can we run around a little less with empty busyness, cancel a few of the talent lessons our children don't really like, and find a little more productive time to do the important things? Can we better prioritize what is most essential in serving the needs and goals of our family? Sometimes our search for less gives us more in our quest for perfection and eternal goals.

Alma counsels his son Helaman, "Now ye may suppose that this is foolishness in me; but behold I say unto you, that by small and simple things are great things brought to pass" (Alma 37:6). Some may still suppose it foolish today, but it is the truth. As we make these words our guide to living, our lives will open up and we will recognize miracles. We will see the lifting that comes from a smile or a kind word, the benefits of simple service. We will understand the true meaning of visiting and home teaching as loving shepherding, without all of the unneeded extras.

I once was told a story of a woman who couldn't do her visiting teaching because she hadn't finished embroidering the cloths that were to go with her homemade bread that went along with her lesson. She missed the whole month. She also missed the simple principle of visiting teaching. The simple acts of listening, discussing gospel principles in solving life's problems, and building trusting friendships are what visiting teaching is really about. Having someone to go to when we need help, having a friend to laugh with, and sometimes having someone to cry with are all parts of the miracles of small and simple things.

In our families, our greatest goals can be accomplished by simple means. By searching the memories of our own childhood and by being a little creative, we can make old-fashioned joys new again. Let's have fun without modern technology and without money. We can turn off the television and the movies. Let's read to our children, all cuddled up on the couch together. We can share the stories we read when we were children and laugh and remember. We could go to the library, come back with armfuls of books, and later tell each other what we've learned. We can take a walk around the block or in the yard and put nature's treasures in a brown paper bag. Let's talk and listen, play a board game, pop popcorn. We should appreciate the blessings that plainness can give our families.

Recently my husband and I made an unannounced visit to the home of a young couple with four small sons. They were all around the kitchen table, decorating cookies to give secretly to neighbors. The mother replenished the cookies and frosting and supplied a wide variety of leftover candy and sprinkles from past birthday parties and baking projects. The father sat with his sons—frosting, decorating, and being creative—sharing the fun and excitement over each treat. The love among them was strong. They enjoyed each other's company. They were best friends. This wasn't anything fancy, expensive, or complicated. It was simple. It was plain. It wasn't terribly unusual, and I'm sure that they have done many of these kinds of projects together before. But it worked. Such simple things build family unity, trust, and love.

Our prophet, President Gordon B. Hinckley, along with other prophets before, has asked us to have family home evening weekly. Clear back in 1915, when the program began, President Joseph F. Smith stated: "If the Saints obey this counsel, we promise that great blessings will result. Love at home and obedience to parents will increase. Faith will be developed in the hearts of the youth of Israel, and they will gain power to combat the evil influence and temptations which beset them."[2] "By small and simple things are great things brought to pass" (Alma 37:6).

Family home evening is the Church's "weapon of mass construction." It builds families. It is the time when families learn the gospel together—sing, play, and pray together. It might seem like a simple thing—one day each week, maybe just an hour—but the benefits from family home evening are great. Our families will become stronger and more unified. I testify of this. My family has grown from the blessings of family home evening. My children, now all moved away, still talk about the lessons we had, the songs we sang, the projects we accomplished, and the memories we made.

The influence from family home evening can continue throughout generations. Our children enjoy and learn from family home evening. They then grow up, make friends, and have families, and the teachings go on. This inspired program not only ties our immediate family together, but the love and memories can bind generations to come.

Family home evening is where parents can bear their most sweet, heartfelt, and personal testimonies to their children. It is where they listen to their children's own first attempts at expressing their feelings for the Savior and their gratitude for blessings. It is a time of trust and acceptance within the family, before they try to express themselves to the world. Children and parents pray for each other and over each others' goals and concerns. Fathers and mothers hold personal interviews with their children, sharing and learning of their lives, goals, and needs. Families plan and schedule together, turning confusion into cooperation and support.

Future missionaries are trained in family home evening. On a mission, it may be hard for young elders and sisters to go to a home where they don't know the people or what to expect, especially when the language and customs are new. It's a different environment, and missionaries are sometimes out of their comfort zones. But if they have been consistently taught in their homes through family home evening, they have resources on which to rely. They know how to pray. They know how to organize and give a lesson. They know how to lead music, how to fix a few treats, and even how to keep a younger, or older, boy or girl interested until the time is up. They have learned how to take turns answering questions and to listen to others with respect. And they understand the basic principles of the gospel as taught by their families. They have a head start in their confidence for a successful mission. From small things come that which is great (see Alma 37:6). That is the power of living with plainness.

The Lord gives us solutions to our problems and ways to accomplish our goals. He has shown us the way through His words and inspiration to our prophets. These ideas may be simple and plain and ones that the world may think foolish, but if we lack the obedience to try them out, we are the ones who lose out. Much like Naaman of old, we may not truly understand the power of simplicity.

As explained in 2 Kings, Naaman was captain of the armies of Syria, "a great man . . . , and honourable, . . . but he was a leper" (5:1). His wife had a Hebrew maid who suggested that he go to see the prophet to be healed from his affliction. He went first to the king of Israel and then to the home of Elisha, the prophet. He came with his riches—horses, chariots, gold, and silver—for he was a very wealthy man. Elisha didn't go out to meet Naaman, but rather sent a messenger to him, saying, "Go and wash in Jordan seven times, and thy flesh shall come again to thee, and thou shalt be clean" (5:10). But Naaman was offended and left angry. How dare Elisha only send a messenger. Wasn't Naaman better than that? And why wash in the Jordan River when there were nicer, cleaner rivers than that in his homeland? Naaman lamented, "Behold, I thought, He will surely come out to me, and stand, and call on the name of the Lord his God, and strike his hand over the place, and recover the leper" (5:11). But Elisha did not. He chose simplicity. Naaman's servants went out to him to console and plead: "If the prophet had bid thee do some great thing, wouldest thou not have done it? how much rather then, when he saith to thee, Wash, and be clean?" (5:13). Naaman was humbled. "Then went he down, and dipped himself seven times in Jordan, according to the saying of the man of God: and his flesh came again like unto the flesh of a little child, and he was clean" (5:14).

Are we sometimes like Naaman? Would we do anything if only President Hinckley would ask us personally or if we were called to some great position in the Church? Do we have a preconceived notion of how it should be? Do we expect the Lord or His prophet to come and do great things in our honor? Is that what it takes for us to obey or understand? Or do we follow the simple authority and instructions given by His messengers? President Hinckley has asked us to have family home evening, family prayer, and family scripture study. He probably has not come to any of our doors to ask, but he has given his instructions to his messengers—the Apostles, stake presidents, bishops, and other leaders. The instructions are simple, but they still work. They are lessons of living with plainness.

Teaching with Plainness

Jesus taught gospel truths with simplicity. He used clear, understandable language for those He taught. His stories and parables came from examples in their own lives: He spoke of shepherds, fishermen, lamps, oil, rocks, water, salt, and bread. His purpose was to clarify, not to confuse. Our Savior was the master teacher. His direct, plain approach was effective. People needed to easily know of His gospel and His teachings, for His time was short.

Is it so different now? Time is of the essence, and there is an urgency in our fast-paced world to understand and apply true gospel principles in this life. As a teacher of any group, teaching with plainness is necessary "that they may learn" (2 Nephi 25:4).

Sometimes in our callings as teachers, we get caught up in the "attraction" of the lesson. I've actually taught lessons when I've had to make three trips to the car just to get all of my decorations and visual aids to the room. There was a time when my handouts were the main focus, and I spent hours and hours on them. They were wonderful! If you haven't done this as a teacher, you've probably seen it in a class. Women seem to do this more than men. We don't see many priesthood lessons full of pictures, statues, flowers, draped cloths, and elaborate table decorations. I think women do it because we are so conscientious in our desire to do well, or maybe it's because we're worried that we won't be as good as the woman who taught before; either way, it really isn't necessary.

I remember a time when Sister Sheri Dew, then a counselor in the general Relief Society presidency, came to our region to train stake Relief Society presidencies. We were so excited to meet her. The stake in charge had beautiful flowers and table arrangements in the room. Sister Dew greeted us and commented on her beautiful surroundings. She noted how lovely the flowers were and thanked the sisters who attended to all of the decorations. Then she picked up the flower arrangement, put it off to the side, and said, "Now, let's get to work."

She continued to teach about the importance of having the Spirit and magnifying our callings. I learned some valuable lessons that day. It wasn't so much what she said as what I saw in myself, and I changed my concept of how I taught. I challenged myself to never again teach without simplicity.

We need to remember for whom we are teaching. We are teaching for our Lord—not ourselves—and we are teaching for the salvation of others. Nephi explains, "We talk of Christ, we rejoice in Christ, we preach of Christ, we prophesy of Christ, and we write according to our prophecies, that our children may know to what source they may look for a remission of their sins" (2 Nephi 25:26).

Our purpose as teachers is simply to help bring others unto Christ.

We need to remember what we are to teach. We are commanded to teach the doctrine. In Doctrine and Covenants 88:77, we are given the words of the Lord: "And I give unto you a commandment that you shall teach one another the doctrine of the kingdom." Part of teaching the doctrine is using proper Church teaching materials—the lesson manuals, scriptures, and words of the prophets. Keep it plain and simple. There is no need to complicate our lessons with outside resources or speculation. I love this quote by President Heber J. Grant: "Teach and live the first principles of the gospel, and let the mysteries of heaven wait until you get to heaven."[3]

We need to remember that only the Spirit can truly teach. We are only humble instruments by which the Spirit works. The Spirit is what touches the hearts and minds of those who listen and causes a change, not us. Nephi states, "When a man speaketh by the power of the Holy Ghost the power of the Holy Ghost carrieth it unto the hearts of the children of men" (2 Nephi 33:1). Our job is to not get in His way, to not distract, so He can do His work. Our job is to try with all our faith, humility, and prayer to have the Spirit for ourselves and for those we teach and to have an understanding of our subject matter. If we don't have the Spirit, our teaching will not be successful. We are plainly told so in Doctrine and Covenants 42:14: "And the Spirit shall be given unto you by the prayer of faith; and if ye receive not the Spirit ye shall not teach."

The gospel is plain, and it makes sense in its simplicity. We should not try to complicate it by "looking beyond the mark." Jacob says of the Jews:

"They despised the words of plainness . . . and sought for things that they could not understand. Wherefore, because of their blindness, which blindness came by looking beyond the mark, they must needs fall; for God hath taken away his plainness from them, and delivered unto them many things which they cannot understand, because they desired it" (Jacob 4:14).

How I hope we appreciate the plainness of the gospel and teach it simply so that its understanding will never be taken away from us. May we always remember that our goal as teachers is plain and simple—to teach the doctrine for the Lord with the Spirit to the people so that they and their families may come unto Christ and return to live with our Heavenly Father.

SPEAKING WITH PLAINNESS

Nephi sets the standard for plain speaking when he declares, "I glory in plainness; I glory in truth" (2 Nephi 33:6). The scriptures have always told us to be honest, truthful, direct, and clear, without pretense, deception, or hypocrisy (see 2 Nephi 31:13). In today's world, where confusion and contradictions abound, it becomes even more important to speak truth in plain and simple terms, especially in our responsibilities to guide and direct our families. The results can bring us our greatest joys. As the Apostle John says, "I have no greater joy than to hear that my children walk in truth" (3 John 1:4).

As parents it is critical that we teach our children to expect and accept simple, honest truth. It starts with open communication in the home, the first training ground. Most of children's social skills, life's expectations, and reactions are started in the home. We taught our children early that they could broach any subject, say or ask anything, as long as it was done in a respectful manner. As a family we have discussed just about every subject imaginable, family members giving their opinions and reasons openly, asking for ideas and solutions from each other. We don't always agree, but we listen and honor each other's right to an opinion. We don't always expect agreement— or even calm conversation—but we always expect honesty. It builds great confidence in individuals and unity for families if we'll just talk—simply, plainly—and keep talking. I know that when a child can come to a parent to ask any question and know that the answer will be honest and complete, he will come again. The comfort and trust level will grow for both.

We have special mantles as mothers and fathers of our children. We cannot give that mantle to anyone else. We should not expect someone else—a teacher, a youth leader, a bishop—to teach our children what we should be teaching. We cannot give up the responsibility. We should not be afraid to be parents.

Part of our responsibility is to teach our families about life, the reality of it all. "The Family: A Proclamation to the World" states:

"Parents have a sacred duty to rear their children in love and righteousness, to provide for their physical and spiritual needs, to teach them to love and serve one another, to observe the commandments of God and to be law-abiding citizens wherever they live. Husbands and wives—mothers and fathers—will be held accountable before God for the discharge of these obligations."[4]

We must teach our families about consequences. That is what our Heavenly Father, the perfect parent, does with us. We must teach them about real life in plain and simple speaking so they can succeed in real life. We like to encourage and tell of all the blessings of life, but we must not neglect the sorrows and hardships as well. We must tell it like it is. How do we know how and what to say? We need to pray for guidance. We need to ask the Spirit to be with us as we speak and counsel our children. Jacob explains:

"The Spirit speaketh the truth and lieth not. Wherefore, it speaketh of things as they really are, and of things as they really will be; wherefore, these things are manifested unto us plainly, for the salvation of our souls" (Jacob 4:13).

Part of our responsibility as parents is to guide, direct, and warn if necessary. We need sometimes to ask the questions we don't want to ask, use the words we don't want to use, find out some things we may not want to know. Some topics must be covered as directly as their consequences are lethal—subjects such as modesty, drugs, pornography, and immorality. We must not be too shy to ask. We will probably be more shocked and embarrassed than our children, but we must have the courage to discuss. We cannot hide our heads and say that something can never happen to us or to ours. It can and it does. If we are to be leading, guiding parents, we cannot be the last to know.

Usually television, movies, and other media do not present reality. Their values don't reflect real-life consequences. They show that sexual activity before marriage is expected. In real life it's called expecting. They show only one side of life and forget to show the sorrows that many of these choices can bring. Is it any wonder that life's decisions have become so difficult for our children? There is much confusion in the world, and almost every choice is laid out before them. We can be catalysts to help our children learn discernment. Through the power of open, honest, plain speaking, we can give them the trust and confidence to know where to go for truth. We can teach them the power of the simple truths of the gospel. By meaning what we say and saying what we mean, we teach what truth is.

Many people say, "I could never speak that directly. I'm afraid I'd offend." Nephi instructs us concerning offenses when he speaks to his brothers: "Wherefore, the guilty taketh the truth to be hard, for it cutteth them to the very center" (1 Nephi 16:2). The offense is usually not meant by the speaker but taken only because it "cutteth . . . to the very center." Why are we so afraid of speaking truth? Is being politically correct so important that we miss opportunities to warn, testify, change, or lift? We do always need to examine our motives when speaking plainly. We must never speak in anger or for revenge. Our purpose cannot be to hurt or gain power; if it is, it is not from the Spirit. If children are raised with plain speaking and expect truth, they have a much easier time accepting it without offense.

Honest speaking is as important in compliments as it is in questions and answers. There is great power in a true compliment. It can encourage and lift to great heights; but we all know the difference between a deserved compliment and one given only out of politeness. Find things that are truly good in people and tell them—plain and simple. We shouldn't wait until people die before expressing how much we love them or how much they've done for us. Eulogies are wasted on the dead. Let's lift the living! Think of the building we could do with more plainness—and our compliments will be believed because we are honest.

Plain speaking is one of the most valuable tools of sharing truth. Think of how missionaries challenge people to change their lives by obeying the Word of Wisdom, reading the Book of Mormon, praying, repenting, being baptized. It works because the challenge is simple, honest, and pure; it is given for the loving benefit of others. It comes from the Spirit, as an expression of true charity. A testimony is the same. "It is a simple, direct declaration of belief. . . . Testimonies are often most powerful when they are short, concise, and direct."[5]

I have a testimony of simplicity, of the power of plainness in living, teaching, and speaking. I believe in honesty and truth. I know it is true that Heavenly Father lives and loves us and that we are His beloved sons and daughters. I know Jesus Christ is His Son and our Savior, who loved us and the plan of salvation so much that He atoned for our sins, opened the doors of resurrection, and gave us the possibility of exaltation. I know Joseph Smith restored this church, the Church of Jesus Christ, upon the earth in the latter days. I know President Hinckley is a prophet today, one who leads with truth. I am grateful for plainness, that I may learn. And I am grateful for this gospel—plain and simple.

NOTES

1. See *Webster's Ninth New Collegiate Dictionary* (Springfield, Mass.: Merriam–Webster, 1987), s.v. "plain."
2. Joseph F. Smith, in *Messages of the First Presidency of The Church of Jesus Christ of Latter-day Saints*, 6 vols., comp. James R. Clark (Salt Lake City: Bookcraft, 1965–75), 4:339.
3. Heber J. Grant, *Teachings of Presidents of the Church: Heber J. Grant* (Salt Lake City: The Church of Jesus Christ of Latter-day Saints, 2002), 5.
4. "The Family: A Proclamation to the World," *Ensign*, November 1995, 102.
5. *Teaching, No Greater Call: A Resource Guide for Gospel Teaching* (Salt Lake City: The Church of Jesus Christ of Latter-day Saints, 1999), 43.

THE POWER AND GIFT OF
THE ATONEMENT

Jana Riess

In his book *Believing Christ*, BYU religion professor Stephen Robinson tells a memorable story from his own family experience about coming to understand the Atonement of Christ. He and his wife, Janet, were active in the Church. They held regular family home evenings with their children and attended the temple as often as they could. He was in the bishopric in their Pennsylvania ward, and she was serving as the Relief Society president. In addition to her Church responsibilities, Janet had just completed her accounting degree, passed her CPA exam, and taken a job with a firm. She had also just given birth to their fourth child.

As you can imagine, all of this activity placed a lot of pressure on her shoulders, and eventually something snapped. Robinson writes, "It was as though Janet had died to spiritual things; she had burned out. . . . When her Relief Society counselors called her, she told them that they could do whatever they wanted to, that she had asked to be released from her calling." After almost two weeks of not wanting to talk about it, Janet finally confessed that she couldn't do it anymore. "My load is just too heavy," she told her husband. "I can't do all the things I'm supposed

---

Jana Riess lives in Kentucky, where she has served as Gospel Doctrine teacher and as a counselor in the Young Women and Relief Society presidencies. A wife, mother, and author of five books, she works from home as an editor for Publishers Weekly *magazine.*

to. I can't get up at 5:30, and bake bread, and sew clothes, and help the kids with their homework, and do my own homework, and make their lunches, and do the housework, and do my Relief Society stuff, and have scripture study, and do my genealogy, and write my congressman, and go to PTA meetings, and get our year's supply organized, and go to my stake meetings, and write the missionaries. . . ."[1]

Are you seeing yourselves at all in this story? I certainly did when I read it, and I felt a breathtaking kinship with this woman I'd never met. Janet felt terribly weighed down by the perfectionistic burdens she was placing on herself. She tried not to yell at her kids, but sometimes she couldn't seem to help it. She tried hard to love everyone, but she failed. "I'm just not perfect," she wailed. "I'm never going to be perfect, and I just can't pretend anymore that I am. I've finally admitted to myself that I can't make it to the celestial kingdom, so why should I break my back trying?"[2]

With her husband's help, Janet came to see that she'd missed the core of the gospel. The very word *gospel* means "good news," yet for Janet the gospel had become an impossible list of demands and soul-crushing responsibilities. Brother Robinson writes, "Who would have thought that after all the meetings and lessons, after all the talks and testimonies and family home evenings, somehow the heart of the gospel had escaped her? She knew and believed everything except the most important part. . . . Janet knew why Jesus can be called a coach, a cheerleader, an advisor, a teacher, the elder brother, the head of the Church, and even God. She understood all of that, but she didn't understand why he is called the *Savior*."[3]

I'm sad to say that I meet a lot of LDS women like Janet. As Latter-day Saints we should be among the most joyful people on the earth. With the Restoration of the gospel, many plain and precious truths that had been lost have been returned. We have the Book of Mormon, another testament of Jesus Christ. We enjoy the gift of the Holy Ghost and the blessings of the priesthood and the temple.

So why don't we have more joy?

I'd like to explore two key applications of the Atonement in our lives. The first is that the Atonement enables us to rest in Christ's grace, knowing that we are forgiven of our sins and also our shortcomings. The second is that the Atonement helps us to deal with the inevitable pain and adversity of our lives. After highlighting these two applications, I'll then review what it means to gain a testimony of the Atonement, drawing on my own conversion experience and exploring the biblical character of the Apostle Peter.

RESTING IN THE GRACE OF CHRIST

Many years ago, shortly before I was baptized into this church, I saw a funny skit about Mormon life, put on by a group of Latter-day Saints in the style of a road show. The key song I remember was to the tune of "Supercalifragilisticexpialidocious," from *Mary Poppins*. This version was called "Super-hyperactive-Mormons-constantly-in-motion," and it featured Mormon men and women getting up from a meeting table to dance and sing about how very busy they were. I found it funny, and I remember laughing hard, though at the time I don't think I appreciated the devastating cultural accuracy of the critique. We are an active people. Some of the sisters at women's conference listen to the talks in service learning rooms, feeding their spirits while their nimble hands make quilts for the needy and activity bags for children all over the world. Talk about multitasking!

I think all of this energy is fantastic. In fact, it was one of the most attractive elements of Mormonism to me, the terrific vitality of people who are committed to a noble purpose. However, I do sometimes worry when I see sisters who feel inadequate in the face of all this feverish activity or who agonize that they are somehow not measuring up. Some of these sisters do what Janet tried to do—they drop out because they feel unworthy. Others raise the bar ever higher, jumping through hoop after hoop to prove to themselves and the world that they *are* worthy. It's interesting that both of these destructive paths are based in perfectionism.

President Ezra Taft Benson quite astutely told us that perfectionism is one manifestation of the sin of pride. When we attempt to save ourselves, we overlook the one who saved us already. As a self-described recovering perfectionist, I can tell you that the times in my life when I've felt closest to the Savior are the times when I have failed, when I've been forced to lean on His merits and not my own. Perfectionism and pride can prevent us from receiving the Atonement and leave us desperately trying to carve out our own salvation. So the first message I'd like to leave with you is that with a proper understanding of the Atonement we can experience the joy of forgiveness, the knowledge that we are not alone. It's not an intellectual understanding. As Janet Robinson's story demonstrates, a person can believe *in* Christ without *believing* Christ. It needs to be a conversion of the heart, a decision to turn our lives over to the Savior, who loves us.

Dealing with Pain and Adversity

The second issue I'd like to touch on is how a knowledge of the Atonement can affect the way we cope with pain. Have you ever had an experience of "pain with a purpose"? When I took a childbirth class shortly before the birth of my daughter, I was told that although the pain would be unimaginably intense, it would be different from other kinds of pain I had experienced through illness and injury. This would be pain with a purpose, with every increasingly difficult contraction bringing me that much closer to the birth of my child.

Now, lest you think I'm a lot more valiant than I really am, please know that after a short time of experiencing the joys of pain with a purpose, I demanded an epidural. Immediately. And this avoidance of pain was a natural human response. After all, who wants to experience agony when there is another way?

Labor is an apt analogy for the pain of our lives. With Christ's Atonement, every pain we experience here on earth can become pain with a purpose. Life can throw us some seemingly impossible blows. Right now in my ward, a couple is coping with their daughter's car accident, an accident that killed her husband and left her in a coma. Her life has been hanging by a thread. Maybe you've suffered through the death of a child. Maybe you had an abusive parent. Maybe you've just been diagnosed with cancer. Or maybe you can't point your finger at any

particular tragedy in your life, but for some reason you just don't feel any joy.

But I testify to you that through Christ's Atonement, all of those trials can be transformed into pain with a purpose. If we allow it to, adversity can refine our spirits and cleanse our hearts, making us more like the Savior. And the knowledge that we gain from those trials is never wasted, but follows us as we depart this life for an eternity with God. Christ's suffering gives meaning to *our* suffering.

What's more, perhaps we should be grateful that we can feel pain at all. If you think I'm crazy, let me tell you a story. In their remarkable book *The Gift of Pain*,[4] Philip Yancey and the late Dr. Paul Brand draw from Dr. Brand's lifetime of experiences as an orthopedic surgeon in India to describe the necessary and highly beneficial role pain plays in our lives. We learn about its necessity by looking at the horror caused when someone can't feel it.

Dr. Brand was a pioneer in the treatment of Hansen's disease, a chronically misunderstood disease that is commonly called leprosy. It turns out that most people have all kinds of misconceptions about leprosy. We imagine that it's highly contagious, for example, and we have historically quarantined and cruelly ostracized those who are afflicted with the disease. In fact, only about five percent of people are at risk for contracting leprosy—primarily children and those who already have compromised immune systems. What's more, leprosy is not contracted by casual exposure.

But perhaps our greatest misunderstanding is in how the disease destroys. Most people realize that leprosy results in the terrible loss of extremities such as fingers and toes. Until the twentieth century, doctors always assumed that those losses stemmed directly from the disease itself, saying that leprosy patients had rotting flesh. However, in the mid-twentieth century they found that leprosy could be treated with sulfa drugs that entirely arrested the progress of the disease. After treatment with the drugs, patients would be tested and found to have no more evidence of the bacteria that caused leprosy—but they would still continue to lose their fingers and toes. Puzzled by this, Dr. Brand followed his leprosy patients closely and discovered that their wounds occurred because

of accidents and not because of their disease. The disease had deadened their nerves and made them entirely insensitive to pain, a natural anesthesia that continued even after the disease itself was successfully eradicated with medication.

All of the normal, everyday injuries that people without leprosy take care of almost automatically—removing shoes that are too tight for our feet, or splinters that drive into our flesh—were never felt by those with leprosy. And then those tiny injuries festered and worsened. Dr. Brand saw that even walking too much in ill-fitting shoes could become catastrophic for a leper: warning blisters would be ignored, and the patient would keep walking. Eventually an infection would set in, the bone might become exposed and start chipping away, and the toe would be shortened or lost. All this was the result of not feeling the pain. Even blindness, one of the eventual horrors of leprosy, was often discovered to be a result of patients' insensitivity to pain: because they could not feel any irritation from dryness or debris in their eyes, leprosy patients weren't blinking often enough to lubricate them.

Reflecting on his lifetime of working with leprosy patients, Dr. Brand quoted the novelist William Faulkner, who said that if he were to choose between pain and nothing, he would choose pain. As a physician, Dr. Brand wrote that lepers' painlessness initially seemed to be a blessing, but he soon realized that painlessness was "the single most destructive aspect of this dread disease." This is all to say that, although it may seem impossible for us to imagine when we are suffering, *pain is God's gift to us.* It is our warning system and our protection. When we have a strong understanding of Christ's Atonement, we begin to see how our pain can be redeemed as our souls are refined through adversity. We can see that pain has a purpose and that suffering can be for our good.

RECEIVING THE GIFT OF THE ATONEMENT

But when do we stop merely believing in Christ, and start believing His promises?

The Atonement is a gift of grace that Heavenly Father has bestowed upon us. As with any gift, we have to open ourselves to receive it.

Recently I had an experience of an unopened gift. This past Christmas, my mother rather sheepishly produced a wrapped present and said it was from my aunt. Well, the strange thing is that this aunt hasn't had contact with us for years, so I was very curious about what she would send me. It turns out that it wasn't what she had sent me this year—it was what she had sent me in 1978. My mom had her attic cleaned last fall, and this old dusty box was discovered up there. So, on Christmas morning of 2003, I opened a gift that was a quarter of a century old. (Just so I won't keep you in suspense, it was a *Charlie's Angels* action figure, still in mint condition.)

For too many Latter-day Saints, the Atonement is like a gift that is sitting up in the attic, unopened and dusty. We can't apply its blessings to our lives because we think we can get along a lot of the time by ourselves, without the gift. But opening the gift of the Atonement is not something that happens in one moment on Christmas morning. This gift unfolds slowly over the course of a lifetime, as we repent of our sins and submit our will to Heavenly Father's.

One person who came to understand this gradual inner transformation was the Apostle Peter. Although we might tend to imagine that Peter had a perfect testimony the moment Jesus called him to follow and made him a "fisher of men" (see Matthew 4:19), close attention to the Gospels shows that Peter's faith unfolded slowly and that he stumbled several times. In the story of the storm on the sea, for example, we find the disciples toiling and straining at the oars so much that they almost miss their Savior passing by. (This sounds a lot like us, doesn't it? Straining so much to save ourselves from the storms of life that we ignore the Savior.) But after Jesus reveals Himself, and Peter sees Him walking on the water, Peter has enough faith to try the unthinkable: walking on water himself. Note that as long as he keeps his eyes fixed on Jesus, he is fine. He begins to fail only when he notices the strong wind, takes his eyes off Jesus, and tries to rely on his own abilities. (See Matthew 14:22–33.)

But still, it's a start. Whereas in an earlier storm Jesus had chastised the disciples for having no faith (see Mark 4:37–40), now He tells Peter he has "little faith." I'm a glass-half-full kind of person, and I'd like to congratulate Peter on his progress! Yes, it's still a rebuke, but Peter has gone from "no" faith to a "little" faith in a short period. And notice that moments earlier, Peter wasn't at all sure about Jesus, saying the equivalent of, "Lord, *if* it's really you . . ." and demanding proof (Matthew 14:28). Now he just begs "Save me!" (Matthew 14:30), fully believing that Jesus can do so. He is growing in faith, line upon line.

I know what it's like to have a faith that grows slowly. I started studying with the sister missionaries in the summer of 1991. We had two months to get through all six missionary discussions, but we barely made it into the fourth one because I had so many questions that we never seemed to make progress. I didn't join the Church until the fall of 1993, after worrying my way through most of the Book of Mormon and exhausting several sets of sister missionaries. My point is that people's faith is not instantaneous. Mine is still growing, and I still have some unanswered questions. What has slowly unfolded, though, is the tremendous sense of guidance I've received from the Lord in gaining a testimony, particularly a testimony of the Atonement of Christ.

This is something that Peter came to understand. If you look at Matthew 16:13–23, you'll see a marvelous moment in Peter's spiritual journey. When other disciples spout their theories of who Jesus is— people say that He is Elijah, or John the Baptist, or Jeremiah—Peter is the only one who quietly voices the truth: "Thou art the Christ, the Son of the living God" (16:16). Jesus responds to this by pronouncing an immediate and very formal rabbinic blessing, using Simon Peter's family name and telling him that Heavenly Father Himself revealed this knowledge. He seals the benediction by reminding Peter that he is a "rock"— a pun on the name Peter—for recognizing the true nature of Christ.

Well, don't get too comfortable with this image of Peter as a paragon of rock-solid faith, because just three verses later he reveals that he still lacks understanding: when Jesus teaches that the Messiah must suffer and die, Peter takes him aside and quietly challenges him. "Be it far from thee, Lord," he says in love. "This shall not be unto thee" (16:22). Again Peter has made a statement of belief, but this time, instead of blessing him, Jesus rounds on him. "Get thee behind me, Satan," He rebukes (16:23). He accuses Peter of savoring the success of the world instead of the things of God. The core of the gospel, He seems to be teaching Peter, is not instant triumph but pain with a purpose.

Peter's setbacks get even more pronounced as we come to the well-known story of his denials of Jesus the night before the crucifixion. After being an eyewitness to healings, miraculous feedings, Jesus's transfiguration, the raising of Lazarus, and the calming of the wind and sea, Peter denies knowing the man—three times. (See Matthew 26:69–75.)

But remember that this is not the end of the story. As we see near the close of the Gospel of John, the resurrected Christ gently gives Peter the opportunity to profess his love three times in restitution. There's a lot more going on in these verses than is evident in our English translation. (See John 21:15–17.) When Jesus asks Peter the first two times if Peter loves Him, the verb that Jesus uses is *agape,* or the pure, charitable love of Christ. "Peter, do you love me in this way—as I love you?" Jesus seems to be asking. Peter affirms his love, but he does so using a different verb entirely: "Yes, Lord, you know I have the deepest friendship possible for you." But when Jesus poses the question a third time, He does so on Peter's own terms: "Simon, son of Jonas, do you love me in friendship?" It's not that Jesus has given up hope that Peter will love Him with the purest love possible, the love of Christ. But it does seem that Jesus is accepting what Peter is able to give at this time. Peter willingly offers everything he can, even though his love is not yet perfect. Despite this imperfection he is given a mission: to feed the lambs and sheep.

What if Peter had become frustrated with himself, saying that because he was not yet capable of perfection and a flawless love for the Savior, he was not worthy as a servant of the Lord? What if his imperfect understanding of the Atonement had prevented him from following the Lord's final commandment to feed the lambs and sheep?

Maybe you struggle at times with your testimony, or with some aspect of living the gospel. Stay on the journey. You are not perfect yet, but that is as it should be. Stay on the journey. One day a woman from my ward, who converted to the Church about thirty years ago, shared with me the tremendous difficulty she had in giving up smoking after she was baptized. For three years she struggled with her habit, even leaving the ward building to have a cigarette on Sunday morning. But this sister continued coming to church because she had a growing testimony that it was true. When the time came for her to choose between going to the temple to be sealed with the rest of her family and continuing what she knew was an unhealthy habit, she was finally ready to say good-bye to her addiction. That woman is now my stake Relief Society president, and she gives so much to the Church. What would have happened if she'd become so discouraged by her inability to quit smoking that she had given up on the gospel altogether? Instead, she courageously put her faith in Christ and in her own gradual transformation. Change does not happen overnight, even when we have a strong testimony. We have to be patient with ourselves and trust in the Lord.

Peter's journey did not end with the ascension of Christ; in fact, it was just beginning. I encourage you to pick up Peter's story some years later, exploring his own writing to see just how far his faith progressed. The man who once denied and misunderstood his Savior became a staunch leader in the Church, a "rock" who could not be moved despite persecution from without and dissension from within. What's more, he finally understood suffering. The whole first epistle of Peter is a treatise on it! Peter now knew the meaning of pain with a purpose. Like Peter, if we persevere in faith and in prayer, we can come to a greater knowledge of the Atonement. We can unwrap that gift and allow its blessings to pour forth into our lives. Ours will not be a perfect knowledge of the Atonement, but it will be enough to equip us to feed the lambs and sheep.

Peter exhorted his flock in 1 Peter 5:10, "But the God of all grace, who hath called us unto his eternal glory by Christ Jesus, after that ye have suffered a while, make you perfect, [e]stablish, strengthen, settle you."

May we, through a greater understanding of the Atonement, endure our sufferings, look forward to a *future* perfection, and feel strengthened and at peace.

NOTES

1. Stephen E. Robinson, *Believing Christ* (Salt Lake City: Deseret Book, 1992), 15–16.

2. Robinson, *Believing Christ,* 16.
3. Robinson, *Believing Christ,* 17; emphasis in original.
4. See Philip Yancey and Paul Brand, *The Gift of Pain: Why We Hurt and What We Can Do About It* (Grand Rapids, Mich.: Zondervan Publishing, 1997).

Repentance: The Great Turning

Mary Jane Woodger

Recently I went through a heart-wrenching experience. I do not need to share the details, but for me it was Abrahamic in nature and left me wondering about the Lord's love for me. I know thinking such a thing is ridiculous, but the experience was gut-wrenching, and I felt I had experienced what Joseph Smith warned about. The Prophet explained:

"'It is quite as necessary for you to be tried as it was for Abraham and other men of God, and (said he) God will feel after you, and He will take hold of you, and wrench your very heart strings, and if you cannot stand it you will not be fit for an inheritance in the Celestial Kingdom of God.'"[1]

During this experience, I felt my heartstrings wrenched. The ram did not appear and the sacrifice had been made. So, one Sunday after sacrament meeting when my stake president walked through the foyer and greeted me, I said to him, "President Hansen, I need you to heal me." He was rather taken aback and a little speechless. He replied, "Well, I have meetings all day. I could meet with you at 11:30 tonight."

Mary Jane Woodger is an associate professor of Church History and Doctrine at Brigham Young University. She has authored and coauthored numerous articles on doctrinal, historical, and educational subjects. Her current research interests include twentieth-century Church history, Latter-day Saint women's history, and Church education.

When I declined that late-night appointment he offered, "Well, I'll have my executive secretary call you."

To give you an idea of how desperately I needed repentance, I thought at the time, "I bet when the Savior was asked for healing He did not reply, 'Well, talk to John and we'll make an appointment for next week.'" The executive secretary called during the week and told me I could have an appointment at 5:00 P.M. next Sunday. I responded, "I have people coming to my house for dinner at 5:00 P.M. next Sunday," The executive secretary then informed me, "It's five or nothing." So I acquiesced. At 5:00 P.M. that next Sunday I had barely begun to open my mouth and tell my stake president my long saga where I could portray myself as a victim when President Hansen cut my story short, quoting this scripture to me: "Return unto me, and repent of your sins, and be converted, that I may heal you" (3 Nephi 9:13). He then counseled, "I can't heal you now; your heart is hardened. If you want to be healed you need to go home and repent. I'll see you next week."

I left his office rather numb. That was not the scenario I expected. Previously, when I have been desperate enough to go to a priesthood leader for counsel, I have experienced great comfort and empathy. Instead, in this instance, I felt my stake president had added to the burden and told me to go home and repent. He had implied I was not a victim, and I needed to change before I could be healed. Being told to repent and then going through the repentance process has never been my idea of a happy day. However, in the last year of my life repentance has become a wonderful blessing, and I now look forward to repenting. It took a few days to humble myself, but I took my stake president's advice and repented. I went back to his office the next week and I was blessed and healed. A situation that had me in tears daily ceased, and I have not shed a tear since. The pain and suffering are gone.

If you have felt negative about repentance, you are not alone. Repentance has taken a "bad rap." Many of us have misunderstood this doctrine of the gospel of Jesus Christ. Part of this misunderstanding is not our fault. The eighth Article of Faith states "We believe the Bible to be the word of God as far as it is translated correctly." Some translators of the Bible erroneously equated repentance with suffering, punishment, confession, remorse, and sorrow. Those conditions may accompany repentance, but they are not the fullness of repentance. Often I have mistaken those adjectives for repentance. In fact, true repentance, like my stake president fostered, is the opposite of those negative synonyms.

By going to the Old Testament we can begin to understand this simple doctrine that translators complicated. The Old Testament was originally written in Hebrew and the word most often used to refer to the concept of repentance was *shub*, which meant "to turn from." Elder Theodore M. Burton taught:

"The message of the Old Testament is to *shub*, or to turn from transgression and turn back to our loving Father in Heaven—to leave unhappiness, sorrow, regret, and despair behind and turn back to our Father's family. There we can find happiness, joy, and acceptance among his other children.

"[Old Testament] prophet after [Old Testament] prophet writes of *shub* to let us know that if we are truly repentant and forsake sin, we can be received with joy and rejoicing."[2]

According to the Old Testament prophets the synonyms for *repentance* were *joy* and *rejoicing*. The concept of *shub* is also found in the New Testament, which was mostly written in Greek, where "writers used the Greek word *metanoeo* to refer to repentance. *Metanoeo* means a change of mind, thought, or thinking so powerful that it changes one's very way of life. . . . The Greek word *metanoeo* is an excellent synonym for the Hebrew word *shub*. Both words mean thoroughly changing or turning from evil to God and righteousness.

"Confusion came . . . when the New Testament was translated from Greek into Latin. Here an unfortunate choice was made in translation; the Greek word *metanoeo* was translated into the Latin word *poenitere*. This word is related to the words *punish*, *penance*, *penitent*, and *repentance*. The beautiful meaning of the Hebrew and Greek words was thus changed in Latin to a meaning that involved hurting, punishing, whipping, cutting, mutilating, disfiguring, starving, or even torturing! It is no small wonder, then, that people have come to fear and dread *repentance*, which they understand to mean repeated or unending punishment."[3]

Elder Burton continued: "The meaning of repentance is not that people be punished, but rather that they change their lives so that God can help them escape eternal punishment and enter into his rest with joy and rejoicing. If we have this understanding, *repentance* will become a welcome and treasured word in our religious vocabulary instead of a word that creates anxiety and fear. . . .

"God is merciful; he has provided a way for us to repent and thus escape the bondage of pain, sorrow, suffering, and despair that comes from disobedience. As the sons and daughters of God, we need to understand the true meaning of repentance, we need to know that it is a beautiful word and a marvelous refuge."[4]

Along with faulty translation, another problem I had was my own misinterpretation of the word *repentance* in scripture. For instance, we find one of the great invitations to repent as follows:

"For behold, I, God, have suffered these things for all, that they might not suffer if they would repent;

"But if they would not repent they must suffer even as I;

"Which suffering caused myself, even God, the greatest of all, to tremble because of pain, and to bleed at every pore, and to suffer both body and spirit" (D&C 19:16–18).

I used to interpret that scripture as you can either suffer a little now or suffer a lot later. I incorrectly thought repenting was suffering. I have since found that it is not repenting that is suffering; it is not being healed and partaking of the Atonement that causes us pain. President Boyd K. Packer concurs:

"We all make mistakes. . . . It is then in our nature to feel guilt and humiliation and suffering, which we alone cannot cure. That is when the healing power of the Atonement will help. . . .

"The Atonement has practical, personal, everyday value; apply it in your life. It can be activated with so simple a beginning as prayer. You will not thereafter be free from trouble and mistakes but you can erase the guilt through repentance and be at peace."[5]

Repentance is the ultimate eraser in life; it is the supreme delete button. For those who completely repent it is as though the act were never committed. That is the miracle of repentance. As Elder Matthew Cowley of the Quorum of the Twelve thought: "That's what I like about it—the erasing. I believe when we repent there is some erasing going on up there so that when we get there we will be judged as we are for what we are and maybe not for what we have been."[6] But for the unrepentant there is no such erasing.

Repentance is the most positive of all doctrines of the gospel of Jesus Christ. Elder Neal A. Maxwell called repentance "one of the most vital and merciful doctrines of the kingdom. It is too little understood, too little applied by us all, as if it were merely a word on a bumper sticker. . . . Repentance is a rescuing, not a dour doctrine."[7]

Elder Richard G. Scott, speaking of repentance, added: "This subject is widely misunderstood and often feared. Some feel that it is to be employed only by those in serious transgression, while the Lord intended that it be consistently used by every one of His children. He has repeatedly commanded His prophets and leaders to proclaim it and to speak of little else. [See D&C 6:9.] I refer to the blessing of true, sincere, continuing repentance, the path to peace and joy. It is a conduit to the reforming power of the Lord and, when understood and used, a dear and precious friend."[8]

Many of us as children learned a three-step, four-step, or seven-step process of repentance. Those steps help us to remember some aspects of the process such as remorse, restitution, or regret. However, as we grow in the gospel, such lists can negate true repentance with a false sense of accomplishment. Repentance is not a mere cessation of wrongdoing, the passage of time, or the expression of sorrow. I found this concept to be true a number of years ago when I had lunch with a friend who had been excommunicated from The Church of Jesus Christ of Latter-day Saints. She made this incredible statement during the course of our lunch about her own *twelve-step program*, "Mary Jane, I have been through the repentance process, and it is just not worth it." She was hurting. She was angry that all her neighbors knew about her sin and treated her differently. She was upset that her opinions were no longer welcomed in the Relief Society class she used to teach.

She lashed out at me, "You don't know anything about repentance because you have never committed a major sin. You've never had to confess to your bishop. You haven't a clue about repentance or what I am going through." At that moment I wondered if I should apologize for not committing more heinous sins. She then suggested I needed to read more about her sin and then I would be educated. However, I have found that it is not deep sinners who are the most educated about repentance. Instead, it is those who repent daily and become more and more attuned to the Spirit. My friend had not experienced godly sorrow, and in many ways she had become immune to the repentance process.

It is ironic that the more we sin, the more we are in need of repentance, but the more difficult it becomes. Save with murder and the unpardonable sin, repentance is always possible but not always probable. Tad R. Callister, explains:

"Just as the physical body weakens with the onslaught of disease, it seems that in the same way we weaken spiritually as we embrace each new sin. Perhaps we lose our capacity or will to absorb light and truth. Perhaps, like an injured muscle, we lose strength and resiliency to confront each new temptation. Whatever the mechanics, spiritual death seems to result in a form of spiritual degeneration or entropy. As with physical death, there needs to be some power to reverse the decaying process, to heal our spiritual wounds, to strengthen our spiritual fiber. Again, the Atonement is the source of that reversing power, that fount to which men 'may look for a remission of their sins' (2 Nephi 25:26)."[9]

If my excommunicated friend had really gone through the repentance process, she would have known it was worth it. She thought she had been through repentance and known remorse, but it was the wrong kind of sorrow. This friend of mine was dwelling on the pain of the sin and consequences. She was experiencing sorrow and suffering, but not godly sorrow. My friend thought that talking about her behavior and others' behaviors toward her would change her behavior. It did not. As President Packer has reminded us on several occasions, "Knowledge of the principles and doctrines of the gospel will affect your behavior more than talking about behavior."[10]

My friend had concentrated on the Latin *poenitere* instead of the Hebrew *shub*. Yes, Alma the Younger talks about being racked, harrowed up, tormented, and in the gall of bitterness, but at the culmination of repentance, he talks of joy (see Alma 36:17–20). My friend was still in process; she had not experienced full repentance.

"True repentance . . . is a melting, softening, refining process that brings about a mighty change of heart. It is manifest by those who come forth with broken hearts and contrite spirits. It is a burning resolve to make amends with God at any cost. Such a change means 'we have no more disposition to do evil, but to do good continually' (Mosiah 5:2)."[11]

If we only dwell on the pain it will inhibit the healing process. Pain is only to help us to remember so we can move forward. King Benjamin told his people to awaken to "a sense of [their] nothingness, and [their] worthless and fallen state" (Mosiah 4:5). Until you and I understand that we are less than dust (see Helaman 12:7), until we are awakened to our nothingness in comparison to the goodness of God, repentance is not complete. In his address to his people, King Benjamin explained:

"Therefore if that man repenteth not, and remaineth and dieth an enemy to God, the demands of divine justice do awaken his immortal soul to a lively sense of his own guilt, which doth cause him to shrink from the presence of the Lord, and doth fill his breast with guilt, and pain, and anguish, which is like an unquenchable fire, whose flame ascendeth up forever and ever" (Mosiah 2:38).

In reaction to King Benjamin's address, his people fell to the earth. These people were not vile sinners; they had placed their tents towards the temple. These were good, righteous men and women. Something happened to them that I have not yet fully comprehended. I have not completely caught my nothingness in comparison to God's greatness. Moses understood that concept when he disclosed, "I know that man is nothing" (Moses 1:10). In that nothingness one understands the full correlation between one's deeds and His pain. President Kimball explained that correlation:

"Repentance can never come until one has bared his soul and admitted his actions without excuses or rationalizations. He must admit to himself that he has sinned, without the slightest minimization of the offense or rationalizing of its seriousness, or without soft-pedaling its gravity. He must admit that his sin is as big as it really is and not call a pound an ounce. Those persons who choose to meet the issue and transform their lives may find repentance the harder road at first, but they will find it the infinitely more desirable path as they taste of its fruits."[12]

So many of us rationalize and excuse our own actions. Many have found that most inmates in prison have one thing in common. It is not that they claim innocence for the crime for which they were convicted. The one common thread instead is a claim that their crime was someone else's fault. They refuse to take responsibility, and until they bear responsibility for their own actions reform is highly unlikely. Likewise, there cannot be a change of heart for many of us until there is a direct correlation between our deeds and His pain. It is His pain that reforms us, not our own. If we at some point can experience that direct correlation, then mercy can take hold, and when it does the joy comes. When King Benjamin's people experienced such an association they "cried aloud with one voice, saying: O have mercy, and apply the atoning blood of Christ that we may receive forgiveness of our sins, and our hearts may be purified; for we believe in Jesus Christ, the Son of God, . . . who shall come down among the children of men.

" . . . The Spirit of the Lord came upon them, and they were filled with joy, having received a remission of their sins, and having peace of conscience, because of the exceeding faith which they had in Jesus Christ who should come" (Mosiah 4:2–3).

Sometimes in repenting we experience remorse, restitution, confession, and resolve but we miss the main course, which is to turn to Him.

When I was a little girl my mother sang the song "Turn Around" to me as she would rock me to sleep. The song describes the feelings a mother has watching her child grow up, how it seems that every time she turns around, her child is older. The mother realizes that one day she will turn around and her daughter will be a mother of her own.

My mother's vision was that one day I would be all that she was and have all that she had. Likewise, our Heavenly Father wants us to turn around. He wants us to become what He is: an eternal parent with spiritual offspring of our own. That won't happen if we do not turn, if we don't *shub*. Most of us turn from sin, but that is just a 90-degree turn, not the full 180-degree turn of coming full circle back to him. Elder Maxwell described that turn:

"When 'a mighty change' is required, full repentance involves a *180-degree turn,* and without looking back! (Alma 5:12–13.) Initially, this turning reflects progress from telestial to terrestrial behavior, and later on to celestial behavior. As the sins of the telestial world are left behind, the focus falls ever more steadily upon the sins of omission, which often keep us from full consecration."[13]

The overwhelming message of the Atonement is the perfect love the Savior has for each of us. It is a love which is full of mercy, patience, grace, equity, long-suffering, and, above all, forgiveness. Repentance requires both turning away from evil and turning to God. Elder Dallin H. Oaks explains, "The purpose of the gospel is to transform common creatures into celestial citizens, and that requires change. . . . Repentance means more than giving up our sin. In its broadest meaning it requires *change.*"[14]

How do you know if you have repented and made the turn the full 180 degrees? Elder Robert D. Hales suggests you will "no longer look back with depression and hurt, but forward to the future with hope and joy and love for God, self, and all mankind."[15] Elder Scott suggests: "When memory of past mistakes encroaches upon your mind, turn your thoughts to the Redeemer and to the miracle of forgiveness with the renewal that comes through Him. Your depression and suffering will be replaced by peace, joy, and gratitude for His love."[16] Those three emotions of peace, joy, and gratitude will be felt if we have fully turned in the repentance circle. With full repentance we are able to look back on our former selves and recall our sins without pain; instead we feel at peace. Tad R. Callister has written:

"When we more fully understand the depths to which the Savior descended, the breadth to which he reached, and the heights to which he ascended, we can more readily accept that our own sins are within the vast sphere of his conquered domain. We then become believers, not only in the Atonement's infinite expanse, but in its intimate reach. The Savior's loving offer, 'My peace I give unto you' (John 14:27), transforms itself from some abstract hope to a profound personal reality."[17]

Along with that peace we also feel great joy. As with Alma the Younger, our happiness and joy will be exquisite. And as we experience that joy our gratitude for our Savior will increase along with our ability to continue to repent. Elder Hales instructs:

"In some quiet way, the expression and feelings of gratitude have a wonderful cleansing or healing nature. . . .

"Gratitude is also the foundation upon which repentance is built.

"The Atonement brought mercy through repentance to balance justice. . . .

"Mormon teaches us that there will always be suffering and sorrow in sin, but to repent only because we feel bad or because we have suffered or because we are sorrowful does not show that we understand the goodness of God.

" . . . When we express thankfulness to God and to his Son, Jesus Christ, we base our faith and repentance upon their forgiveness and their goodness."[18]

I knew my excommunicated friend had not experienced the true joy of repentance because she never expressed any gratitude to the Son of God for His suffering in my friend's behalf. When we have truly repented, that gratitude becomes so deep it almost feels like it will consume our flesh.

In a treatise on repentance two other questions should be considered: "How do I know that I need to repent?" and "What do I need to repent of?" Pretending everything is okay when it is not is a great drain on our energy, emotionally, spiritually, and physically. I would rather have my iniquities be known now than go on for forty or fifty more years trying to pretend to myself and others that I don't really have any. Thomas Carlyle observed, "The greatest of faults is to be conscious of none."[19]

One of the reasons that the last year of my life has focused so much more on repentance is because I have started a new practice in my life that has made a difference. Let me introduce this practice I have incorporated into my life from the annals of Church history.

I would like to talk of Martin Harris. As you know, Martin had a hard time realizing when he needed to repent. Through the Prophet

Joseph Smith the Lord would call him to repentance on numerous occasions, even calling Martin a wicked man, and yet Martin still did not get it. What did it finally take before Martin Harris was willing to humble himself and understand the correlation between his deeds and the Savior's pain? When the Lord called the three witnesses together to pray, Martin finally understood he needed to repent and told the others he was the reason they were not receiving the promised manifestation. Martin then left, repented, and was forgiven. A revelation did not bring Martin's repentance. Joseph verbally reprimanding Martin did not do it. What did it? What brought about Martin's true repentance? It was praying aloud with others. If you want to know if you need to repent of something, participating in vocal prayer with someone else will give you that information. I call this practice the repentance meter. It is then that sins, including little inconspicuous things that harden our hearts, will come to the forefront. Joseph Smith told us of Martin's experience, with repentance:

"I now left David and Oliver and went in pursuit of Martin Harris, whom I found at a considerable distance fervently engaged in prayer. He soon told me however that he had not yet prevailed with the Lord, and earnestly requested me to join him in prayer, that he might also realize the same blessings which we had just received. We accordingly joined in prayer, and ultimately obtained our desires, for before we had yet finished, the same vision was opened to our view, at least it was again to me, and I once more beheld and heard the same things, whilst at the same moment, Martin Harris cried out apparently in ecstasy of joy, ''Tis enough; mine eyes have beheld,' and jumping up, he shouted hosannah, blessing God, and otherwise rejoiced exceedingly."[20]

We too can cry out in ecstasy of joy, the ecstasy of experiencing true repentance. Full repentance, the kind of repentance that Martin Harris experienced, will put your life together. It can solve all of our complex spiritual, emotional, or physical weaknesses, even those that have been passed down from our upbringing. Through repentance, we can become the transitional figure in a family. We can absorb the effects of sin and break the cycle of whatever weaknesses our families gave us. The scriptures tell us that if we repent, turn to the Lord, and "restore four-fold for all [our] trespasses," then the Lord will revoke His vengeance (see D&C 98:47).

Like many of us, most of my weaknesses I struggle with are inherited. I had wonderful parents; they did wonderfully well, but, I still inherited some tendencies, some false core beliefs that cause problems in my present relationships. Isn't part of turning the hearts of the children to the fathers (see D&C 2) neutralizing any inherited ancestral sin? We can reach back to our fathers and mothers and repent of whatever they passed down to our generation and stop the consequences. We do not have to have grandmother's temper or mother's shyness, grandfather's alcoholism or dad's abuse. We truly become their saviors on Mount Zion as we turn to the Savior of all mankind. I can see my mother, father, and grandparents peeking through the veil, thinking, "Where are you going, my precious little child? Are you going to repeat my same mistakes and weaknesses?" And I also picture Him at the veil, imploring:

> *Where are you going, my precious little child?*
> *Turn from sin, you'll have peace.*
> *Turn to them, you'll find joy.*
> *Turn to me, and you're on your way to repent evermore.*
>
> *Where are you going, my precious little child?*
> *Just repent and you'll see.*
> *Turn from sin, turn to Him,*
> *Just repent and you're exalted,*
> *With them and me eternally.*

NOTES

1. Joseph Smith, as quoted by John Taylor, in *Journal of Discourses*, 26 vols. (London: Latter-day Saints' Book Depot, 1854–86), 24:197.
2. Theodore M. Burton, "The Meaning of Repentance," *Tambuli*, November 1988, 10.
3. Burton, "The Meaning of Repentance," 10–11, 13.
4. Burton, "The Meaning of Repentance," 11, 13.
5. Boyd K. Packer, "The Touch of the Master's Hand," *Ensign*, May 2001, 23–24.

6. Henry A. Smith, *Matthew Cowley: Man of Faith* (Salt Lake City: Bookcraft, 1954), 295.

7. Neal A. Maxwell, "Repentance," *Ensign*, November 1991, 30.

8. Richard G. Scott, "The Path to Peace and Joy," *Ensign*, November 2000, 25.

9. Tad R. Callister, *The Infinite Atonement* (Salt Lake City: Deseret Book, 2000), 175.

10. Boyd K. Packer, "Washed Clean," *Ensign*, May 1997, 10.

11. Callister, *The Infinite Atonement*, 178.

12. Spencer W. Kimball, "The Gospel of Repentance," *Ensign*, October 1982, 4.

13. Maxwell, "Repentance," 30; emphasis in original.

14. Dallin H. Oaks, "Repentance and Change," *Ensign*, November 2003, 37, 40.

15. Robert D. Hales, "The Lord Offers Everyone a Way Back from Sin," *Ensign*, November 1976, 26.

16. Scott, "The Path to Peace and Joy," 26.

17. Callister, *The Infinite Atonement*, 197.

18. Robert D. Hales, "Gratitude for the Goodness of God," *Ensign*, May 1992, 65, 63–64.

19. Thomas Carlyle, quoted in David O. McKay, *Gospel Ideals* (Salt Lake City: The Improvement Era, 1953), 13.

20. Joseph Smith, "History of Joseph Smith," *Millennial Star*, October 1843, 98.

"With . . . Utmost Assurance"

Kathleen H. Hughes

Doctrine and Covenants 123:17 states: "Let us cheerfully do all things that lie in our power; and then may we stand still, with the utmost assurance, to see the salvation of God, and for his arm to be revealed." I want to look at that sentence rather carefully, because I find several important concepts in it.

As I thought about our early sisters and their circumstances when Joseph wrote this counsel to them, I wondered how many of those who had been forced from their homes by Governor Lilburn Boggs's extermination order were cheerful—at least in the way we usually think of the term. I suspect that none of them tramped across the state of Missouri singing and smiling. They might have felt a little the way we do when we look at our monstrous "to do" lists or face the tantrum of a two-year-old in a busy supermarket. Are you like me? Sometimes do you say, "OK, I'll persevere, but please, don't ask me to be *perky* while I'm doing it"?

But maybe that's not what Brother Joseph had in mind. If *cheerful* doesn't necessarily mean a smiling face or a bubbly personality, then what was he asking of his people? Certainly attitude comes to mind. Our outlook on events makes a significant difference in how we respond. But

---

Kathleen H. Hughes was called as the first counselor in the general Relief Society presidency in 2002. She is a wife, the mother of three children, and the grandmother of nine.

is there more to cheerfulness than just an attitude? Are there different meanings we can apply to the word? As I thought and prayed about that question, two words kept coming to me: *courage* and *obedience*. In the context of the scripture, both seem to fit: "Let us courageously do all things that lie in our power" and "Let us obediently do all things that lie in our power." I even checked my dictionary and the transitive verb "to cheer" can be defined as "instilling courage." "Cheerful obedience" is listed as a common phrase referring to an ungrudging willingness.

With this expanded definition, I began to apply the Prophet's counsel to the Saints in a different way. Certainly, crossing Missouri in the winter and early spring—trudging through snow and mud and feeling the cold penetrate their scantily covered bodies—took amazing courage, along with tremendous faith and obedience. It would have been easy for our early sisters to have given up this religion that had already required so much of them. Of course, some did give up. But the ones we honor—many of them our progenitors—persevered through those and many other hardships to follow.

Sisters, so must we. Today we live in what President Hinckley has called "perilous times." In January of 2004, he went so far as to say, "I do not know that things were worse in the times of Sodom and Gomorrah."[1] That is a frightening thought to me. And I hope it is to you as well. As women of The Church of Jesus Christ of Latter-day Saints, the prophet has put us on notice that we must "stand strong and immovable." We, like our early sisters, must act with courage and respond obediently to the prophet of the Lord if we are to withstand the challenges of these difficult times.

And we might as well smile as we do it—at least as often as we can! Let's not forget that President Hinckley also reminded us at our recent general conference that these are *also* marvelous times when committed Latter-day Saints are doing great things. We may worry about our young people, but look at them. In spite of all they are facing, most are carrying on this great work, often at a higher level than we did at the same age. We should look to President Hinckley's optimism about our world, in spite of his concern about its sinfulness, and we should always remember the good humor, the wittiness—and, yes—the almost ever-present smile of dear Sister Hinckley. She taught us well the importance of enjoying the simple experiences of life without taking ourselves too seriously in the process.

Let's remember, it's part of the nature of this life that we face challenges. We must each find our ways to deal with them. Let me describe the circumstances of three women who are doing just that. Each woman is a composite of several sisters I have met. Do you hear elements of your own story in theirs?

Susanne is the mother of six children, ranging from preschool to missionary age. She and her husband made the decision many years ago to have Susanne remain a stay-at-home mom. Now that the children are older and the financial needs more pressing, they see this decision as a greater challenge than they ever expected. Still, after prayer and discussion, they feel they can continue to find ways to manage.

Louise is getting to be what we call a senior citizen. (I'll let you decide what age that is, but I've noticed that I keep pushing it back a little more each year.) She and her husband raised their family and, as they approached retirement, were excited about the opportunities that lay before them. But sadly, after a prolonged struggle, Louise's husband passed away. Now, left by herself to recreate a future left vacant by the death of her husband, Louise has determined that with the money from insurance, retirement, and savings, she can move forward. All the things they had planned as a couple are still possible—even a mission— although now she may have to do those things alone.

Finally, we meet Tamara. She is a young woman, now single because of divorce, and the mother of small children. She married prior to completing her education, but now she must work, and the opportunities for well-paying employment are not readily available. Child-care costs take much of her meager income. She knows she needs more education, and so, with support from family and friends, she has now enrolled at a community college to begin the daunting task of finishing school.

For me, these women represent the "everywoman" in each of us. Do the experiences each is having result in them being cheerful? Not if we define *cheerful* as "bubbly" or "effervescent." But in their lives—and in each of our lives as covenant women—I do see courage and the desire to be obedient to covenants made. And let me add that other decisions are possible in each of these examples. The point is that each has looked at her own circumstances, made a decision about what to do, prayed and received confirmation from the Holy Ghost, and now is following through—without looking back. I find a kind of deep-seated optimism in the trust required to do that, and that, to me, describes *cheerfulness.*

As women—sisters in Zion, if you will—I think it is also important for us to focus on the next phrase in D&C 123:17: "do all things that lie in our power." There are circumstances in our lives over which we may have little or no control, and I think this is difficult for many of us to accept. I happen to be a "fix-it" person. When something is wrong, my immediate response is to try to figure out a solution. But, I am slowly but surely learning, there are many things I cannot fix. I cannot convince some of today's entertainers that they are setting a bad example for my grandchildren, but I can teach my grandchildren not to follow their examples. I can't, all by myself, stop television networks from airing sitcoms that are frivolous at best and disgusting at worst, but I can turn those shows off and teach my children to do the same. I can't force my children and grandchildren to ignore the influence of all the evil this world offers them, but I can teach them to love the Lord and to obey His commandments. Certainly, our children must gain their own testimonies of the gospel and choose their own paths, but as a mother I will never give up on them, even when they make choices that give me pain.

Does this mean we don't try to change the world—that we don't let our voices be heard in defense of those principles of righteous living and behavior? Of course not! President Hinckley has told us that we must try. As covenant women, we are one of the last defenses in a world that is spiraling downward. But at the heart of the word *cheerful* is the idea of hope. Being cheerful, in that sense, is continuing to fight the good fight, no matter how frustrating and disappointing the effort becomes.

Remember our scripture—"do all things that lie in our power." In this context, I like to recall the Lord's admonition to Oliver Cowdery when he wanted to do some of the translating of the Book of Mormon plates. In Section 9 of the Doctrine and Covenants, the Lord counsels him to be patient, not to murmur, and then chastises him: "Behold, you have not understood; you have supposed that I would give it unto you, when you took no thought save it was to ask me. But . . . I say unto you, that you must study it out in your mind; then you must ask me if it be right" (vv. 7–8). This message is for each of us in many life circumstances. We are not helpless people who only react. There is much we can and must do as individuals and as groups to proclaim our beliefs and commitment to righteous behaviors and actions. But we should not act in ignorance. We should study the issues and concerns we have—all sides of them—to understand thoroughly what we should and can do. And then, I believe we ought to ask our Heavenly Father to *confirm* our thinking—our plan, if you will. Brashness and rashness too often bring anger and foil our attempts for doing good.

Finally, sisters, we must listen to the Prophet Joseph's other reminder: "stand still, with the utmost assurance, to see the salvation of God." Stillness is a dwindling commodity these days. As the world becomes louder and louder, we must consciously invite quiet into our lives. It is not usually discovered as we drive our children to lessons and sports; nor is it found in television or videos, or as we take care of the myriad chores that every woman faces each day. But it has never been more needed. A sister from Australia I met recently said that she often sees women in her area who are so busy they neglect their emotional and spiritual lives. We cannot do that, sisters, and survive in our world. We need to seek stillness to hear the whisperings of the Holy Spirit as we seek guidance for our lives and the lives of our families. We need stillness to feel the peace promised by the Savior as we deal with the vagaries of our lives. We need stillness to understand the meaning of the scriptures, our patriarchal blessings, and the blessings of the Atonement in our lives.

To find stillness, we usually have to *create* quiet for ourselves. It doesn't come looking for us. Do we, sometime during the day, perhaps before we go to bed, simply turn off the TV and radio? Do we help our children understand that quiet is needed in our lives (and in theirs) each day in order to give us opportunity to rest and feel refreshed? Do we, after we have prayed, continue to kneel, giving Heavenly Father His chance to speak to us? I know a woman who has taught her children that when they find her in her bedroom, kneeling, they must understand that she is talking to her Father in Heaven. It is not a time to interrupt. Her children have learned to respect that time (although occasionally her three-year-old will whisper in her ear, "When you're done talking to Heavenly Father, I need some apple juice"). The woman hopes and believes her children will, in time, learn their own need for that same peaceful time of communication.

Let me present two other thoughts that, at least in my mind, are related. Many years ago, my husband and I faced a dilemma and a decision that some of you may face. I was offered a grant to return to college to work on a graduate degree. The grant would not only pay my tuition and fees but would also provide a small living allowance as well. The dilemma we faced was that I was six months pregnant and we had two preschoolers at home. But would this opportunity ever be available to me again if I didn't act on it then? Dean and I talked about this for days. We made lists of the positive and negative sides to the question: Money we desperately needed would be available. My educational dream would not only be realized, but paid for as well. But I would have to leave my children more than I wanted to.

Dean agreed that he could stay home with the children for the summer while he wasn't teaching. (And by the way, I wasn't about to tell him what he was offering to get himself into.) During the school year, he could take care of the children in the evenings while a babysitter could take the kids *for a couple of hours a day* two or three times during the week *if we needed additional help*. But was it right to leave a new baby home for two or three nights a week, even if he was with his father? Was it right to leave my children with a babysitter at other times? Could we manage this new experience with all of its attendant unknowns—the things we could not even anticipate? How much stress would all this busyness place on our family? After we wrestled with these and other questions and determined solutions to the questions, we made our decision.

We decided not to pass up the opportunity. Then we took our decision to the Lord, asking Him to confirm the rightness of it *for us*. Now, sisters, that is the key phrase here: it was a decision for *our situation*, not for anyone else. We received our confirmation and moved forward. But for me, the decision sometimes brought pain. Women boldly asked, "Shouldn't you be home?" I began to doubt. And in doubting, I experienced sadness and, sometimes, just plain anger. In retrospect, perhaps I didn't fully trust the answer we had received. And yet, Dean and I had received our answer, and our confirmation had been strong.

We criticize each other for too many kinds of things—how we wear our hair, how we raise our children, whether we work or don't work. We must stop doing this to one another. There is a commandment and a principle in operation here. "Judge not, that ye be not judged" (Matthew 7:1) is the commandment, and the principle is that we do not have inspiration for another's life if it is not within our stewardship. President James E. Faust reminded us of this principle in a recent message: "Latter-day Saints, having received the gift of the Holy Ghost by the laying on of hands, are entitled to personal inspiration in the small events of life as well as when they are confronted with the giant Goliaths of life. If worthy, we are entitled to receive revelations for ourselves, parents for their children, and members of the Church in their callings. But the right of revelation for others does not extend beyond our own stewardship."[2] We should not have to announce to each other that we have prayed about our decisions. We certainly can assume that about one another.

One last thought. President Packer has admonished us to keep a sense of humor as we go about the tests in our lives.[3] I was reminded of the situation of a young mother I know. Her husband was out of work and had been for several months, and then she got in an accident and totaled their car. In the midst of all this she caught cold and *on her birthday*, her mouth broke out in canker sores—lots of them. She was in a lot of pain. In frustration, she told her husband, "I am a modern-day Job. I'm Jobette!" And they both began to laugh. After all, they knew that their lives were good, that they had great family and ward support, and things would get better. Her husband is back to work now, and things are better, and now she has a fourth little baby to keep her awake half the night. See, things did get better!

A dear friend once told me, "This is so hard that if we don't laugh, we'll cry. We're choosing to laugh." So should we!

Cheerfulness, courage, obedience, action, stillness, trust. That is a big order. But what comes of it? *"Utmost assurance"*—that calm, confident knowledge that God is with us, that trials have a purpose, that we have done all that is within our power—and that is enough. Then we will see the Lord's salvation at work in our lives and His arm will be revealed. Or in other words, we will know that we are not alone, that God's great strength is supporting us. There is no greater assurance than that, no better reason to feel cheerful.

I believe we can meet the expectations given us. We are covenant daughters of our Heavenly Father. He has promised us His peace, His presence in our lives. I like to think about President Spencer W. Kimball's comment to the women of the Church over twenty years ago. He said, "Much of the major growth that is coming to the Church in the last days will come . . . to the degree that the women of the Church reflect righteousness and articulateness in their lives and to the degree [they] are seen as distinct and different—in happy ways—from the women of the world."[4] We are different. We are becoming more so as we avoid the dress and language and behavior of the world. We will be more distinct as we demonstrate through the way we live and treat others that we are truly daughters of God.

Ask yourself whether you have enough "stillness" in your life, and if you do not—as most of us don't—look into your daily routine and see whether there isn't a little more room for the Lord. Be practical and specific about this. Don't schedule an hour of contemplation every day when you know that simply won't happen. But find some minutes, some strategies, and try to make a change. And when you reach the decisions that come from this time you spend with the Lord, will you take comfort in the source—and not spend so much time and energy doubting yourself? Finally, will you ask whether you are not only too hard on yourself but on your sisters as well? May I ask you to spend some minutes thinking about each of the women around you and letting go of any harsh judgments you may feel, whether you have ever communicated them or not? I honestly believe you'll find peace in this process—and good cheer.

Oh, and one last thing. Let's all smile a little more.

NOTES

1. Gordon B. Hinckley, "Standing Strong and Immovable," *Worldwide Leadership Training Meeting,* January 10, 2004 (Salt Lake City: The Church of Jesus Christ of Latter-day Saints, 2004), 20.
2. James E. Faust, "Communion with the Holy Spirit," *Ensign,* March 2002, 4.
3. See Boyd K. Packer, "Do Not Fear," *Ensign,* May 2004, 79.
4. Spencer W. Kimball, "The Role of Righteous Women," *Ensign,* November 1979, 103–4.

"Joy Cometh in the Morning"

Gayle Clegg

Our daughter Emily was in the hospital in another state caring for her two-month-old baby, who had an upper-respiratory infection, and her two-year-old, Ella, who had come to visit her little sister.

It had been a difficult five days for Emily. Her husband was in the middle of final exams in a rigorous graduate program. Two children under two years of age is a large enough challenge under the best of circumstances. Finances were limited, and no extended family lived nearby for support. Emily had been wearing the same clothes, sleeping in the hospital by her baby, passing the two-year-old back and forth to her husband as he was able to break away from school. She was fatigued and frightened and lonely.

Ella could not stay happy long in the confines of her baby sister's hospital room, so our daughter took her to the children's playroom. Ella was delighted with the toys and puzzles. Unfortunately, the attendant came soon after Ella arrived to close the playroom. Ella threw herself on the floor in a full-fledged two-year-old tantrum. Can you imagine her mother's embarrassment as she looked around at the other children,

Gayle Muhlestein Clegg has served as second counselor in the Primary general presidency. A graduate of the University of Utah in history and secondary education, she has served in various stake and ward leadership positions. She served with her husband, Calvin C. Clegg, as he presided over the Lisbon North Mission. They are the parents of five children and grandparents of fifteen.

who were very sick in contrast to Ella's robust countenance, leaving obe-diently, dragging IV poles behind them? Emily picked up her distraught child and hurried out of the hospital. They sat down somewhere on a bench far from the eyes and ears of strangers. Emily let Ella finish out the tantrum but was unable to contain her own emotions, which she had kept pent up for five days in the hospital. She gave way to her own good cry. Imagine Emily's surprise to have Ella look up at the tears now streaming out of her mother's eyes and say, with remarkable two-year-old compassion, "I'm sorry, Mommy. Don't cry. Ella happy now."

In our later phone conversation, we talked about how difficult it is to handle a tantrum, especially when it happens outside of our homes, where we have established some sense of routine for these breakdowns. Emily was grateful she didn't try to redirect Ella in the middle of a diffi-cult day. Emily was blessed with a moment of joy, even though she had miles to go in resolving the immediate concerns of her family.

So often joy is realized only in hindsight, in subtle, surprise interac-tions or through simple conversations each of us has had with our chil-dren, with ourselves, and with our Heavenly Father. In myriad ways daily, each of us can be "surprised by joy."

Our lives are a combination of disappointment, loneliness, and sor-row interspersed with memorable joyful moments. We can feel over-whelmed and discouraged and happy all in the same day or even the same hour. Joy and sorrow are twinborn, as is reflected in a scripture from Psalms: "Weeping may endure for a night, but joy cometh in the morning" (Psalm 30:5).

In late December I received a letter asking me to speak at Women's Conference. This wasn't the first time I had been asked to speak. The minute an invitation like this comes into your life, things are different. The topic is with you at the grocery store, as you go to sleep, as you push grandchildren on swings in the park, even as you work on Church assignments. In January and February I browsed the Church Web site, entering the word *joy* into the search engine. Talks with titles like "Finding Joy in Life" and "Joy in the Journey" came up. I took them to bed with me at night, usually finding them all crumpled in the covers in the morning. I looked in the Topical Guide, read each scripture suggested, and even wrote them all out on paper with my own observations and impressions. I felt good. I was learning and loving the time spent researching and pondering the topic of joy, and the deadline was far away—or so it felt.

But after returning from a training trip to Africa, on March 1, I found a letter from the First Presidency notifying me that I was assigned to speak in general conference a few weeks later. The Women's Conference talk left my mind—so did joy. After conference I saw that we were now into April, and there were just days left until the deadline for turning in a finished talk to the Women's Conference committee. My talk in general conference was about finishing, and I wondered if I could finish my Women's Conference talk, which was almost three times longer than the conference talk and which took several weeks to complete. I now had four days to the deadline.

Now what would you do? I am sure you would start writing. But not me. I looked at my home office, which is also my husband's home office, and saw stacks of papers, books, mail, candy wrappers, cups, and bedroom slippers. I thought, *I can't write in this mess.* In our mission we regularly told the missionaries in zone conference that the Spirit can't work in a dirty living space. So I proceeded to purge, clean, and organize. In this cleaning frenzy I found a number of notes and letters that I wanted to respond to from kind friends and neighbors, wedding invitations that needed attention, an overlooked bill in the stacks of paper, and much more. As I organized I started becoming distraught. I found tears running down my face as I thought of all the important things I needed to do, and now I was adding more necessary, good things to do to that long, impossible list.

After I had my meltdown, I remember talking to Heavenly Father just as though He were on the couch next to my piles of unorganized matter. I felt He was close and aware of my dilemma. He knew my heart and all my good intentions, and I knew the thank-you notes and even missed wedding gifts could wait for another time. He wanted me to start writing right where I was and, well, basically finish the message I had tried to deliver in conference. Why was I the last to learn?

I felt renewed, even though it was late at night. I knew joy could come in the morning. Off to bed I went and the next day—in the middle of the stacks—I wrote the fragments of conversations I'd had with people who smile through tears of frustration, sorrow, or difficulty.

A dear friend and I talked about her struggles with her grown children. She said that one morning she walked alone along the lakefront near her home in downtown Chicago. She was thinking about her children, her busy schedule, and a new Church calling. She was also thinking about a gospel lesson taught in Relief Society the previous day. The lesson was on joy. She began to wonder when she had last felt real joy in her life. She couldn't remember a recent time when she had not felt burdened and at her wit's end. As she walked she began to pray that she might remember when joy had lifted her spirit. As soon as this prayer formed in her mind, the sun burst from behind the overcast clouds in the sky to light up the lakefront and the beautiful Chicago skyline. As the sun lit the day, she experienced a deep and sudden affirmation that she was loved. That awareness gave her the power to cope with the problems at hand. Joy came quietly on a gray fall morning in Chicago to Mary.

Jesus Christ came into this world not only to suffer for our sins but to take upon Himself our struggles and pain. "And he shall go forth, suffering pains and afflictions and temptations of every kind; . . . he will take upon him the pains and the sicknesses of his people" (Alma 7:11). Why did He do this? "That his bowels may be filled with mercy, according to the flesh, that he may know according to the flesh how to succor his people according to their infirmities" (Alma 7:12).

He knows how we struggle, how we feel, and He knows how to send His love and comfort. He will do this as often as we are in a position to receive those messages. Joy comes from knowing He loves us and from seeking His help. Then we can experience those exquisite moments of joy when we are "encircled . . . in the arms of his love" (2 Nephi 1:15).

As mothers we raise our children to one day become worthy and righteous parents. Our little daughters cuddle and care for dolls. We catch them mothering, sometimes with our very own words. Now that can be embarrassing! They can't wait to become mothers. I have four lovely daughters and one daughter-in-law. All of them pursued professional careers at the university level, but their one great desire was to become mothers.

Imagine the devastation felt throughout our family when one of our daughters was told after years and years of medical procedures that she would not be able to bear children. I remember well that Easter morning when the last procedure failed and the diagnosis was given that she and her husband would be childless. My husband and I felt our own hearts breaking. We had been to the temple earlier and felt such love and confidence that this sweet daughter and her dear husband would have a family. So the contrary news that day was difficult. Easter seemed tainted. Our belief had not changed or been shaken. But our joy in the magnificent patterns of seasons and the glory of rebirth and spring buds and blossoms had temporarily drained away.

Soon after that dismal Easter Sunday, armed with the sweet reassurance from the temple, our daughter and son-in-law began the adoption process. Later we found out that a courageous unmarried young girl was struggling with a difficult decision about what to do with her pregnancy at the same time we were in the temple praying for a child. This young girl felt an answer to her prayers. She knew she would be giving her baby the gift of both a mother and a father who were sealed in a temple of the Lord. She knew she could be a mother, but she unselfishly decided that was not enough for this little one she was carrying. Our daughter and son-in-law now have two adopted children. Joy comes in waiting patiently on the Lord and trusting in His own patterns for fulfilling promises. We don't know how the answers will come to our prayers. But the Lord does, and His comfort is "joy in the morning."

Some months ago another one of our daughters wanted to make and keep a commitment to read her scriptures daily. She had heard a motivational and inspired speaker from an earlier Women's Conference say that just having them open in a conspicuous place would be an impetus for keeping this kind of a goal and a wonderful example for her children. She began reading in the Book of Mormon and after some days was in 2 Nephi chapter 11, pondering Jacob's testimony of his Redeemer. She left her scriptures open right on the end table by the couch, basking in the joy of reading the scriptures and in her heart thanking the speaker who had given such good advice.

She went to the laundry room and had begun sorting and loading the wash when her four-year-old boy, Logan, came running to find his mom—carrying the entire chapter 11 of 2 Nephi in his hands. He knew what his sixteen-month-old sister, Ashlyn, had done would be of grave importance to his mother, and that's why he reacted so quickly, just not quickly enough. Now what do you do to teach a sixteen-month-old not to tear up scriptures? Nothing, except put them in a spot where this won't be a possibility in the future. Did my daughter have good intentions? Yes. Was she trying to put into practice basic gospel habits? Yes. Was she trying to let her children see her reading the scriptures daily? Yes.

"Why is it so hard to do the right things?" she asked me in a conversation later that week. She told me that this was the chapter most marked in her scriptures. (She meant before the baby colored on it.) We talked about other attempts at keeping the commandments and all the things that can happen to impede our efforts. Think about going to the temple regularly. If a tire is going to go flat, it happens then. We both decided that the best we can do is to adjust and just keep trying to live each and every commandment. I don't think that it is the plan to have righteous intentions and desires be fulfilled easily or without obstacles. But we know that when the restored gospel of Jesus Christ and the blessings of living it are our focus, joy comes. Our conversation ended in a happy place—thinking about diligent Logan, who at least knew how important the scriptures were to his mom. Now that counts for a lot! The moment of the incident was painful to Tina, but after some time we could talk, we could laugh; we found ourselves surprised by joy.

Joy is a gift from God. Thinking back to Emily—crying right beside Ella and acknowledging her own emotions allowed for a sweet moment. Why? Because Emily did not try to control or force perfection in a two-year-old or in her own vulnerable self. The result was a joyful moment, a gift from God, a gift from the Holy Ghost. As we become joyful mothers, and it will take a lifetime to do this, our children can experience and become part of those moments. Becoming a joyful mother of children is what we are about, and making sure our days have as many joyful moments as possible is a righteous goal. The ripping apart of chapter 11 by little Ashlyn was a painful experience for her mother, but a conversation with someone who loved her and understood her and had experienced similar situations helped. Conversations with loved ones, friends, and, most important, Heavenly Father help us find joy. I was blessed by my conversation with Him several weeks ago when He helped me prepare for Women's Conference and create order out of chaos.

Think about learning a new skill. For me this was learning how to use a computer while in my fifties. I learned in the mission field when it became a necessity. Our numbers of missionaries dropped so dramatically when visas to enter Portugal became a challenge that the only answer to having enough missionaries in the field to preach the gospel was to put me right into the mission office. My skill level on the computer increased dramatically with each new task I had to assume.

Maybe we shouldn't whine about life becoming too hard. Maybe we are being given new opportunities to move to higher skill levels. I can now send documents with attachments, highlighted, edited, and so forth. I couldn't even turn a computer on a few years before. In our parenting, with every child we add to the mix in our family, the skill level of our mothering goes up a notch. And just as the difficulty of using a computer increases with new technical capabilities, so every obstacle you successfully overcome builds your ability to parent. The parenting challenges escalate as you safely navigate through the childhood years to arrive at the ultimate test of living with teenagers. If you keep learning and don't give up, you will get better and better. And then before you realize it, your teenagers turn into wives and husbands, mothers and fathers.

At the same time, your own parents, who have looked forward to those golden years, are finding them "laced with lead." Recently, a call came from one of my daughters telling us that my mother had fallen and broken her hip. Mom was in an ambulance and on her way to the hospital, and my father, whose short-term memory has disappeared, was with some kind strangers. For the winter Mom and Dad were in southern California, far from family members. My husband and I were with a daughter for the blessing of her newest baby in northern California. We quickly rented a car and started driving. All the way during the six-hour drive, we talked by cell phone to my father, his Samaritan helpers, and my mother in the hospital waiting for X-rays.

Upon arriving, we found Dad with a kind couple from the ward, who just happened to be the Relief Society president and former bishop. How relieved we were as they said Dad was doing well and had related in considerable detail his sweet two-year courtship with Mom. My husband stayed with my father, and I drove immediately to the hospital. I found Mother alone and in so much pain. But all she could talk about was her dear companion of sixty-five years. I spent my days and nights with my mother, coordinating two surgeries, transfusions, and reactions to medicine. My husband spent his days and nights with my father, reassuring him over and over that his Lillie would be all right. The transfer after a six-day hospital stay to the rehab center was difficult, and the drive home to Salt Lake with my father but without my mother was even more difficult. But as we prayed for direction and help, it came in surprising ways.

Our daughter Lisa said, "Mom, we will pack up the four children and come," and they did. Her strong and capable husband helped my mother return to Salt Lake City on the airplane so she could rehabilitate closer to family. Help came as we prayed with Dad and saw the anxiety disappear even before the "amen" was uttered. Help came as my husband and father gave a blessing of healing and comfort to Mom.

I have thought over and over again, *Why is life so complicated?* Why is there so much "unearned" suffering? Consequences are one thing, but old age is another; who earns that? In our heart of hearts we think we should be immune to some of our deepest heartache because we are trying so hard and contributing so much. Sometimes I think suffering is the answer to that arrogance. Do we search for food and water and firewood every day in a parched desert or seek safety in a crime-infested, concrete inner city? We do not. In some ways these trials reinforce how blessed our lives really are. Hospitals with tubes and tests and insurance tangles and all the things that kill the spirit outright while trying to heal the body are nevertheless a gift to us.

Joy comes through misery and heartache, through having a husband to love and protect your father through the night while you sit in a chair accumulating two days of body odor. It comes in the memories of childhood and your admiration for a remarkable, resilient mother whose caretaking you only now begin to comprehend. Joy comes in sharing these things with your children, who have learned much about making and keeping commitments from their grandparents.

The joy is not in arriving, but in getting better each time a new challenge is thrown your way, each time you learn in a new situation. Joy comes not from having a pain-free life but from conquering the obstacles, even when they are painful. If our children can see us enduring well and finding laughter, humor, and joy in the process, I think some of this will rub off on them. It will take many conversations, sometimes late at night, early in the morning, and all the times in between, but it is worth it. And as was prayed for in the temple dedication at Kirtland, we can pray that Heavenly Father will send us forth from our homes armed with His power, with His name upon us, with His glory round about us, and strengthened by His angels (see D&C 109:22). We pray through the night and joy comes in the morning in the form of a new perspective, a new energy and resolve, a conversation with someone who validates or mentors or just remembers.

Joy comes in the form of the natural world bursting with sunlight and patterning resurrection and rebirth just as we imagine birth will not be part of our life's experience. Joy comes through crying with the toddler whose tantrum pushed us to the limit in the first place. Joy comes in cyclical patterns and seasons. I find more humor in my daughter's dealing with a tantrum than in my own tears of frustration over wanting to help my father understand that I have not kidnapped him. Joy comes through our own gratitude for the Holy Ghost teaching and testifying of the plan of salvation.

PRAY NOT FOR LIGHT BURDENS
BUT FOR STRONG BACKS

———◆———

Ardeth G. Kapp

I have come to understand that to honestly pray for a strong back is a very courageous thing to do. The spiritual exercise required is not an easy course, but the promised blessings make it worthy of our total commitment—whatever the cost.

I learned of the importance of a strong back when I was about ten years old.

In the summertime after we had put in a full day's work, my father would take me down to the Belly River near the edge of our small Canadian town, Glenwood, not far from the Alberta Temple in Cardston. There he taught me to swim, and not only to swim but also to eventually jump off the pier into the cold water and swim upstream against the current. It wasn't easy. It took a lot of courage and determination—yes, and a lot of encouragement from my dad. As I recall, the water was always cold and it seemed very swift to me. What made it possible was my father swimming along beside me. I can hear his voice in my mind even today: "You can make it. Keep going." By the end of the summer, my back was stronger from the consistent effort and

---

Ardeth Kapp, an author and speaker and former member of the Brigham Young University faculty, served as the Young Women general president from 1984 to 1992. She accompanied her husband while he served as president of the Canada Vancouver Mission. Later, she served as matron of the Cardston Alberta Temple.

constant encouragement. The water in the river had receded, and the swiftness of the current had subsided considerably—but only after I had learned the lesson. There must be opposition if we are to develop strength. The river had served the purpose my father had in mind.

Today we must be prepared to swim upstream against the current. We face tremendous opposition. President Hinckley recently spoke of the challenges we face:

"In the Church we are working very hard to stem the tide of . . . evil. But it is an uphill battle, and we sometimes wonder whether we are making any headway. But we are succeeding in a substantial way. . . .

"We must not give up. We must not become discouraged."[1]

We must be strong enough to take a stand and to defend our values and courageous enough to speak up and speak out, to register our vote and stand firm for truth and righteousness under all circumstances. We are swimming upstream against a river of opposition. Our families need our constant encouragement, reassurance, love, and faith. We will never be given more than we can handle with the Lord's help.

When we pray for a strong back, we learn that it is through our covenants with the Lord that we are strengthened far beyond our natural ability. The testimony of President George Q. Cannon explains this relationship:

"When we went forth into the waters of baptism and covenanted with our Father in heaven to serve Him and keep His commandments, He bound Himself also by covenant to us that He would never desert us, never leave us to ourselves, never forget us, that in the midst of trials and hardships, when everything was arrayed against us, He would be near unto us and would sustain us."[2]

Honoring our covenants is the only way to swim against the escalating opposition of our day. When we are baptized and confirmed members of The Church of Jesus Christ of Latter-day Saints, we are given the gift of the Holy Ghost. Each week we have the blessing and opportunity to strengthen our backs and fill our spiritual reservoirs. We renew our covenants by partaking of the sacred emblems of the sacrament. We hear in our minds and hearts the words of the covenant to "*always* remember him and keep his commandments" so we can "*always* have his

Spirit to be with [us]" (D&C 20:77; emphasis added). This should be our most earnest desire. Nothing will prepare us to stand against the opposing forces like the blessing and power of the gift of the Holy Ghost.

The Holy Ghost is the messenger who provides personal revelation, communication, and connection with our Father in Heaven and our Savior, Jesus Christ. Suppose we were to make a pledge to do all within our power to keep the communication lines open. Suppose there were no compromise, no justification, and no excuse to tolerate any entice-ment of the world—in our entertainment or other activities—that would lessen the Spirit. Let us strive every day to avoid anything that could weaken our spirit and extinguish the light. Let us simply give it up, turn our backs, and walk away.

Elder David B. Haight helped us understand the strength that can be found in our temple covenants, not only for our backs but for every fiber of our soul. He said:

"A temple is a place in which those whom [God] has chosen [that's all of us] are endowed with power from on high—a power which enables us to use our gifts and capabilities with greater intelligence and increased effectiveness in order to bring to pass our Heavenly Father's purposes in our own lives and the lives of those we love. . . .

"Come to the temples worthily and regularly. . . . Freely partake of the promised personal revelation that may bless your life with power, knowledge, light, beauty, and truth from on high, which will guide you and your posterity to eternal life."[3]

A very significant chapter in the Book of Mormon tells of Father Lehi explaining to his son Jacob the need for opposition. "For it must needs be, that there is an opposition in all things. If not . . . , righteous-ness could not be brought to pass" (2 Nephi 2:11). The very purpose of this life is for us to be tried and tested in preparation for receiving all the blessings the Lord has promised to those who love Him and keep the commandments (see D&C 136:31).

We can expect trials and tribulation—they are an essential part of the great plan. Some we will experience because of our own mistakes—our sins—others merely as a part of living in mortality, and others because the Lord loves us and provides experiences that tend to our spiritual growth. "Whom the Lord loveth he chasteneth" (Hebrews 12:6). It doesn't seem so hard once we understand the purpose for the trials. There are times when we must trust in the Lord with all our hearts even when we don't understand (see Proverbs 3:5).

As Elder Bruce C. Hafen teaches: "If you have problems in your life, don't assume there is something wrong with you. Struggling with those problems is at the very core of life's purpose. As we draw close to God, He will show us our weaknesses and through them make us wiser, stronger."[4]

Some years ago, Sister Jana Taylor, one of our faithful sister missionaries who committed to be totally obedient and strive to have the Spirit with her always, had some very difficult, discouraging, and challenging times—not unlike a typical mission. If we are committed to really make a difference, it seems the adversary is right there to increase the swiftness of the current, to increase the opposition that would, if possible, carry us downstream away from our goal. The last day before Sister Taylor was to return home from her mission, she stood before her peers to testify. She had a glow about her, a confidence different than when she arrived. "I'm thankful," she said, "for the challenges and the trials. I'm thankful for every single hard day." She paused, then added, "And every day was hard. If it hadn't been, I wouldn't be who I am now. I am not the same person I was when I came out." And because of those hard times she will never be the same person again. She had, as the scripture says, grown up in the Lord (see D&C 109:15). And her growth will continue.

The writings of Orson F. Whitney help us understand the need for adversity:

"No pain that we suffer, no trial that we experience is wasted. It ministers to our education, to the development of such qualities as patience, faith, fortitude and humility. All that we suffer and all that we endure, especially when we endure it patiently, builds up our characters, purifies our hearts, expands our souls, and makes us more tender and charitable, more worthy to be called the children of God . . . and it is through sorrow and suffering, toil and tribulation, that we gain the education that we came here to acquire and which will make us more like our Father and Mother in heaven."[5]

While serving in the Alberta Temple the past three years, I witnessed many people with strong backs. Some were stooped with age, and others had traveled long distances to enter into the walls of the temple. I'm not talking about the physical distance of miles or kilometers, but about the inward desire, about their priorities and commitment.

One day a young woman, Annae Jensen, came to the temple to receive her endowment. I could feel the radiance of her spirit. This young woman was born without any arms—nothing beyond her shoulders. However, it was almost as though she had lost awareness of her physical limitation and had been spiritually compensated.

Recently, my husband and I received a call from Annae and Garath Jones telling us of their blessing and excitement. They are expecting their first baby in just a few months—the beginning of their posterity. Into my mind I saw this faithful young mother without arms and thought of her desire to cradle and love this special little spirit.

I asked Annae, knowing she would respond positively, "How have you learned to handle the hard things in life?"

In her usual happy, upbeat tone, she said, "I just say, 'Heavenly Father, what am I supposed to learn from this?' And if I don't learn it, I've missed an opportunity." While Annae is without arms, her back is strong. She has developed spirituality under what would appear to be adversity. There is no question—that baby will be enveloped in its mother's love.

We have many examples in the Book of Mormon that show us how the Lord intervenes when we turn to Him and how trials and tribulation turn to our good. When Alma and his people were being persecuted by Amulon—the leader of the priests of the wicked King Noah—they began to pray "mightily to God" (Mosiah 24:10). The voice of the Lord came to the people of Alma, just as it will come to us. The Lord said, "I know of the covenant which ye have made unto me; and I will covenant with my people and deliver them out of bondage" (Mosiah 24:13).

From this record we learn several very significant lessons. The steps toward the complete delivery from bondage did not happen all at once.

Alma's people were told that the Lord would first ease the burdens on their backs, even to the extent that they wouldn't even be able to feel them. The Lord did not take them away completely. There was a reason. It would not have allowed for the growth that took place as they learned to trust in Him. The Lord explained this when He said, "This will I do that ye may stand as witnesses for me hereafter, and that ye may know of a surety that I, the Lord God, do visit my people in their afflictions" (Mosiah 24:14). Learning to carry the burden with ease allowed them to testify from personal experience that the Lord does watch over us in our adversities.

We can follow these steps as we apply the pattern in our own lives.

"And now it came to pass that the burdens which were laid upon Alma and his brethren were made light; yea, the Lord did strengthen them that they could bear up their burdens with ease, and they did submit cheerfully and with patience to all the will of the Lord" (Mosiah 24:15).

And the lesson continues. Because of their great faith and patience through their trials, the Lord spoke to them again. He would not only ease their burdens, but as He had promised in the beginning, He would deliver them. "Be of good comfort," He said, "for on the morrow I will deliver you out of bondage" (Mosiah 24:16).

We know about our Savior, but it is often in our adversities that we truly find Him and know Him and love Him. In our times of trial, if we turn to Him, the Spirit bears witness that our Savior not only can, but will, ease our burdens. I can testify from my own experience in life that some of our heaviest burdens, disappointments, and heartaches can in time be replaced with "the peace of God, which passeth all understanding" (Philippians 4:7) while we "wait upon the Lord" (Isaiah 40:31).

In the words of Elder Neal A. Maxwell: "We can say: 'I know that [God] loveth his children; nevertheless, I do not know the meaning of all things' (1 Nephi 11:17.)

"There have been and will be times in each of our lives when such faith must be the bottom line: We don't know what is happening to us or around us, but we know that God loves us, and knowing that, for the moment, is enough."[6]

We have a work to do. Our trials and tests are an important part of our preparation. The Lord is counting on us.

Now let us consider the possibility of burdens on our backs of our own making. Some would think that filling up their daily planners with activities, events, and lists of good things to do defines them as being successful. But the burden slowly gets heavier and heavier, and without noticing it, they are in danger of being hunched over with osteoporosis. "Oh, my aching back" or "My back is breaking" might be the shout for relief at such times.

President Kimball's statement about life invites some thoughtful contemplation. He said, "Since immortality and eternal life constitute the sole purpose of life, all other interests and activities are but incidental thereto."[7] Now does that suggest there should be no time for fun, sports, scrapbooking—yes, shopping—and fancy parties? Of course not! We need to make time to do other worthwhile things, as long as they do not distract from what matters most, the very purpose of life.

Deciding what we really want is a very significant and powerful tool. It gives us a sense of being in control of our life, rather than being controlled. You see, the feeling of being controlled, or being out of control, is contrary to our divine nature. We cannot feel the Spirit or the peace and joy of each day when we are burdened beyond our ability to handle it all. I believe that, if it were possible, the adversary would keep us busily engaged in a multitude of good things in an effort to distract us from the few vital things that make all the difference.

Now this task of cutting back on some of our activities is really the hard part. It may seem as painful as cutting off an arm or a leg. It requires determination. Pruning is hard. It can come only after pondering and praying to know what we're willing to cut out to provide more time for what we really desire. I love Michael McLean's song "Hold On, the Light Will Come." As we look at our busy lives, we might sing, "Let go of some things so the light can come."

In the Book of Mormon, the writings of Zenos teach us the need for pruning, cutting back, and thinning the branches. The Lord of the vineyard looks at his dying trees and says to the dedicated servant what we might say when we have concerns for the welfare of our family: "What could I have done more in my vineyard? Have I slackened mine hand, that I have not nourished it? Nay, I have nourished it, and I have digged about it" (Jacob 5:47). We might echo his lamentation, saying, "I've worked all day long, even into the night. What else might I have done?" (see Jacob 5:47, 49). Sound familiar? It sounds like complete dedication, doesn't it? The servant then explains the problem. It wasn't a lack of dedication or hard work. The branches of the tree—like our over-crowded lives—had "overcome the roots," or grown faster than the roots, "taking strength unto themselves" and leaving the roots under-nourished (Jacob 5:48). We are not left to wonder what nourishes our own roots. It is time spent together. It is in following the words of the prophet—including the guidance given in "The Family: A Proclamation to the World."

The first responsibility to ease the burden on our backs rests with us. We must take time to *ponder,* to *pray,* and to *prune.* Perhaps it would be a good idea to ponder the question Nephi was asked when he was swept away by the Spirit in chapter 11 of 1 Nephi. We learn that Nephi must have spent some time thinking and pondering, because when the Spirit said to him, "What desirest thou?" Nephi was prepared with an answer. If we were asked in answer to our prayers, "What desirest thou?" would we be ready with an answer? Do we know what it is we really want? Not only what we want, but more importantly, what we want to have happen and why?

I can hear one of my darling nieces say something like, "What I most desire is to make it through the whole day without being impatient or raising my voice. Or just to catch my breath for a few moments before the troops come home. Or just to feel loved, appreciated, and in con-trol." Certainly those desires are reasonable and real, but when time is provided to get an eternal perspective and see beyond the urgencies of the day, our perspective changes. We are willing, even anxious, to do some pruning, some cutting back, if that would provide more time for the things we most desire.

I have been impressed with the moving account of Emma Smith's most earnest desires at a very challenging time in her life. We read that when her husband decided to return to Carthage:

"Emma asked [him] to give her a blessing. The Prophet told her to write the best blessing she could desire. He promised her that upon his return, he would sign it for her."[8]

That tells us something about the confidence the Prophet had in the desires of Emma's heart. He never returned from Carthage. But we have a record of her desires at that fateful time in her life. She wrote ten things she most desired. The first sentence used the words "I . . . crave," and the following nine, "I desire." I would like to share with you her first and last statements.

"First of all that I would crave as the richest of heaven's blessings would be wisdom from my Heavenly Father bestowed daily, so that whatever I might do or say, I could not look back at the close of the day with regret, nor neglect the performance of any act that would bring a blessing."

She completed her list of ten with this statement: "Finally, I desire that whatever may be my lot through life I may be enabled to acknowledge the hand of God in all things."[10] Under the most severe testing during that crucial time in the history of the Church, Emma Smith's desires tell us something of the strength of her back.

There are courageous women among us today and those who will follow after us when we do our part. In the poetic words of a Mormon pioneer, Vilate C. Raile, we see this legacy of faith passed from one generation to the next.

> *They cut desire into short lengths*
> *And fed it to the hungry fire of courage,*
> *Long after—when the flames died—*
> *Molten gold gleamed in the ashes.*
> *They gathered it into bruised palms*
> *And handed it to their children*
> *And their children's children.*[11]

We are on the Lord's errand. We can have His Spirit to be with us always, with angels round about us to bear us up. I honor my great-grandmother Susan Kent Greene and her unwavering testimony.

In 1835 Susan married Evan M. Greene and soon after went to

Kirtland to live. They were among the first of the Mormon fugitives at Mount Pisgah, Iowa, in the early spring of 1846. We read:

"As soon as Evan pitched the tent he left his wife and their little ones while he went with his team and wagon to aid in bringing forward some of the saints who were without means of their own. Unfortunately for Susan she had no near neighbors. Almost as soon as her husband had gone the eleven-month-old baby became ill. The baby rapidly grew worse, and after a few days died in its mother's arms. This occurred on a dark and stormy night accompanied by loud thunderbolts and vivid lightning flashes. All she could do was to pray that the Lord would not forsake her, but would send someone to help her, which prayer was answered. A young man came to the door and spoke words of pity and comfort. In the morning he made a coffin and dug a grave for the baby and buried it. Susan had to prepare the little body for its last rest, herself."[12]

This was only the beginning of the tests that were to follow.

Evan and Susan arrived in Utah, having endured much. She wrote the following on the first page of her journal dated February 3, 1875:

"I make this covenant to do the very best I can, asking God for wisdom to direct me in that I may walk with Him in all righteousness and truth. I much desire to be pure in heart that I may see God. Help me, Lord, to overcome all evil with good. Signed: Susan K. Green.

"This covenant with the writings on this page is written with my blood and I have not broken my covenant and trust shall not. Signed: Susan K. Greene."[13]

I look forward to one day meeting my great-grandmother and pray that I can tell her that I have followed her path and kept the faith and all of the covenants.

With an understanding of the purpose of life, of our promised blessings as women of the covenant, and of the need for opposition, let us be grateful that God allows us to struggle, to cry, and to feel pain. Else how could we comfort others in their tribulation? (see 2 Corinthians 1:6).

Let us be grateful to know about hurt and healing. Else how could we know the Healer, the Great Physician, who invites us to come unto Him and be healed? (see D&C 42:48).

Let us be grateful to know about fear and faith. Else how would we recognize the light of faith after the dark night of fear? (see D&C 6:22–23).

Let us be grateful to know about discouragement and encouragement. Else how could we reach out and take another's hand in empathy, understanding, and love? (see John 13:34).

Let us be grateful to know about offenses and forgiveness. Else how could we ever begin to appreciate the Atonement? (see Alma 7:11).

Let us be grateful for His infinite love and hear in our minds and hearts His words of comfort: "What I say unto one I say unto all, be of good cheer, little children; for I am in your midst, and I have not forsaken you" (D&C 61:36).

I testify that in those difficult times, when our crosses seem unbearable, He who carried the cross for all of us—our Lord and Savior Jesus Christ—will sustain us, be with us, and will be the strength in our backs when we turn to Him in earnest and fervent, sincere and humble prayer.

NOTES

1. Gordon B. Hinckley, "Standing Strong and Immovable," *Worldwide Leadership Training Meeting,* January 10, 2004 (Salt Lake City: The Church of Jesus Christ of Latter-day Saints, 2004), 20.
2. George Q. Cannon, *Gospel Truth: Discourses and Writings of President George Q. Cannon,* ed. Jerreld L. Newquist (Salt Lake City: Deseret Book, 1974), 134.
3. David B. Haight, "Come to the House of the Lord," *Ensign,* May 1992, 15–16.
4. Bruce C. Hafen, "The Atonement: All for All," *Ensign,* May 2004, 97.
5. Orson F. Whitney, quoted in Spencer W. Kimball, *Tragedy or Destiny* (Salt Lake City: Deseret Book, 1977), 4.
6. Neal A. Maxwell, *"Not My Will, But Thine"* (Salt Lake City: Bookcraft, 1988), 119.
7. Spencer W. Kimball, *The Miracle of Forgiveness* (Salt Lake City: Bookcraft, 1969), 2.
8. In *Relief Society Courses of Study, 1985* (Salt Lake City: The Church of Jesus Christ of Latter-day Saints, 1984), 199.
9. In *Relief Society Courses of Study,* 199.

10. Cited in Asahel D. Woodruff, *Parent and Youth* (Salt Lake City: Deseret Sunday School Union Board, 1971), 124.

11. Lula Greene Richards, "Life Sketch of Susan Kent Greene," typescript, in author's possession.

12. Quoted in Ardeth Greene Kapp, " 'I Shall Know They Are True': Susan Kent Greene," in *Heroines of the Restoration*, ed. Barbara B. Smith and Blythe Darlyn Thatcher (Salt Lake City: Bookcraft, 1997), 87–88.

"Peace Like a River"

Heidi S. Swinton

A few years ago, a film crew and I climbed into a rented green van at the Boston airport and set off up the coast to trace the unfolding of the Restoration. It was March—cold and blustery, with sheets of ice and snow. We started in Topsville, Massachusetts, where Joseph Smith's ancestors settled and had a pew in the church on the commons. Taking each historic site in sequence, we then drove to Sharon, Vermont, the birthplace of the Prophet Joseph. It was a serene, somewhat isolated setting.

Next we went to Palmyra to that grand stand of trees—the Sacred Grove. I had been there several times. With each visit I felt the spirit of that setting. There, young Joseph Smith spoke to the Father and the Son, face-to-face. And reality changed forever. Church President Joseph F. Smith described it as "the greatest event that has ever occurred in the world, since the resurrection of the Son of God from the tomb and his ascension on high."[1] Think about it. From that moment Joseph Smith

---

Heidi Swinton is an award-winning author and screenwriter of LDS life and history, including America's Choir: A Commemorative Portrait of the Mormon Tabernacle Choir; American Prophet: The Story of Joseph Smith; Sacred Stone: Temple on the Mississippi; *and* Trail of Hope: The Story of the Mormon Trail. *She is a wife, mother, and grandmother and currently serves as a member of the Relief Society general board.*

knew more about our Father in Heaven and our Savior, Jesus Christ, than anyone alive.

The Restoration is marked by significant settings like the Sacred Grove that string across America. But it is much more than rebuilt cabins, monuments, and places on a map. Joseph Smith described the Restoration as "a work that God and angels have contemplated with delight for generations past; that fired the souls of the ancient patriarchs and prophets; a work that is destined to bring about the destruction of the powers of darkness, the renovation of the earth, the glory of God, and the salvation of the human family."[2]

There is grandeur in the Restoration.

Elder Jeffrey R. Holland has taught:

" 'The simple truth of the matter is that without the Restoration, the great Plan of Salvation would be forever thwarted . . . and the full blessings of the Atonement . . . would have been lost to almost all of God's children, past, present and future.

" 'Almost all the work for the living and for the dead falls on the shoulders of the Dispensation of the Fulness of Times. Not Adam's time, or Noah's time, or Abraham's time . . . nor Peter's or Paul's in the Meridian of Time. Those churches and those efforts ended in disarray and decay, and they ended quickly.

" 'Without the Prophet Joseph Smith, we . . . would be left with fragmented scripture, unrelated doctrine, conflicting opinions, uninspired practices that over time became binding traditions.

" 'This is what existed prior to 1820.' "[3]

As it falls on our shoulders, our responsibility in the Restoration is sobering. We have work and responsibility that is ours alone. And, increasingly, we are standing alone. In my earlier life I was a news junkie; but I can hardly stand to watch or listen to the rancor today. Crisis management has become a profession; there are few if any happy endings at the movies; television sitcoms herald what is clearly the underbelly of society; power has become a commodity brokered, sold, and abused; and recent studies show that stress is the reason we are fat. I thought it was the brownies I eat for breakfast.

President Harold B. Lee said: "We have been called to difficult tasks in a difficult age. . . . The converging challenges posed by war, urbanization, dilution of doctrine, and domestic decay surely provide for us the modern equivalent of crossing the plains, enduring misunderstanding, establishing a kingdom throughout the world in the midst of adversity."[4]

No war, threat of terror, disappointment, absence of decency, morality, or civility can penetrate the peace promised by the Lord. That peace came with the Restoration of the gospel of Jesus Christ. The ancient prophet Elisha understood peace and tumult. When he and his young servant arose early and went forth, "an host compassed the city both with horses and chariots. And his servant said unto him, Alas, my master! how shall we do?" (2 Kings 6:15). Can't you just see the servant thinking, *This is not good. Two of us, so many of them?* Elisha responded with calm: "Fear not: for they that be with us are more than they that be with them" (6:16). And then he asked that the Lord open the young man's "eyes, that he may see. And the Lord opened the eyes of the young man; and he saw: and, behold, the mountain was full of horses and chariots of fire round about Elisha" (6:17). So it is with us. As members of the Church of Jesus Christ, we gather in wards, stakes, and districts around the world, and we are promised, "My Spirit shall be in your hearts, and mine angels round about you, to bear you up" (D&C 84:88). With a testimony of the Lord and His ways comes peace.

I learned much more about peace in Harmony, Pennsylvania, during the tour of Church sites I mentioned earlier. I was not particularly interested in going to Harmony. In my mind I had already jumped ahead to Kirtland, Ohio. Kirtland was a happening place: Joseph saw the Lord Jesus Christ standing upon the breastwork of the pulpit in the temple at Kirtland; angels walked on the roof of the temple in the middle of the day.

But first the trip to Harmony. Harmony was a quiet little burg when Joseph Smith lived there and translated the gold plates. Today, it's not even a town. Its name, though, holds great significance, for here it was that heaven and earth came into harmony. A statue stands alone on a grassy plot—no Church missionaries, no visitors' center. It is isolated from the world. There is nothing but the Susquehanna River. When we left the highway in the van, we rumbled down a potholed dirt road past the cemetery where Joseph and Emma's infant son is buried, crossed railroad tracks, and stopped in a marshy field. We got out and walked to a thicket of trees that edged the river.

And then we walked down to the water.

I wasn't prepared for Harmony. In ancient times Moses heard the voice of God from the burning bush: "Put off thy shoes from off thy feet, for the place whereon thou standest is holy ground" (Exodus 3:5). The Susquehanna setting is also holy ground. In another dispensation, Saints had stood at the waters of Mormon and were "baptized in the name of the Lord" and felt His Spirit pour out of the heavens upon them (Mosiah 18:10). It was the same for me at that river.

There, the Aaronic Priesthood was conferred by John the Baptist upon his "fellow servants." That priesthood "holds the keys of the ministering of angels, and of the gospel of repentance, and of baptism by immersion for the remission of sins" (D&C 13:1). Not long after, the Melchizedek Priesthood was restored with the authority to bestow the gift of the Holy Ghost, ordain, heal, bless, comfort, and seal for the eternities. Oliver Cowdery referred to that time as "days never to be forgotten" (JS–H 1:71, footnote).

Today, peace still ripples down the Susquehanna. I felt it—I who had my eyes on Kirtland. And isn't that the way it is? The Lord's ways are "not in the wind" but in the "still small voice" (1 Kings 19:11–12). I had been looking for what I thought were the grandstand moments of the Restoration to compete with the grandstand actions of the adversary. Instead, I found "peace . . . like a river" (Isaiah 66:12)—steady, directed, clear, catching and reflecting the light from above.

These words of Isaiah point clearly to our source of peace: "For thus saith the Lord, Behold, I will extend peace . . . like a river."

The Restoration is all about that peace. It is about knowing that, notwithstanding the anxieties afloat in the world, Jesus Christ, our Savior, suffered and atoned for our sins. He lives. He loves us and He knows us. He has gone "to prepare a place for [us]" (John 14:2). The holy priesthood of God has been restored to the earth, and we are blessed beyond earthly measure by that authority. We have covenanted to take His name upon us. Many of us have made further covenants in the holy temple, the house of the Lord. With this knowledge comes peace. Jesus Christ said, "My peace I give unto you: not as the world giveth, give I unto you. Let not your heart be troubled, neither let it be afraid" (John 14:27).

Peace comes from the Spirit testifying to our spirit, "Happy day! All is well!"[5] Think of the context of that familiar phrase. The Saints were crossing the plains; they were burying family members and walking on. I can't imagine the challenge. And yet they "press[ed] forward with a steadfastness in Christ" (2 Nephi 31:20). They relied on the words of the Lord: "Let not your heart be troubled, neither let it be afraid" (John 14:27). Why? Because of revealed truth—that He lives.

President Boyd K. Packer described looking at a two-year-old grandson and thinking:

"'What kind of a world awaits him?' . . . Everywhere we go fathers and mothers worry about the future of their children in this very troubled world. But then a feeling of assurance came over me. My fear of the future faded."[6]

Assurance and peace, they are the same.

Still, the adversary is attacking the very heart of God's plan for His and our family. When our prophet, seer, and revelator Gordon B. Hinckley presented the "The Family: A Proclamation to the World" in 1995 at the general Relief Society meeting, he calmed our fears for the family with these prophetic words:

"Sacred ordinances and covenants available in holy temples make it possible for individuals to return to the presence of God and for families to be united eternally. . . .

" . . . The sacred powers of procreation are to be employed only between man and woman, lawfully wedded as husband and wife. . . .

" . . . Parents have a sacred duty to rear their children in love and righteousness. . . .

"The family is ordained of God. Marriage between man and woman is essential to His eternal plan."[7]

Jesus Christ said, "In the world ye shall have tribulation: but be of good cheer; I have overcome the world" (John 16:33). Think about it. Peace comes in having a witness of the Spirit that He, the Lord Jesus Christ, has already overcome the world—for us. In knowing that, we know the adversary is fighting a losing battle. This work will march on just as the Susquehanna flows to the ocean.

What gets in the way of our peace? For many of us it is busy lives. We have perfected marathon mothering—the daily race of getting to the finish line, one step in front of the other, grabbing a drink before we pass out, not thinking about our time because we know we are so off pace. So we just plan to run faster and, next time, get running clothes that match the number so we'll look better. We are all too busy: too busy to "meet together oft" (Moroni 6:5) as the scriptures say; too busy to read the scriptures; too busy to ponder their meaning in our lives and to find the direction, solace, and peace that we so desperately need. President Gordon B. Hinckley has counseled us, "There is a better way than the way of the world. . . . It is so tremendously important that the women of the Church stand strong and immovable for that which is correct and proper under the plan of the Lord. . . . They must begin in their own homes."[8]

Does the Spirit of peace abide in our homes? The Susquehanna River was home to the Lord's restored peace. We invite the Spirit into our homes by the way we live the Lord's commandments, by our priorities, and by the way we follow the prophet. He has asked us to hold regular family prayer, to have family time at dinner, to hold family home evening and counsel together, to study the scriptures and the words of our living prophets as a family, to bear testimony to our children and grandchildren, nieces and nephews. We need to help them know that we know that Jesus Christ is the Redeemer of the world, that we are accountable to the Lord for our actions, that our Father in Heaven loves us, and that through the mission of our Savior Jesus Christ we can return to Him. My question is this: How are we doing? What can we do differently so that peace abides in our homes?

We are counseled in the scriptures to "lift up an ensign of peace" (D&C 105:39). We are that ensign. People watch us and they will be watching more if, as President Spencer W. Kimball counseled, we are "different—in happy ways."[9] They will watch more if we distinguish ourselves by dressing modestly and being examples to our daughters, who also watch our ways. They will watch more if we are treating one another with charity, forgiving and then forgetting, acting with integrity and honor, and living providently. These bring peace.

Peace comes by inspiration. When the Lord said to troubled Oliver Cowdery, "Did I not speak peace to your mind?" (D&C 6:23), He taught us a great lesson. We must learn to hear and feel the language of the Spirit. Then we will know when prayers are answered and when the Spirit is directing us.

A few years ago I was writing about the Prophet Joseph Smith. I did not view myself as the obvious choice for that assignment, as servants of the Lord go. My credentials were more being "steadfast and immovable" (Mosiah 5:15) than being an expert on the Joseph Smith story. I had to become an expert—on the job. When you think about it, most of our work for the Lord is like that. He calls us to do things so that we can learn how to do them. I gave days and nights for more than two years to study and write about Joseph Smith. It was consuming. I love him as the prophet of the Restoration. I came to understand his single-minded devotion to the cause of Christ, his willingness to give his life for the work of the Lord. I testify to you that he was and is a prophet of God.

I wanted, more than anything, to get the story of his life right—for him. I wanted to tell of his nobility, goodness, devotion to the Savior. I could almost hear him testifying of the work of the Lord. But here's the rub. When I finished with my writing and watched it move forward to print and screen, there was an ache in my soul. I felt it wasn't good enough.

Day after day I walked in the cemetery near my home thinking that all those pioneers buried row upon row could somehow help me. (It was an odd place to search for peace.) I struggled with the thoughts that I had let Joseph Smith down. Worse, I had let the Lord down. Yet I had tried so hard. Perhaps some of you identify. You too may have unresolved issues or efforts in your own life. You've done all you can do. Your desires are righteous. You've put them before the Lord and hoped for resolution.

And there's the lesson. We seek resolution, saying, "Fix this, Lord," instead of seeking peace.

To the beleaguered Saints clutching to life in tents and dugouts along the bank of the Mississippi in 1840, the Prophet Joseph Smith said, "I obligate myself to build as great a temple as ever Solomon did if the Church will back me up." And then this personal desire: "And if it should be . . . [the] will of God that I might live to behold that temple completed and finished from the foundation to the top stone I will say, 'Oh Lord it is enough. Lord let thy servant depart in peace.'"[10] It seems a fair request from a man whose whole life was given to the Restoration, who had faced mobs, been tarred and feathered, experienced repeated financial reverses, had friends turn against him, and been unjustly jailed time and again. Would he live to see the temple completed and the power of the priesthood used to unite families for the eternities? No.

Two years later, in May 1842, with the temple not yet above ground and baptisms for the dead being conducted in the cellar font, Joseph Smith knew the Lord was not going to grant him his worthy wish. Without waiting to complete the temple, he invited nine men into his red brick store and gave them the endowment. Over the next two years, nearly sixty men and women received their endowments from the Prophet Joseph. Bathsheba Smith, my third great-grandmother, was one of them. She wrote at the time, "[We felt privileged] to be led and taught . . . by the prophet himself who explained and enlarged wonderfully upon every point."[11] The work of the Restoration would roll on without him. Peace is often spoken in these words: "Not my will, but thine, be done" (Luke 22:42).

So there I was, walking in the cemetery, weeping as I talked out loud to the Lord, and knowing it was too late for Him to fix the book or documentary. The men mowing the lawns were looking at me. They thought I was talking to myself. They thought I was crazy. And then in this obscure and unlikely setting, a thought came to me. (Isn't that the language of the Spirit?) It was this: *Joseph Smith wanted more than anything to see the temple completed. He had to give the endowment in the red brick store. It wasn't the way he wanted it, but it worked.* It worked for the Restoration. It worked for Joseph—he did all the Lord asked of him. So had I. "My peace I give unto you" (John 14:27) still sounds in my soul. As Joseph Smith rode to Carthage, he turned in his saddle to catch one last glimpse of Nauvoo from up on the bluff, the half-finished temple before him, the Mississippi River winding along. Then he rode on to Carthage, "calm as a summer's morning" (D&C 135:4). Circumstances had not overwhelmed his soul. Peace was his. It can be ours.

Our prophet has asked us to do the very best we can;[12] and the Lord has urged us to "be still and know that I am God" (D&C 101:16). I knew my offering had worked because I had felt it. Faced with the reality of his shortened tenure, Joseph Smith did the very best he could in the unfolding of the Restoration. And it worked.

The Lord has called us to "stand . . . in holy places, and be not moved" (D&C 87:8). The Restoration has made a mark in places all over the world, through temples, in particular. Elder Dallin H. Oaks "borrow[ed] a metaphor from the familiar world of athletic competitions" in describing the latter days. "We do not know when this game will end, and we do not know the final score, but we do know that when the game finally ends, our team wins."[13]

If anyone should be at peace in their souls, it is us. We know the Lord is on our side. He has overcome the world—for us. Not everything in our lives will turn out the way we want it, but if we give place for and honor to the Restoration in our lives, it will work. And we will have peace—flowing from us—like a river. As the Apostle Paul said, "The peace of God, which passeth all understanding, shall keep your hearts and minds through Christ Jesus" (Philippians 4:7).

NOTES

1. Joseph F. Smith, *Gospel Doctrine* (Salt Lake City: Deseret Book, 1939), 495.
2. Joseph Smith, *History of The Church of Jesus Christ of Latter-day Saints*, ed. B. H. Roberts, 2d ed. rev., 7 vols. (Salt Lake City: The Church of Jesus Christ of Latter-day Saints, 1932–51), 4:610.
3. Jeffrey R. Holland, "Quotes by members of the Twelve during new mission presidents seminar," *Church News*, July 6, 2002, 13.
4. Harold B. Lee, *Teachings of Presidents of the Church: Harold B. Lee* (Salt Lake City: The Church of Jesus Christ of Latter-day Saints, 2000), 214.
5. William Clayton, "Come, Come, Ye Saints," *Hymns of The Church of Jesus Christ of Latter-day Saints* (Salt Lake City: The Church of Jesus Christ of Latter-day Saints, 1985), no. 30.
6. Boyd K. Packer, "Do Not Fear," *Ensign*, May 2004, 77.
7. "The Family: A Proclamation to the World," *Ensign*, November 1995, 102.

8. Gordon B. Hinckley, "Standing Strong and Immovable," *Worldwide Leadership Training Meeting,* January 10, 2004 (Salt Lake City: The Church of Jesus Christ of Latter-day Saints, 2004), 20.

9. Spencer W. Kimball, "The Role of Righteous Women," *Ensign,* November 1979, 104.

10. *The Words of Joseph Smith: The Contemporary Accounts of the Nauvoo Discourses of the Prophet Joseph Smith,* comp. and ed. Andrew F. Ehat and Lyndon W. Cook (Provo: Brigham Young University, 1980), 418.

11. Bathsheba Smith, in "Latter-day Temples," *Relief Society Magazine,* April 1917, 185–86.

12. See Hinckley, "Standing Strong and Immovable," 21.

13. Dallin H. Oaks, "Preparation for the Second Coming," *Ensign,* May 2004, 10.

AWKWARD PRAYERS

Louise Plummer

A few summers ago I taught in a BYU children's writers' workshop with other writers from diverse places and backgrounds. One of these writers was a woman from New York named Joan, whose books I admired for their spunky characters and comic timing. Over the week Joan and I became friends. The night before the last day, all the workshop faculty and staff, including Joan, gathered at a professor's house for dinner. When we were seated, I was called upon to say the blessing over the food. I don't like to pray in public, if the truth be known. I always feel like I've been trapped into an assignment for which I'm completely unprepared. Give me ten minutes and I could write a really eloquent blessing over the food, but when I'm asked off the cuff I feel like a fool. I blundered through that particular prayer, knowing from experience my main job was to be grateful for the food and the hands that prepared it, then ask God to bless it for our good, and get on with it. If I had to grade my prayer that night, I would give it a B-minus.

I think that prayer was important for what followed the next day. The workshops ended and I gave Joan a ride to the hotel. We began talking and ended up sitting in my car with the motor and the air

Louise Plummer is a writer and an associate professor of English at Brigham Young University. She is married to Tom and has four grown sons. She lives in Salt Lake City, Utah.

conditioning running. We talked about writing, about publishers and editors and money. We talked about our families. We talked for an hour, and then Joan said to me. "Let's pray together."

Now is the time to mention that I think prayer is more intimate than sex. I only pray about anything I care about with Tom, my husband. Sometimes I pray with my visiting teaching companion before we visit, but only if she suggests it, and I haven't had a visiting teaching companion in ten years.

"Okay," I said to Joan. "How do you want to do it?" I was hoping that she'd offer to say the prayer—it was her suggestion after all—and I would simply listen. I am good at passive prayer. This was not to be.

"I'll say a prayer," she said, "and then you say a prayer."

I nodded dumbly.

She grasped my hand, closed her eyes, and addressed God. I closed my eyes and listened as she thanked God for our new friendship and for our lives and then asked Him to bless me with every blessing I could imagine wanting. She prayed for my career and for my family. She spoke easily with God. She spoke fast and confidently. It was, as I told Tom later, like a laying on of hands. I knew I'd been blessed.

When it was my turn, I stepped into the breech as best I could and prayed for her. She was worried about selling her house to move to another. I prayed that the move would go smoothly. It seemed to me that I wasn't speaking with the same ease with the English language that she did; indeed, that I wasn't as practiced at prayer as she was. I gave it my best shot, because I wanted the best for my new friend.

A year later, I wrote Joan and told her I was coming to New York, and asked her if she would like to have lunch with me. First, we were going to meet at a restaurant in Manhattan but then she called me at my hotel and suggested I come to her house, "That way," she said, "We can pray."

"Okay," I said. "That would be nice." This time I had time to prepare what I wanted to say, what I wanted for Joan and for our friendship. I felt more comfortable.

I asked her if she had always prayed this way and if it was attached to any religion. She said that she had grown up as a Methodist, but that the church affiliation didn't matter as much as her need to have the Holy Spirit with her at all times.

I asked her if she attended church on Sundays, and she said she did, because she needed to be reminded of God's way. Then she told me this story:

She said that when she was in her thirties, she lived in Chicago with a man and had a really wonderful job and made a lot of money. "I thought I was living the perfect life," she said.

At about the same time, her mother was diagnosed with cancer and joined a prayer group. Joan explained that her mother and several other women met in the basement of a church each Wednesday night where each woman would talk about her life, and when they were finished, each woman said a prayer. They prayed for each other.

One week, Joan's mother told her that the prayer group was praying for her—for Joan. Joan was incensed. She didn't need any prayer group praying for her. She was fine without their prayers, thank you very much. "Don't pray for me," she told her mother.

Several weeks after this, Joan was home alone when she was overcome with religious feeling and fell to her knees realizing that she must live differently than the way she had been living. "It's hard to describe," Joan told me. "It was like being born again, although I don't like that term."

She called her mother to tell her of this overwhelming experience that she had had. Her mother said, "That's because we were praying for you."

"No, you weren't," Joan said. "This happened on Thursday and your prayer group meets on Wednesday."

"Not this week," her mother replied. "This week, we met on Thursday."

Since Joan's "born again" experience, she has prayed constantly for her own life and her family and for others as well. "I can't live without praying."

Do I need prayer this much? I wondered. Do I care this much about having the Spirit of the Lord with me? Or do I take prayer and the Holy Ghost for granted. I'm a Mormon, so I have it, don't I?

Thirty years ago, I published my first short story, "Wallflower," with the *New Era,* which was then a brand-new magazine. The story was narrated by a young teenage girl at a ward dance hoping that specific boys would ask her to dance, but, of course, none of them do. Finally, her father, the bishop, asks her to dance. As we all know, this is not exactly what we want at fourteen. We're glad our fathers love us, but we'd rather dance with Mike Mason or Buster Cahoon. Dancing with your father is like dancing with your girlfriend. You're out on the dance floor, no longer a wallflower, but you're still pathetic.

I received a lot of mail from readers, but I only remember one letter. It was from a young high school girl who wrote that she loved my story. She loved my story so much that she wrote a similar story and handed it in as an assignment to her English teacher. Her teacher loved the story as well and submitted it to the school literary journal for publication. When this young girl saw that her story was in print, her conscience was tweaked and she went to the teacher with the *New Era* in hand and showed her my story saying that she must have *unconsciously* memorized the story and written it down word for word as her own. The teacher didn't buy this excuse and accused the girl of plagiarizing. And this is where the letter gets interesting. Her teacher is now angry with her. "Would you," this young girl asks me in her letter, "Would you write my teacher and tell her that I am a Mormon and Mormons don't plagiarize!"

Here was a girl who couldn't reconcile her own behavior with her belief system.

I'm no different from her.

If I was more immature than I already am, I might have written my friend Joan and said, "It's not possible that you could have the Holy Ghost. You aren't a Mormon. It's not possible that you are more comfortable speaking to God than I am. The gospel was restored through Joseph Smith, a fourteen-year-old boy's prayer to God. Mormons invented prayer. How could you pray with such feeling? How could God strike you to your knees and make a believer out of you? And by the way, how come you have more money than I do, and have written more

books than I have, and received more awards than I have? How come you're skinny and I'm not?"

When I am in my whole mind, however, I realize that prayer is not about competition. It might be an ongoing struggle, but it is never about competition; although I have sometimes over the years treated it like a competition. This is especially true with public prayers. I listen to articulate people pray in church—people who are called at the spur of the moment. Dignified four- and five-syllable words of gratitude fall from their lips, and I think, I wish I could pray like that. When I'm called on to pray in church, I'm horrified. I become a cabbage. I try to remember the four rules of prayer: open with a salutation, give thanks, ask for what is needed, and close. Or are those the four rules of writing a business letter that I learned in ninth grade typing class? I am the prayer cabbage: Heavenly Father, We thank thee for our blessings. We ask thee to bless us and take us home in safety. In the name of Jesus Christ, amen.

Even a cabbage knows that this prayer doesn't quite cut it.

Worse than being asked to pray in church is to be called to pray in a BYU meeting. I often don't know what the meeting is about, so I have no idea what to pray for. This is an ongoing problem for me. If I have advanced notice, I actually organize a prayer in my head or even write it down and memorize it. If I have no advanced notice, I stammer out sentence fragments. I become grammatically challenged and clichés spill out of my mouth like cornflakes.

I don't think I'm the only woman in the Church with these feelings of inadequacy about public prayer. I have been in enough Relief Society presidencies to know that one out of twelve of you, when asked to pray, will flutter your hands up and down in front of you and whisper with panic in your voice, "Oh—oh please don't ask me. I can't pray. I just can't." I have done this myself a couple of times, especially if I've just had a fight with a member of my family (who will remain nameless) or when I was too depressed to have a positive thought. Once or twice I have balked at having to pray over the food for a dinner party where I have done all the preparation. You shouldn't have to cook and pray over the food in the same afternoon. But over the years I have made this rule: I will always say yes when asked to pray. I will be okay if the words are a little thin, if I feel

a little awkward, or if I just feel little. I need the practice. I don't ever want to feel as spiritually shallow as I did the first time my friend Joan asked me to pray with her. I'm not so good yet that I volunteer to pray, but I'll never say no again. This I learned from my friend who is not Mormon and probably never will be. Prayer is good for me. For us.

Now comes a second confession: I haven't been all that confident with personal prayer either. When I was young, up to my marriage in fact, I prayed nightly, but then I began thinking about prayer, how I was supposed to pray "with a sincere heart, with real intent" (Moroni 10:4), and felt that I was probably wasting God's time with my narcissistic prattlings. "Let them cease wearying me concerning this matter," He says to Joseph Smith in the Doctrine and Covenants (90:33).

I don't want to weary the God of this universe.

Let Tom pray for both of us. Tom is good with three- and four-syllable words. And yet Tom praying for me is not good enough. What if I need to pray about Tom? What if I have my own issues, separate from Tom, to pray about? Why is prayer so hard?

I think it's hard because I have allowed other people's comments and rules of prayer to intimidate me. Well-meaning people read verses about prayer in sacrament meeting and we nod our heads and smile without thinking. Here's one that doesn't help me a bit:

An Answered Prayer

I asked for strength,
And God gave me difficulties to make me strong;

I asked for wisdom,
And God gave me problems to learn to solve;

I asked for money,
And God gave me brain and brawn to work;

I asked for courage,
And God gave me dangers to overcome;

I asked for love,
And God gave me people to help;

I asked for favours,
And God gave me opportunities.

I received nothing I wanted—I received everything I
  needed.

My prayer has been answered![1]

If I hear too many poems like this, I'm not likely to want to ask God for anything. It's taken years—I'm a late bloomer, I admit—to realize that God does *not* give us difficulties, problems, and danger. They are simply a given in this lone and dreary and exhilarating world we live in. This poem and others like it contradict the scripture in Luke, chapter 11, verses 11–13: "If a son shall ask bread of any of you that is a father, will he give him a stone? or if he ask a fish, will he for a fish give him a serpent? Or if he shall ask an egg, will he offer him a scorpion? If ye then, being evil, know how to give good gifts unto your children: how much more shall your heavenly Father give the Holy Spirit to them that ask him?"

I wonder if we don't sometimes misinterpret what God gives us. When I lived in Minnesota, I remember a new young couple with their small children moved into the ward from Utah and were asked to speak in sacrament meeting. Both of them spoke about how the man had lost his job more than a year before and how they had been praying to the Lord for work. Finally, a wonderful job opened up in Minnesota that matched this young man's skills and abilities. In the same talks this couple expressed their bewilderment at why they were in Minnesota. Why did God bring us here, they asked aloud. What does He want us to do here? It seemed pretty clear to me why they were there. They had prayed for work and found it in Minnesota. That's why they were there. There was employment and money for them to raise their family. They had received a very direct answer to their prayers, but didn't recognize it.

Another reason why I have had a difficult time with personal prayers is that I'm afraid that God will scold me, as He does with William McClellan and Sidney Gilbert in the 90th section of the Doctrine and Covenants. "I am not well pleased with many things," He says. "And I am not well pleased with my servant William E. McLellin, neither with my servant Sidney Gilbert; and the bishop also, and others have many things to repent of" (90:35). Earlier the Lord calls to everyone's attention that William McLellin has been tempted to commit adultery (see 66:10). I find this kind of public pronouncement frightening. I want to say here and now that I have committed adultery in my heart, before God booms it from the rooftops (I expect you have too).

Once in my effort at personal prayer, I told the Lord that I had this fear of Him. I told Him that I thought He had a scary voice in the scriptures, and I found it intimidating. I got an answer to that prayer. He said, "Louise, your voice is pretty scary sometimes too." That answer made me smile.

G. K. Chesterton wrote that the one thing that God has hidden from us is His sense of humor. I think it depends on what you bring to the conversation.

Can you be mad with God and say it aloud? I think so. If we have to pretend to emotions we don't feel, then the prayer can't be sincere. Years ago, I got a call from a member of the stake presidency asking me to meet with him on a Sunday afternoon. I hung up the phone and said to Tom, "He's going to call me to some stake job. Why else would he be calling? I hate stake jobs. I don't want to work in the stake. The ward is where things happen, not the stake. I'm not going to do it. They can't make me."

Tom, who knows better than to argue with me in these hot moments, said, "You won't know until you see him."

"Well, I already know what he wants and I'm going to say no."

"Fine," he said.

When it was time to leave I got in my car and ranted and raved at God aloud. "I know you have given me all these blessings, but I don't want a stake job. This is blackmail. Just because everything I have that is good came from you, I have to do this silly stake job, whatever it is. I'm not going to. Do you hear me? I'm not going to do it. Are you listening?"

I arrived at the stake center and waited outside the stake president's office, growing crankier by the minute. Soon, the counselor greeted me and asked me to sit down. I tried to look pleasant.

"Deanne Francis is going to be the new stake Relief Society president," he said. "And she wants you to be one of her counselors."

"Really?" I said with raised eyebrows. I liked Deanne Francis. I liked her a lot. It would be fun to work with her. "I'd love to," I said. And I meant it.

On the way home in my car, I spent the time apologizing to the creator of the universe. "I'm very sorry," I said. "I shouldn't have forecasted that way. I should have known it would be something I wanted to do. Please forgive me. Thank you, thank you for letting me work with Deanne. Thank you."

I find it easier to thank God for my blessings than to ask Him for anything. I am almost constantly grateful for my life, for my family, for my friends, for my satisfying work, for good food and a warm house. I thank Him aloud when I'm driving in my car or when I'm swimming at the gym, pushing the water with my hands and listing off the blessings: Thank you for Tom and Charles and Erica and Anne and Harrison, and Sam and Sarah and Lucy. Especially Lucy. Thank you for Ann Cannon, my best friend. Thanks for my sisters. They make me laugh. Thank you, thank you.

Finally, the hardest thing about prayer is asking for something that seems impossible, because asking means believing. It means having faith that the Lord can bring it about. Jesus says in Mark 11:

"Whosoever shall say unto this mountain, Be thou removed, and be thou cast into the sea; and shall not doubt in his heart, but shall believe that those things which he saith shall come to pass; he shall have whatsoever he saith.

"Therefore I say unto you, What things soever ye desire, when ye pray, believe that ye receive them, and ye shall have them" (vv. 23–24).

God wants us to have the desires of our hearts. He can help us find work, go back to school, write a book, give a talk, buy a new house. There is nothing so mundane in our lives that He will not grant it. Nor is there anything as impossible as moving mountains that He cannot grant us.

At this moment I live with a strange dichotomy: I have a granddaughter, Lucy, who was born fourteen days ago without a diaphragm. This means that her stomach and intestines and even her liver have drifted into the chest cavity. She has made it through her first surgery but remains in very critical condition.

Then I have an 82-year-old mother in the last stages of Alzheimer's. She can't walk, talk, smile, or even sit up. She is the woman who cannot die. I'm not sure how to pray for her. Someone has suggested that we pray for her to pass on, but I can't do this. She is my mother and still loves to eat ice cream when I spoon it into her mouth. Maybe that's worth living for: Baskin-Robbins chocolate chip ice cream. Pretty good comfort food.

I know what I want for Lucy. I want her to wear all those new shoes waiting for her. There's nothing like new shoes. I want her to play ring around the rosie with her cousin Mira and after the "all fall down," to say "Again!" And then repeat it. I want her mother, Sarah, to be able to hold her in her arms, which she has not yet been able to do. I want her to hear her father, Sam, sing in that great baritone voice of his. I want her alive and well for all of us. I don't want to wait until the next life to know her. I don't want her to have some other mission. I don't want her martyred so that the rest of us can learn some cosmic lesson. I want her here. Now.

"What things soever ye desire, when ye pray, believe that ye receive them, and ye shall have them."

Can I ask God to heal my granddaughter? Yes, I can. And here's the scripture that allows me to do it: In Mark, chapter 9, a father brings a son with a "dumb spirit" for Jesus to heal. The father says, "And wheresoever he taketh him, he teareth him: and he foameth, and gnasheth with his teeth, and pineth away" (v. 18).

And Jesus asks the father, "How long is it ago since this came unto him? And he said, Of a child.

"And ofttimes it hath cast him into the fire, and into the waters, to destroy him: but if thou canst do any thing, have compassion on us, and help us.

"Jesus said unto him, If thou canst believe, all things are possible to him that believeth.

"And straightway the father of the child cried out, and said with tears, Lord, I believe; help thou mine unbelief" (vv. 21–24).

Have compassion on our family, Lord. You healed the blind man, the woman with the issue of blood. You cast the devil out of a boy; you healed ten lepers; and you raised Lazarus from the dead. Please Lord, heal Lucy. Make her whole.

Lord, I believe; help thou my unbelief.

What if Lucy dies? Will I still believe? Yes, I will. Behind every prayer for a miracle we must include the thought: "Thy will be done."

My struggle with prayer and faith continues on a daily basis, but I have learned about prayer from Joseph Smith and from my friend Joan, a lapsed Methodist. I have learned prayer from Deepak Chopra, who tells me the universe is filled with goodness and light and that I must connect with all that is positive. I have learned prayer from the Buddha, who tells me to sit still and listen. I have learned prayer from Norman Vincent Peale, who taught me the phrase, "If God [is] for us, who can be against us?" (Romans 8:31). I got my first job at age sixteen by repeating that phrase over and over.

I pray in my car and when I swim. I write positive statements on cards and stick them on the bathroom mirror where I am forced to read them. I write them in present tense: Lucy lives to a ripe old age, or Louise finishes her book, January 30, 2004. When my children need something big from God, they say, "Put me on the mirror, Mom." Once I made a prayer tree for my husband when he had brain surgery. I wrote little prophecies on small sheets of paper and tied them to the tree branches. "Tom catches large trout in the Provo River," "Louise and Tom take walks well into the 2020s."

While I still struggle with prayer, I am not in the same spot I was five, ten, or fifteen years ago. I continue to learn that prayer is not a performance nor is it a competition; God is not grading on a curve. Prayer is an intimate conversation with a loving Heavenly Father, who listens when I'm crabby, when I'm sleepy, when I'm rebellious, and even answers with a little humor. I've learned that God doesn't speak in English or German or Swahili; He teaches us through His own divine language. And for me to worry whether I'm speaking eloquently or grammatically is of no concern to Him. It doesn't matter if I stammer my way through a prayer with awkward phrasing. The Lord has borne our sorrows and griefs, our rage, our imperfection, and our weaknesses so that we can be with Him.

I'm going to heaven. And I'm going to be in a celestial choir conducted by Lorraine Bowman, my high school a cappella teacher. I'll sing second alto instead of third alto because the tenors won't need my help in heaven. See you there!

NOTE

1. From Azriela Jaffe's "Create Your Own Luck" newsletter, issue 37.

"My Soul Delighteth in the Scriptures"

Jan Godfrey

I do love the scriptures. My soul does delight in them. But it was not always so. I do not remember being without a testimony. Even as a child my membership in the Church made perfect sense to me; it was logical and reasonable. I attended church willingly and I obeyed the commandments. I believed what my mother told me. I read the *Relief Society Magazine* and lesson manuals. As I grew older, I accepted callings, and I even took classes as part of my BYU requirements. I had the witness of the Spirit that the Church was true. But I did not regularly, daily, faithfully spend time with the scriptures. My knowledge of the scriptures was secondhand.

Then the Brethren began telling us that as a Church, and individually, we should study the scriptures. They even told us to get our own copy. I did get my own copy. But I still didn't "study." I began feeling very guilty about not obeying this particular direction, but it seemed to be such a formidable task. Where was I to begin? At a ward conference the assigned stake visitor pointedly encouraged us to "study" the scriptures. I was a mother with five little children. I lived "in the country," which

Jan Bingham Godfrey graduated from Brigham Young University in 1956. She is a former fifth-grade teacher and currently serves as a Church Service missionary with the Timpview Seminary. She is mother to five children and grandmother to five grandsons.

necessitated time in the car. I was busy with Relief Society and Primary and Mutual three times a week, not to mention piano, soccer, meals, and laundry. How could I squeeze it in? I asked the speaker for suggestions, and he said, "If you can't 'study' the scriptures perhaps you could just 'read' them." It was a simple solution but it was one I had missed. His encouraging suggestion made sense. I could do *that*. It was the idea of reference books and commentaries that had intimidated me. That year the new LDS Bible had just been completed so I got a copy and began reading. I read at night when the children were asleep and the house was quiet. I started in Genesis and read every word. I loved the new foot-notes. They actually explained the information. I checked the maps and devoured the dictionary. I marked words I found unusual or interesting. I cross-referenced and began to keep my own lists and connections. Lo and behold! I was "studying" the scriptures! It was superficial at first, but the collection of study aids all in one handy volume made it easy to pur-sue some things in more detail. I began to write in the margins. I dia-grammed my own genealogy charts. I underlined. I finished the Bible and eagerly awaited the publication of the second volume of LDS scrip-tures. It was a time of great personal satisfaction.

I first read the Bible for information. Who were the principle char-acters? Why was their story important enough to be included in the scriptures? Why were some stories repeated twice, even three times? My curiosity was aroused. I read about Ruth and Esther and King Saul and Joshua. I loved the details of their lives. I loved those giant characters with their tremendous talents and their human flaws and family struggles.

Then I began to notice that one particular scripture kept reappear-ing. If the page fell open at random, there it would be: "Ask, and it shall be given you; seek, and ye shall find; knock, and it shall be opened unto you: For every one that asketh receiveth; and he that seeketh findeth; and to him who knocketh it shall be opened" (Matthew 7:7–8). I thought that passage must be the most frequently repeated scripture in the book. But I didn't think of it as personal advice. I know now that I was being prompted to pray about what I was reading, but I didn't take the hint.

Then I had a dream that was repeated several times. In the dream I was standing on a stage behind a closed curtain. As the curtain started to open I realized that I was the star but as I began to see the audience I remembered that I had not been to any practices. I thought, I am not prepared! I don't know my lines! What am I going to do? When I mentioned my dream to a friend, he told me that he had had the same experience. His perception was that it meant he should increase his study of the scriptures because he needed to be prepared. About that time Elder Nelson suggested that we should understand the Abrahamic covenant. By now I was familiar with the characters and the format and I began to read to understand the ancient promises given to the House of Israel and the individual responsibility that I bore as a descendant of Ephraim.

The triple combination was not yet available, and I could hardly wait for it to be published. When I got a copy I continued "reading." I was reading one night in Section 6 of the Doctrine and Covenants, which is a revelation given to Joseph Smith and Oliver Cowdery. Suddenly the scripture warnings and instruction became very personal. I felt the Lord was speaking not just to Oliver and the Prophet but also to me. It was as if He had whispered in my ear, "I know everything about you and I am watching you." It was electric. The next time I opened the scriptures I was subdued. I was filled with great reverence. I knew the scriptures contained great accounts of important events in the lives of prophets and kings and the people they led. But they also held the key to personal heavenly communication to me—and about me.

Why didn't I understand about the power of likening the scriptures before? I do not know. But my focus shifted. I began reading with all my senses alerted, watching for that moment when I would know that a particular verse contained something very personal for me. I had some amazing experiences. My discovery that the scriptures were personal as well as general was a pivotal event in my life. As I was reading the scriptures, and just absorbing the information in a routine way, suddenly a passage would seem to be in bold print telling me things I needed to know about my own life or witnessing that a particular doctrine was true. The witness of the Spirit would send a peculiar electric tingle through my body. I read more often. I was still a busy mother, but now I was awakened spiritually. I had formerly read for information; now I read for inspiration.

Very unexpectedly I had a calamity in my life. As a result of that, I really held onto the scriptures. They were essential to me. I was lost without them. Now I understood about hungering and thirsting for the word. I could hardly wait to plug in to the constant stream of inspiration I received. I had scriptures in the car, more in the kitchen, and additional copies throughout the house. I read them every moment that I could. I was ridiculed for spending so much time in the scriptures, so I read secretly. I read by the roadside. I read in the doctor's office. I read while the mechanic changed the oil. I needed explanations and I ached for comfort. I did get explanations and I did get comfort. I was enlightened by the true doctrine of Jesus Christ. Through the scriptures I was told time and again that I was loved. I would be cared for and sustained. I got counsel on how I was to act and told to be patient. I was advised that revenge belonged to the Lord and He would administer justice but that mercy and forgiveness were his gifts, too. I was even told that my debts would be paid. And they were.

Adversity provokes the greatest need but also provides the greatest opportunity for growth. The experience of having great personal need drove me deeper into the scriptures, and since that time they have remained my true and unfailing friend. I wish I could tell you that I have become a gospel scholar through these experiences and that I remember every suitable passage relating to a particular topic. It isn't true. The more I study the more I discover the things I don't know or can't remember. I sometimes rediscover a particular truth. There it is in my very own scriptures with my notes and exclamation marks. I have certainly been on this page before, yet the message is fresh and meaningful. How could I not have remembered that passage? Though a meal of the scriptures doesn't always stick in retrievable ways, I can tell you that generally I have become more knowledgeable and certainly my testimony has been strengthened and expanded. "There is a law, irrevocably decreed in heaven before the foundations of this world, upon which all blessings are predicated—And when we obtain any blessing from God, it is by obedience to that law upon which it is predicated" (D&C 130:20–21).

From that small beginning, that little surge of guilt and desire, has come a powerful blessing in my life: "And out of small things proceedeth that which is great. Behold, the Lord requireth the heart and a willing mind; and the willing and obedient shall eat the good of the land of Zion in these last days" (D&C 64:33–34). I nibble, I snack, I gobble, I feast. The scriptures are a delightful source of nourishment and satisfaction. And, like physical nourishment, a daily portion is best.

I also wish I could tell you I lead a perfect life because I know the gospel secrets. That isn't true either. Mistakes and inadequacies plague me. Every turn in life brings new challenges. The learning curve shoots upward. The scriptures give me hope and I keep going. Occasionally I notice a small change for the better. Progress is slow.

Some years ago I began to notice that the scriptures themselves advise us to study. Numerous verses speak of benefits and blessings. I started a list simply to see how many reasons I could find to read the scriptures. At first I only listed the benefit as one word, such as *comfort*. But then I began adding the scripture notation because I found so many I couldn't remember their location. Soon I had a list that covered a whole page. Here is one of those passages: "And for this very purpose are these plates preserved, . . . that the *promises* of the Lord might be fulfilled, . . . and that [they] might come to the *knowledge of their fathers*, and that they might *know the promises* of the Lord, and that they may *believe the gospel* and *rely* upon the merits of *Jesus Christ*" (D&C 3:19–20; emphasis added).

I had not used that particular set of scriptures for some time, so I had actually forgotten about the list; but when I pulled out my old worn scriptures I found the list. As I reviewed it I no longer saw a simple tally of rewards, I noticed that it was a list of promises that had been fulfilled in my own life. I *had* received comfort. I *did* know about the Lord's promises. I *do* know more about the fathers. I believe in the gospel—those laws about repentance and baptism and forgiveness. I am coming more and more to submit my will to my Father's and rely on the merits of Jesus Christ. The promises are sure, but recognition of the fulfillment of them came only after a considerable investment of effort over a long period of time. If I had not learned of the promises certainly I would not have known when they were fulfilled.

I read or study the scriptures in a variety of ways:

I read randomly. With no real goal in mind, I simply open the book and start reading, perhaps in the middle of a verse. Sometimes it is instant messaging. An answer appears even before I ask the question (See D&C 100:4–8).

I read by subject. I read to understand a doctrine or know more about a topic that is not familiar. Or I may just read all the references in the Topical Guide under a particular subject heading.

I read a large section. Reading large sections gives an overview that is useful. We claim that the people in the Book of Mormon were Hebrew in origin and lack of proper names starting with *W* can be used to authenticate the Book of Mormon as Hebrew in origin. That probably would not have been noticed if only small sections were read. It takes a larger bite to reveal certain patterns.

I read to compile a chart, a diagram, or a genealogy. I had difficulty with all the wanderers in Mosiah and Alma until I charted their comings and goings in a visible format. Other people have done this and published their versions, so I could have used their research, but I found that digging it out myself was more beneficial. My margins are filled with sketches and scratches. I always read with a pen in my hand.

I read to concentrate on a very narrow area. I once spent an inordinate amount of time on the word *vanity* while I was reading Ecclesiastes. My original understanding of this word was that it identified a person unusually concerned with personal appearance or accomplishments. But that didn't make total sense in Ecclesiastes. I discovered that "temporary" was one of its multiple meanings. Now when I read that word, *vanity*, I think of all the unnecessary things we value that are temporary and of use in this life only. I have a lot of them stored in my basement. I need a sign down there saying, "Vanity of vanities; all is vanity" (Ecclesiastes 1:2).

I read to teach. This means I must reorganize and select information for presentation to others to accomplish a specific purpose. I take notes. I shuffle the order. I leave out unnecessary events in order to grasp the pertinent information for the point I am trying to teach. I try to get the whole picture straight in my mind before I offer it to others. I look for pictures or make visual aids that portray my mental image. I use a standard dictionary to better understand the origin and meaning of individual words.

There are other ways, no doubt better ways, to study the scriptures but these are the ones I use most frequently.

I have told you how I *began* to study the scriptures, how I began to draw water from the well. I have told you how that water sustained me. I have told you how I *continue* to study the scriptures. Now I'd like to tell you of the *delight* I find in them. "And upon these I write the things of my soul. . . . For my soul delighteth in the scriptures, and my heart pondereth them" (2 Nephi 4:15). What are "the things of [the] soul"? I think they are the eternal things. They are those intense feelings that transcend the present and connect us to God, the intuitive recognition that we are more than our bodies, more than our minds, and more than the material surroundings in the physical world. We had an earlier existence, we have a divine purpose here, and we have been promised future glory.

Reading the scriptures stirs my soul. I cannot speak all that I feel (see Alma 26:16). It reminds me of the covenants and promises, the pitfalls and rewards, and tells me of my ultimate destination. There is a plan for the world. There is a plan for me. I have discovered some of the rules. I love finding encouragement when I struggle to comply.

I love the history of the composition, compilation, and preservation of the scriptures. I love all those ancient prophets and kings, scribes and translators, reformers, martyrs, and priests that had a hand in that tremendous task. I love to read about their efforts and remember that angels were participants, too.

I love the sound of the words. I take pleasure in the rhythm and the archaic forms: "Beareth all things, believeth all things, hopeth all things, endureth all things. Charity never faileth" (1 Corinthians 13:7–8). I love the poetic imagery, the meaning behind the words: "He maketh me to lie down in green pastures; he leadeth me beside the still waters. . . . My cup runneth over" (Psalm 23:2, 5). I love the contrast of power and tender concern implied in "When I consider thy heavens, the work of thy fingers, the moon and the stars, which thou hast ordained; what is man, that thou art mindful of him?" (Psalm 8:3–4). Or: "Consider the lilies of the field, how they grow; they toil not, neither do they spin: And yet I say unto you, That even Solomon in all his glory was not arrayed like one of these" (Matthew 6:28–29).

I love knowing about ancient Hebrew literary forms, such as chiasmus, that have survived translation. I love knowing that a language construction that is unusual or repetitive in English is actually a deliberate effort by a Hebrew writer to communicate his intense feelings about the saving truths of the gospel.

I love the conversational style of the Doctrine and Covenants. Joseph inquires of the Lord, and God gives him a revelation. I can ask a question and the Lord will answer me, too.

I love the pure doctrine of the Book of Mormon. I know about "other sheep." I know that I am one of many but that I am loved and saved individually. I know about the Fall and the Atonement. I know that the plan of salvation is the great plan of happiness and my eternal happiness requires that I understand the purpose of a mortal existence and the rewards of repentance. I know that Christ suffered and died for me and I must serve others for Him. His appearance, in His body, to the ancient Nephites is a second witness of the actuality of resurrection.

I love the characters. I love Queen Esther's response to Mordecai's question, "And who knoweth whether thou art come to the kingdom for such a time as this?" (Esther 4:14). I love young David when he faced Goliath: "For who is this uncircumcised Philistine, that he should defy the armies of the living God?" (1 Samuel 17:26). I love Abinadi, unyielding, demanding more time from his accusers: "Touch me not, for God shall smite you if ye lay your hands upon me, for I have not delivered the message which the Lord sent me to deliver" (Mosiah 13:3). I think of Moroni, all alone, still faithfully writing: "Now . . . I had supposed not to have written more, but I have not as yet perished; and I make not myself known to the Lamanites lest they should destroy me" (Moroni 1:1). And Mary, completely submissive and obedient: "Behold the handmaid of the Lord; be it unto me according to thy word" (Luke 1:38).

I love all the Josephs connected by divine and mortal DNA.

I love seeing the volumes on my bed at night. They are tangible evidence that I am obedient in at least one thing.

I love the fact that they are divided into small sections. I can read a verse or consider a page. I can stop and start conveniently and always relocate.

I love the economy of the writing. It takes more time to paraphrase a few verses than it does to read it straight from the scriptures themselves.

I love the intellectual growth, the stimulation of curiosity, and the element of discovery that is available in a compact portable library that is deep and often unfathomable.

I love to visualize the beautiful creations described in the scriptures: the architecture of the great temple at Jerusalem, the portable tabernacle in the wilderness. What was the actual design of the fabric and the furniture? How did the artisans, some mentioned by name, complete all their tasks in a wilderness? (see Exodus 38). What satisfaction did they find in hanging the curtains or stitching the ephod? What tools did they need for setting the precious jewelry with the stones representing the tribes of Israel? What were the patterns for the weaving of the wool, and what skill is necessary to make fine-twined linens? (see Alma 1:29). I like thinking of a pomegranate as a motif in the ceremonial cloths (see Exodus 39:24).

I love the comfort in the companionship of the Spirit. When I am diligently, willingly searching the scriptures, I am blessed to have the companionship of the Spirit. I am more alert, more sensitive, more intuitive, more grateful, and more obedient. I am less demanding, less self-centered, less irritable. The Spirit witnesses of truth and the fulfillment of prophecy—in general and specifically in my own life. I am less disturbed at temporary distress. I know I can trust in the Lord.

Do I have a favorite scripture? I have many, but my all-time favorite is from Hebrews. The verse is speaking of the faith of Abraham and Sarah: "Through faith also Sara herself received strength to conceive seed, and was delivered of a child when she was past age, because she judged him faithful who had promised. Therefore sprang there even of one, and him as good as dead, so many as the stars of the sky in multitude, and as the sand which is by the sea shore innumerable" (Hebrews 11:11–12). There is ultimate faith. *He* was "as good as dead" and *she* was "past age." And God gave them life.

I love the inspiration, the insights, the cautions, the instruction. I have been nurtured and admonished by prophets. I have been advised by kings. I love the obvious directions, such as the Ten Commandments, stated so clearly. And I love the not-so-obvious mysteries I have uncovered with persistent effort. They are personal discoveries and connections that are mine alone. It is oil I cannot share. I have profited by knowing the truth and following the still small voice with its whispered advice. In my heart I know that I am blessed to come to earth in this dispensation and have the scriptures in my life. My soul delighteth in the scriptures and my heart pondereth them. And with joy have I drawn water out of the wells of salvation.

"Jesus . . . Sat Thus on the Well": The Activity of Immobility

John R. Rosenberg

It has been four hundred years since the publication of Cervantes' *Don Quixote*. Even today we are inspired by Quixote's pursuit of an impossible dream; we have our own windmills that rise up like menacing giants during our daily routine; we root for the Don each time he struggles to his feet after being thrashed by the evil enchanter. We cheer when, in Dale Wasserman's *The Man of La Mancha*, Quixote rises from his deathbed one last time and in a frenzy of chivalric enthusiasm shouts, "What is sickness to the body of a knight-errant? What matter wounds? For each time he falls he shall rise again—and woe to the wicked! Sancho . . . My armour! My sword!"[1]

However, Wasserman's version of the novel is unjustifiably optimistic. He allows us to forget that one thing, perhaps the only thing, which the characters of the novel agree on is that Don Quixote is mad. And his madness is cured not by running around incessantly doing what he perceives are good deeds, but by returning home and coming to rest. It is then he can declare, "I am no longer Don Quixote of La Mancha, but Alonso Quixano . . . the good." From madness to goodness, not by journey, but by rest. Wasserman was fundamentally a romantic;

John R. Rosenberg is a professor of Spanish literature and associate dean of the College of Humanities at Brigham Young University. He is married to Gaylamarie Green Rosenberg and is the father of two daughters, Marie and Eliza.

Cervantes was a Christian Aristotelian and his work is grounded in Aristotle's dictum: "God always enjoys a single and simple pleasure; for there is not only an activity of movement but an *activity of immobility.*"[2]

In Lewis Carroll's famous poem, a loving father bids farewell to his son, warning him to "beware the Jabberwock." The son leaves the safety of his home, he takes his "vorpal sword in hand," and for a "long time" he seeks the "manxome foe." Significantly, "then *rested* he by the Tumtum tree, and *stood* a while in *thought.*" This thoughtful standing suspends the journey in order to better understand the journey. It is Aristotle's "active immobility." And "while in uffish thought he stood," he is prepared to defeat *his* evil enchanter, which he does, and is welcomed back to the tender arms of his father.[3]

Robert Frost arrives at that famous fork in the yellow woods. We think his poem is a journey poem. Perhaps it is. But what we often forget is that the poet says, "long I stood and looked." Eighteen of the poem's twenty lines deal with thinking about the journey, with his reflections that lead to his decision of which path to follow—with his active immobility. It is the reflection "that has made all the difference."[4]

Of course, the greatest example of active immobility is the Savior. The breathtaking pace of the Lord's three-year mission is punctuated with moments of stillness. One brief example: The Savior makes wine of water; he attends Passover, cleanses the temple, performs miracles, instructs Nicodemus, and travels to Galilee through Samaria. And then, as John states in the fourth chapter of his gospel, "Jesus therefore, being wearied with his journey, sat thus on the well" (v. 6). He drinks and is restored. Being restored, he offers living water to the woman who has greeted him. She becomes the first "missionary" of Christ's witness and brings "many of the Samaritans of that city" (v. 39) to drink with her deeply "out of the wells of salvation" (Isaiah 12:3).

Scripture is the Lord's medium for inducing active immobility. It contains the living water that cleanses, refreshes, and restores. When we open scripture, time stops. By definition, we cannot reflect and act at the same time. Meditation allows us to step back from the river of history. Here timelessness begins; the journey is suspended—change ceases and we can reflect on the changeless, and this is the beginning of how we are changed ourselves. The irony of the way most of us read scripture is that the reading is measured by the clock. We aim to read for a half hour and then dive back into the river of history. But mechanical clocks were invented by thirteenth-century monks for precisely the opposite purpose: to make sure that history (the chores of the world of contingency) did not encroach on the tasks of eternity: prayer, scripture study, and meditation.[5]

In addition to sacred time, the scriptures also usher us into sacred places: we exchange our busy streets, businesses, and homes for gardens like Eden and Gethsemane, the waters of Mormon, and the Sacred Grove. By offering sacred time and holy places, scriptures are like portable temples. There is an insightful play on words in Latin: *fructa inter folia*, fruit among leaves. The leaves are the leaves of a tree and the leaves or pages of a book. The fruit of the word is available to gleaning readers. Alma explains, "Ye shall pluck the fruit . . . , which is most precious, which is sweet above all that is sweet, and which is white above all that is white, yea, and pure above all that is pure; and ye shall feast upon this fruit even until ye are filled, that ye hunger not, neither shall ye thirst" (Alma 32:42). Could there be a more explicit definition of the methods and promises of gospel literacy?

Yet often we transfer the methods of journeying to what should be the restfulness of the scriptures. The journey emphasizes the *telos* (end point), the getting there. Parents hear this every time they load the children into the car: "Are we there yet?" "How many more miles?" Laman and Lemuel asked essentially the same thing of their father. We often read like they journeyed. "When will I be done with the Book of Mormon?" "Come on, kids, we have to finish this chapter." Nephi, on the other hand, paused like Robert Frost on the road, desiring to know. "I *sat* pondering," he says (1 Nephi 11:1). Only by interrupting the journey could he understand its meaning. The words are nearly identical to those used by Joseph F. Smith to describe his active immobility. Grieving over the loss of his apostle-son, anticipating his own death (which would occur in a few short weeks), wondering about the awful mortality rates of the last weeks of World War I and the pandemic of the Spanish flu, he "sat in [his] room pondering over the scriptures" (D&C 138:1). His posture is suggestive. He ponders *over* the scriptures, not *under* them as many of us do. And he receives a revelation that brings comfort to his personal mourning and clear doctrine about the spirit world to the rest of grieving humanity. Note the parallel with Christ, whose resting refreshed him and then allowed him to enlighten others. Or Enos, whose active immobility first led to an epiphany regarding his relationship with God and then turned his attention to others.

So what does restful reading look like? It prefers contemplation to coverage. Its greatest enemy is the speed-reading class. It hovers, lingers, and savors. Let's use as an example an especially restful passage, the Twenty-third Psalm.

The Lord is my shepherd.

This well-known metaphor expresses a comforting doctrine. It suggests that the Lord himself is a not just a person but a *place* of refuge for his people as a whole. He is the sheepfold where we will find rest during the journey. As Amulek puts it, he "encircles [us] in the arms of safety" (Alma 34:16). Isaiah uses a tender version of this metaphor:

"He shall *feed* his flock like a shepherd:

"He shall *gather* the lambs with his arm,

"And *carry* them in his bosom,

"And shall gently lead those that are with young" (40:11).

The promise of the Good Shepherd to lead those that are with young to a resting place must be reassuring to those exhausted ones among us who are trying to feed, gather, and carry their own lambs.

We might emphasize the first line differently. The *Lord* is my shepherd (and none other). This is relevant for times when rulers and false gods claim ownership of the flock. Psalm 146 tells us, "Put not your trust in princes" (v. 3); other places remind us not to trust the arm of the flesh, or the bow, or any other manifestation of earthly power because the refuge they provide will always be transient. Only the Lord's rest is reliably omnipresent.

Or we might read the verse this way: The Lord is *my* shepherd. Now we move from theology to personal witness, from the abstract notion that Israel is God's chosen people to the testimony of one who amid all the ups and downs of daily life has found rest. This is the ever-resilient

Job who, drowning in adversity, can still assert, "I know that my redeemer liveth" (Job 19:25). In a single line, the psalmist has defined God's attributes, has taught that the Lord is the one God, and has shared his personal witness.

I shall not want.

Desire is the most fundamental of human motivations. In literature and art it usually is the justification for the action. A character known as the protagonist pursues the fulfillment of a desire. Another, the antagonist, does his best to interrupt that quest. Most literature explores the conditions and reasons behind frustrated desire. Many of our greatest creations, like Don Quixote or Faust or Willy Loman, are left wanting. What they want may range from food to love to power to fame to immortality.

Significantly, the psalmist does not tell us what is wanted; he says simply, "I shall not want." The line is an expression of mature hope. Following the faith-full affirmation, "The Lord is my shepherd," comes the declaration of hope: because he is my shepherd, whatever I might desire that is eternally relevant will be supplied (see Proverbs 11:23). The Savior, who defines Himself as the "good shepherd," explains the basis for this hope: "Your Father knoweth what things ye have need of, before ye ask him" (Matthew 6:8). The perfect shepherd anticipates our desires; indeed, He promises that He will share with us all that He has.

In contrast, when we allow someone other than the Lord to be our shepherd, our wants are only magnified: "Because thou servedst not the Lord . . . thou [shalt] serve thine enemies . . . , in hunger, and in thirst, and in nakedness, and in *want of all things*" (Deuteronomy 28:47–48; emphasis added).

He maketh me to lie down in green pastures:
he leadeth me beside the still waters.

The abstraction of not wanting in the previous verse is made more concrete here: the shepherd provides food and water (see D&C 104:17). But the place of nourishment is here as significant as the substance. The watered pasture stands out against the arid Judean wilderness. This is the well in Samaria or Joseph F. Smith's quiet room. It makes the journey possible by suspending the journey. We are in the archetypal *locus amoenus:* the pleasing place. It is a common motif in world literature: the grove, garden, or oasis that allows us to pause during our exile in the wilderness called mortality. It has clearly defined boundaries; one is keenly aware of pausing the forward movement of the journey to enter a place of active immobility. While activity in the wilderness wears us down, active immobility in the oasis is restorative. Just as the green pastures surrounding the still water frame the oasis and mark it as different from the wilderness, the covers of the book of scripture separate the sacred from the profane and timelessness from time. The words of the book are the still waters, gently cleansing and healing, washing away the journey's dust. "And the Lord shall guide thee continually, and satisfy thy soul in drought . . . : and thou shalt be like a watered garden, and like a spring of water, whose waters fail not" (Isaiah 58:11). The psalm makes clear that the oasis is not a gas-and-go on time's interstate. The Lord "maketh me to lie down"—He invites me to linger. He does not have me cross a bridge spanning the still waters; He leads me *beside* them, extending as long as possible their cool and calming influence. This, I believe, is the posture suggested by President Hinckley when he counseled us to read the scriptures "quietly and thoughtfully and introspectively."[6]

He restoreth my soul.

Architects restore historical buildings. Preservationists restore old books and paintings. With patience, steadiness, sure knowledge, and genuine love for the worn object, they gently scrape away dirt and wear, mend broken pieces, thoughtfully replace missing ones, and straighten crooked ones. In each case the expert hand knows what has been and what potential the future might reveal. The psalmist speaks of an *intimate* restoration carried out by the "finisher of our faith" (Hebrews 12:2) whose perspective on what we are is sharpened by His perfect understanding of who we were and what we might become. I love the way Isaiah uses oasis imagery to describe how the Messiah takes crooked things and makes them straight: "To give unto them beauty for ashes, the oil of joy for mourning, the garment of praise for the spirit of heaviness; that they might be called trees of righteousness, the planting of the Lord, that *he* might be glorified" (61:3; emphasis added).

Though I walk through the valley of the shadow of death,
I will fear no evil.

We typically read this line literally: we can approach death with confidence. The original can also be read "even though I should walk in the midst of total darkness."[7] This might suggest trials of faith or any adversity or opposition to the satisfaction of our righteous desires. Read this way, we descend into this valley almost daily as we confront the effects of our failures or the impact of other's weaknesses on us, or simply struggle under the gravity of mortality. In the face of this existential antagonism comes the quiet affirmation, "I will fear no evil"—evil being that which would separate us from our proper "wants."

I like the way Patrick D. Miller puts it: This "is the gospel kernel of the Old Testament, that good news that turns the tears of anguish and fear into shouts of joy, that glad tidings given by the angelic choir to the shepherds which itself echoes a word first given to the patriarchs and repeated to Israel again and again in moments of distress and fear: you don't have to be afraid."[8]

The Lord does not promise Joseph that he will be shielded from evil; He does ask him: "What power shall stay the heavens? As well might man stretch forth his puny arm to stop the Missouri river in its decreed course . . . as to hinder the Almighty from pouring down *knowledge* from heaven" (D&C 121:33; emphasis added). What a powerful passage! We strike back at the opposition that is in all things not with force, but with knowledge. And where does that knowledge come from? In Joseph's case, it was from a most curious *locus amoenus,* the Liberty Jail. God was able to use the Prophet's active immobility to transform for a time the squalid conditions of his prison into a place of spiritualized rest and a temple of instruction. He can do the same for us: He who makes red things white and crooked things straight can make a *locus amoenus* out of any of our daily spaces: the pause at a stoplight, the market line, or even the garden space choked with weeds. The Restorer of Souls responds to Joseph's anguish: "My son, peace be unto thy soul" (D&C 121:7). Once again the Shepherd offers consoling constancy. To those gathered in the topographically ravaged Bountiful, He says: "For the mountains shall depart and the hills be removed, but my kindness shall not depart from thee, neither shall the covenant of my peace be removed, saith the Lord that hath mercy on thee" (3 Nephi 22:10).

Thou preparest a table before me . . . : thou anointest my head with oil; my cup runneth over.

Here the imagery changes. The rural shepherd is now the generous host. We are no longer sheep, but honored guests at the Lord's table. The simple sustenance offered to the sheep is now a thanksgiving banquet, the Lord's supper. The overflowing cup reminds us of Malachi's promise of blessings in excess of our need or wants (see 3:10); or of the thousands who ate the miracle fish and loaves and were filled (see Matthew 14:16–21); or of the disciples invited to the first sacrament at the last supper (see Luke 22:15–20); or of Cleophas and his companion in Emmaus who ate, then said one to another: "Did not our heart burn within us, . . . while he opened to us the scriptures?" (Luke 24:32); or of those served at the altar in Bountiful: "He gave unto the disciples and commanded that they should eat. And when they had eaten and were filled, he commanded that they should give unto the multitude" (3 Nephi 18:3–4). Here again we have the pattern of Jesus at the well: once filled, we are able to serve others. The most transcendent example of this pattern? Christ purchased the overflowing cup for us with another: "Father, if thou be willing, remove this cup from me" (Luke 22:42). Grace for grace.

Surely goodness and mercy shall follow me all the days of my life.

Goodness is wise and consistent fairness, also called justice. We think of justice as the bad news. We want mercy and we shrink from justice. Yet justice is also the divine antidote to our cries of "It's not fair!" Of course, it *is not* fair. God's gift of agency also created endemic unfairness because of the way we would employ that agency. But the law of justice guarantees that at some point everything will be restored to its proper balance. The Psalmist tells us that justice (goodness) joins mercy and that they *follow* us each day of our life. We cannot avoid them; they are tireless and persistent pursuers.[9] Earlier in the psalm we had the impression of being hounded by evil and affliction. We now realize goodness and mercy are our rearguard. "Behold, I will go before you and be your rearward; and I will be in your midst, and you shall not be confounded" (D&C 49:27). We are literally surrounded by goodness and mercy, insulated not from the presence of evil, but from its eternal effects.

I will dwell in the house of the Lord for ever.

We return to the beginning, to the *locus amoenus*. The green pasture and still water are now the house of the Lord—the temple. The temple is the architectural manifestation of the green pasture and still waters. It is the well and the garden. It is the place most conducive to active immobility. It is three-dimensional scripture. The temple teaches how to read: we rest, we linger, and we hover over familiar things until they are freshened with new meaning.

Please permit one final analogy. We respond with enthusiasm to reports of archaeological discoveries that seem to verify events and places described in scripture: the location of Zarahemla or of Noah's ark. A far more relevant and rewarding archaeology is the digging we do in the scriptures during our moments of active immobility. These spiritual excavations uncover intimate evidence of God's covenant with each of us. This scriptural archaeology can be done in small pieces during short seasons: we need not excavate God's plan in a day. An artifact here, a vessel there; line upon line, one verse at a time. In a solitary verse we find shards of providence. They require assembling, by first looking at each piece, thinking deeply about it, then seeing how it fits together with another. Sometimes we hold a single piece in our hand for days or weeks. Contemplating its shape and texture can signal the proper choice at each fork in the road. Returning to an earlier image: savoring a single verse is more satisfying than gorging a chapter. The point is in the pausing; the coming to rest. By reading the Twenty-third Psalm we have lingered over a testimony of how the Lord brings us rest. We have read it restfully, savoring and hovering, increasing our chances of being filled.

We do not need more time; we do need to slow down for whatever amount of time we have so that the living water of each verse has time to seep in. This is what is meant, I believe, by drawing deeply out of the wells of salvation.

NOTES

1. Dale Wasserman, *The Man of La Mancha* (New York: Random House, 1966), 79.
2. Aristotle, *Ethics,* trans. by J. K. A. Thompson (London: Penguin, 1953), 14.7.27ff.
3. Lewis Carroll, *Alice's Adventures in Wonderland and Through the Looking Glass* (New York: Grosset and Dunlap, 1996), 164.
4. Robert Frost, *Collected Poems of Robert Frost* (New York: Halcyon House, 1940), 131.
5. Stewart Brand, *The Clock of the Long Now* (New York: Basic Books, 1999), 42.
6. Gordon B. Hinckley, *Teachings of Gordon B. Hinckley* (Salt Lake City: Deseret Book, 1997), 608.
7. Mitchell Dahood, *The Anchor Bible: Psalms I. 1–50* (New York: Doubleday, 1966), 145.
8. Patrick D. Miller, *Interpreting the Psalms* (Philadelphia: Fortress Press, 1986), 115.
9. See Miller, *Interpreting the Psalms,* 116.

JOY IN THE DIVINE ROLES
OF MEN AND WOMEN

Cecil O. Samuelson

While my wife, Sharon, and I enjoy doing much together, we have learned that some differences can be enriching and very helpful, rather than competitive or conflicting. Largely because of my career and callings, we have also learned to do some things on our own without feeling any minimization of our love or relationship. This is clearly a matter of attitude and choice. Let me give you just one example. Years ago when I had regular responsibility for groups of medical students, I would ask Sharon to speak to their spouses. She did a wonderful job, and her counsel always seemed to be very helpful. In fact, on occasion I still have these former student families mention how helpful her advice and example have been.

She would say something to the effect that being married will make you either a better or a worse student, and it depends on your attitude. She would also say that the potential opportunities and traumas of school and training could be either joyful or depressing. One frequent

Elder Cecil O. Samuelson, twelfth president of Brigham Young University, is a member of the First Quorum of the Seventy for The Church of Jesus Christ of Latter-day Saints. Prior to his call to full-time LDS Church service, he was senior vice president of Intermountain Health Care. In addition to his career as a physician of rheumatic and genetic diseases, he served at the University of Utah as a professor of medicine, dean of the School of Medicine, and vice president of health sciences. He and his wife, Sharon Giauque Samuelson, have five children and five grandchildren.

example was that if you are focused on how terrible and lonely it is to be alone (and young doctors' spouses are alone a lot!), then you will often be sad. On the other hand, if you choose to focus on how wonderful it is to have some time together and not really expect that you will have too much or that it will occur too often, then those moments, however few, can be most joyful. I can report that her reactions to me over almost forty years have almost always been positive but also always truthful!

Even bad news or difficult counsel is better received in an atmosphere of optimism and positivity. Necessary changes and adjustments will lead to more joyful living in a generally happy environment when they are nonthreatening and supportive.

Our family has had wonderful and touching experiences at Martin's Cove and traveling over Rocky Ridge. These gave us much more insight into our responsibilities and opportunities to find joy even in the face of almost overwhelming adversity. It also gave us renewed and enhanced appreciation for courageous ancestors who traveled with handcarts, wagons, and on foot, as well as other pioneer Church members who understood the principles of real joy in the face of the daunting disappointments and challenges of mortality.

This trip also demonstrated for me again the principle that those of us who are married can find joy and satisfaction in doing things together even when we might contribute in different ways or see some of the particulars with divergent perspectives. As we went over Rocky Ridge in our aged family vacation vehicle, I took great pleasure in the capacity of our 4-wheel drive to navigate up and over the very rough terrain. Sharon took equal pleasure in carefully and frequently directing and correcting my driving.

We have done other things together—differently. When we built our home thirty years ago, I delighted in drawing plans, pouring concrete, framing, and doing other carpentry work. Sharon used her talents in selecting and staining much of the finish woodwork and cabinetry. I enjoyed calculating the electrical circuits and stringing the wires, and she assumed the heavy task of choosing the light fixtures and other finishes and furnishings. She was wise enough not to counsel me much about the sizes or routes of the plumbing pipes, and I happily left to her entirely the choice of basins and sinks.

We even have gardened together over the years. Sharon has a green thumb, and I have green stains on the knees of my jeans. She knows for sure what shrubs to plant and where, and I know how to dig the holes the right depth! I installed the sprinkler system, but she is the one who understands the timer and when the water should come on and go off. We have even found joy in gourmet cooking! Sharon prepares it with great enthusiasm, and I, with equal glee, eat it. This could go on and on, but I think you get the point. We enjoy being together and also enjoy our differences, which we believe are real but also are compatible and complementary. Thus we, with you, can understand the doctrinal and scriptural basis, as well as the experiential, for finding joy in the God-ordained differences between men and women, husband and wife.

It does seem important to understand that within the framework of the gospel, which includes the priesthood and sacred roles unique to women and men, considerable room exists for individual choice and preference as well as capacity to adapt to necessary personal and family circumstances. For example, I know devoted and exemplary Latter-day Saint women who are able to hang sheetrock, lay beautiful wood flooring, and program their VCRs! Likewise, I know a wonderful priesthood leader, father, and patriarch who enjoys knitting. I have never felt that a man who can sew on a button, iron a shirt, or run a vacuum cleaner is demeaned in any way.

Understanding these joyful differences is also possible and necessary for those without companions or those yet to be married. Again, the combinations of preference and necessity are given great latitude in God's plan for His children when we understand who we really are.

These significant but wonderful differences also apply in our Church assignments and experiences. Think of bishops and Relief Society presidents as they attend to the welfare needs of their wards. Neither has the experience nor the insights possessed by his or her counterpart, and both are necessary to bless the members to the fullest. Likewise, we see the wisdom in Heavenly Father's plan, which provides the optimal situation for rearing children under the loving stewardship of both a faithful mother and a faithful father who complement and support each other in their unique responsibilities. Gratefully, provisions are often made to compensate when the ideal does not occur or is interrupted. Sadly, in the world today, there are those voices who suggest that the ideal is not possible and also that it is not desirable. More than ever before, we need to understand that the unique roles of women and men are both necessary and joyful.

In our current world—where religion and devotion to God are often thought, if considered at all, to be synonymous with sacrifice and stultifying sobriety, restrictions, and restraints—one of the most stunning doctrinal assertions of the Restoration is that "men [and women] are, that they might have joy" (2 Nephi 2:25). What is this joy and how are we to obtain it?

I believe most of us would not be surprised by a dictionary definition of *joy*. One of the best describes joy as a feeling of happiness (or contentment) that comes from success, good fortune, or a sense of well-being.[1] Sadly, none of the dictionaries with which I am familiar seeks to identify the real source of real joy. There are additional words that others may consider to be synonyms but that might not quite match the mark from our perspective. Examples include words like *pleasure, fun, gratification,* and the like.

The scriptures use a phrase—*a fulness of joy*—that provides clarifying and useful insights. Some general and doctrinal principles seem evident that we might apply to our consideration of finding joy in our unique roles as women and men. Let me mention a few.

The Psalmist said, "In thy presence [meaning the Lord's] is fulness of joy" (Psalm 16:11). A definition of the fulness of joy, then, is being in the presence of the Father and the Son, and the promise of the scriptures to us is that we were created to be able to return to Them and experience this fulness of joy. Fundamental to the entire plan of salvation is that we might achieve joy—real joy—and experience it in its fulness.

Jesus Himself adds assurance and clarity. As He taught the Three Nephites, who desired to remain on earth until the Second Coming, He commended them for their desires to "bring the souls of men unto me."

He also explained, "For this cause ye shall have fulness of joy; and ye shall sit down in the kingdom of my Father; yea, your joy shall be full, even as the Father hath given me fulness of joy; and ye shall be even as I am, and I am even as the Father; and the Father and I are one" (3 Nephi 28:9–10). The fulness of joy includes not only proximity or propinquity with Deity, it means a oneness with the Father and Son. What a distance in time, place, attitude, and behavior we have yet to go to truly have and experience a fulness of joy!

Through the Prophet Joseph, we receive some additional understanding and clarification that shed light on the essentiality of the Resurrection and its relationship to our potential joy. We are dual beings. Our spirits have existed for a very long time, long before we came to earth in mortality. Our bodies, essential to our progression and return to the Father and the Son, are made of the "elements." When our bodies and spirits are separated, we cannot receive a fulness of joy, but when our spirits and bodies are "inseparably connected," or we are resurrected, we can "receive a fulness of joy" if we have otherwise qualified (see D&C 93:33). Thus, the Atonement is key and even more magnificent when we consider it is really about making a fulness of joy possible for us.

Special Enoch, blessed of the Lord with uncommon and most sacred insights because of his remarkable goodness and almost limitless faith, was privileged to be a witness of a panorama of the plan of salvation from the beginning to the end. Enoch "received a fulness of joy" (Moses 7:67) as he and "his people walked with God" (Moses 7:69) and were taken into His presence.

Clearly, then, joy means more to us than momentary comfort, no matter how comfortable we are or may be! When we understand the basic and broader dimensions of joy, pleasure must be seen in context. Proximate gratifications are often antithetical to real, lasting joy that leads us to a fulness.

One of the wonders of joy is that it can be limitless in the sense that one person's fulness does not subtract from another's. In fact, as we were reminded in the examples of Enoch and the Three Nephites, they received a fulness of joy in large part because of their exemplary efforts to bring a fulness of joy to others. Just as Jesus models His love for us by what He has done and continues to do for us, so must we be what we should and do what we must for others to truly achieve the joy that is fully possible for all of us. Think of these encouraging words of the Redeemer as He expresses His love in the context of His instruction: "If ye keep my commandments, ye shall abide in my love; even as I have kept my Father's commandments, and abide in his love. These things have I spoken unto you, that my joy might remain in you, and that your joy might be full" (John 15:10–11). Jesus has joy, and He wants us to have His joy remain with us—to feel it, savor it, experience it, and share it—all to the effect that our "joy might be full."

What are some other applications of the doctrine of joy that we might consider in our special, unique, and God-given roles as women and men? We know that our individual identities are neither accidental nor unknown to God. Further, our mortal circumstances are a constellation of challenges that may share commonalities with others and also unexpected dimensions unique to ourselves. While we are hopefully willing to acknowledge absolute fairness in the overall plan, most feel at least sometimes, often with apparently good reason, that in the fine print of our lives stark unevenness occurs in advantages and blessings, disappointments and difficulties.

In addition to issues such as health, prosperity, geography, and opportunity, special challenges may occur in matters pertaining to the most significant parts of the plan designed to lead us to a fulness of joy. In spite of best efforts and intentions, some do not have eternal companions or children. Some have horrible difficulties in family relationships that make a future fulness of joy seem so remote as to be inconceivable. Physical, mental, emotional, and spiritual challenges vex the afflicted and those who love them. You can add many more seeming limitations, but to all—everyone—is the promise that the Savior's Atonement can fully apply to them and that a fulness of joy is eventually possible for everyone, save those relatively few who have consciously chosen to reject the Redeemer's gift. Nephi understood this principle as he explained the clear urgency of his own efforts: "For we labor diligently to write, to persuade our children, and also our brethren, to believe in

Christ, and to be reconciled to God; for we know that it is by grace that we are saved, after all we can do" (2 Nephi 25:23).

Our Father in Heaven and Jesus Christ make our personal salvation and exaltation with a fulness of joy possible by their grace through the Savior's Atonement, "after all we can do," whatever our limitations. Gratefully, the compensations of the eternities equalize the limitations of mortality when we do what we should and can. While some apparent deficiencies or handicaps are more obvious than others, we all have them to such a significant degree that a large measure of meekness and humility, in addition to unbounded gratitude and faith, should be pervasive in us.

For those of us who are married or who will have the privilege of marriage in this life, the Preacher in Ecclesiastes gives some good counsel in which, incidentally, is couched a significant promise or insight: "Live joyfully with the wife [or husband] whom thou lovest all the days of the life . . . which he [meaning God] hath given thee" (Ecclesiastes 9:9). I admit I do not know exactly how it is that the Lord gives husbands to wives and wives to husbands, except in the temple sealing ordinance. I have, like you, watched the matchmaking process all of my life. I do not believe God makes our choices for us, nor do I believe that He will instantaneously remodel any of us or our mates into that person we fantasized that we would be or marry before we got down to the practical issues at hand. He does help us with attractions, hormones, and opportunities; hopefully, the positive examples of parents, other loved ones, and leaders and, most significantly, the promptings of the Holy Ghost can assist us regarding when to proceed and when to back away. I do know that marriage is sacred, vital to God's plan, and essential to an eventual true fulness of joy in the eternities. Happily, whatever our current circumstances, we are assured that "all things must come to pass in their time" (D&C 64:32).

When we keep in mind what it really means to live joyfully, we will understand that marriage means much more than we or others may have supposed. It is not just a useful or pleasant or convenient arrangement between two people who enjoy being together and who have genuine affection and concern for each other, as significant as this may be.

Marriage is described in "The Family: A Proclamation to the World" as being "ordained of God" and vital to the eventual achievement of a fulness of joy.[2] Anything, however seemingly attractive, pleasant, or useful, that detracts, delays, or derails the pursuit of a fulness of joy must be avoided or discarded if the antonyms of true joy are not to be achieved.

Should we be surprised that so many are apparently confused about these issues or that there is so much effort being made by some to distract people from the path to a fulness of joy? I think not. These dynamics have been in operation for a long, long time and have had an impact on God's children ever since Lucifer was expelled for his rebellion and began his campaign to make as many others as possible "miserable like unto himself" (2 Nephi 2:27).

Listen to these words of Lehi to Jacob:

"For it must needs be, that there is an opposition in all things. If not so, . . . righteousness could not be brought to pass, neither wickedness, neither holiness nor misery, neither good nor bad. . . .

"And if ye shall say there is no law, ye shall also say there is no sin. If ye shall say there is no sin, ye shall also say there is no righteousness. And if there be no righteousness there be no happiness. And if there be no righteousness nor happiness there be no punishment nor misery. And if these things are not there is no God. And if there is no God we are not, neither the earth; for there could have been no creation of things, neither to act nor to be acted upon; wherefore, all things must have vanished away. . . .

"Wherefore, the Lord God gave unto man that he should act for himself. Wherefore, man could not act for himself save it should be that he was enticed by the one or the other" (2 Nephi 2:11, 13, 16).

Clearly, the obtaining of a fulness of joy is not easy work nor an activity for the fainthearted woman or man! Opposition is an essential part of the plan, but so too is the magnificent gift of moral agency. Elder Neal A. Maxwell taught beautifully in a recent BYU devotional that agency is among the greatest blessings a loving Heavenly Father has bestowed upon His children, but it is also unavoidably accompanied by great responsibility. Wonderfully, we can choose to be joyful now and achieve a fulness of joy in the eternities.

Often we hear those making poor choices in their lives say, "I'm only hurting myself." That is such a great lie that even the adversary should blush, were he able to do so. What we do individually, and this is particularly true in families, has an impact upon those around us to a great degree, whether it be positive or negative. If my path is not leading to a fulness of joy, these nearest and dearest of necessity have their own joy and future possibilities severely impacted negatively.

Little wonder then that this simple but carefully targeted sentence from 3 John resonates so clearly with those who are beginning to understand what the business of joy is really all about: "I have no greater joy than to hear that my children walk in truth" (3 John 1:4). Likewise, we should experience little surprise when we discover that prophets like Lehi, King Benjamin, and Alma have recognized that their first duties were to their families or that others like the Prophet Joseph and his closest associates have been reproved by the Lord when they were distracted away from family responsibilities by even very important considerations. (See D&C 93:41–50.)

While we may all be very familiar with these scriptural references, there is a verse following the counsel and rebuke to Joseph Smith that we may usually ignore: "What I say unto one I say unto all; pray always lest that wicked one have power in you, and remove you out of your place" (D&C 93:49). Our place in the Church or in the world can be in jeopardy, but also, and especially, our place in the only precincts where a "fulness of joy" can be experienced.

Emma Smith learned some important things when Doctrine and Covenants section 25 was given, but I suspect that Joseph, her husband, did also! I used to believe the words "this is my voice unto all," which conclude this section, were to all women or sisters (D&C 25:16). As has often been the case, my view was too constricted. I believe now that it also applies to me and to all men as well as to all women. This section is fully inclusive in its basic message, even in the face of some important details included for Emma alone. I believe that it has some truths or secrets, which, if understood and applied, will help us all live more joyfully. Let me mention a few of these. I invite your careful study of these verses, and you will find others.

First, Emma and the rest of us are daughters and sons of God. We need to be very careful about whose relatives we offend!

Second, if we are "faithful and walk in the paths of virtue" (D&C 25:2), our lives will be preserved and we will receive a fulness of joy. This does not tell us how long we will dwell in mortality. It does promise our outcome if we live as we should.

Third, our sins can be forgiven. Each of you sisters, like Emma, can be "an elect lady" (D&C 25:3).

Fourth, the Lord is free with His counsel to bless us if we will listen. Here are two concrete examples that may apply more broadly than just to Emma Smith:

"Murmur not because of the things which thou has not seen, for they are withheld from thee and from the world, which is wisdom in me in a time to come.

"And the office of thy calling shall be for a comfort unto . . . thy husband [or wife], in his [or her] afflictions, with consoling words, in the spirit of meekness" (D&C 25:4–5).

Fifth, if we are called to teach or serve, we can be set apart and use the scriptures effectively as directed by the Spirit. The best teachers in the home are almost always the mothers—both because of their special endowment as mothers and because they get of necessity the most constant practice! It is also true in my experience that often the best instructors in the ward or branch are the women, whether in the Gospel Doctrine class or in the Primary. For this reason, the Lord has emphasized that for all of us, but especially for women, "thy time shall be given . . . to learning much" (D&C 25:8). This learning does not exclude the scriptures!

Interestingly, as the Lord gives assurance and guidance to the sisters and wives, He also gives direction to husbands—not just prophets or bishops, but to all men and husbands: "And thou needest not fear, for thy husband shall support thee" (D&C 25:9).

Some of the particulars mentioned in this verse apply to the Prophet Joseph, but the direction that husbands need to support their wives is very clear, whatever the unique personal circumstances: "And verily I say unto thee that thou shalt lay aside the things of this world, and seek for the things of a better" (D&C 25:10).

"Things of a better." Does that sound like a fulness of joy?

I hope that each of us can understand a little better and a little more clearly both the possibilities and the promises that lead to a fulness of joy. Joyful living in the here and now is an important antecedent to the complete joy that we know can be ours in the eternities, which is made possible by the presence with us of our families in the company of the Father and the Son.

"Wherefore, lift up thy heart and rejoice, and cleave unto the covenants which thou hast made.

"Continue in the spirit of meekness, and beware of pride. Let thy soul delight in thy husband, and the glory which shall come upon him.

"Keep my commandments continually, and a crown of righteousness thou shalt receive. And except thou do this, where I am you cannot come" (D&C 25:13–15).

Let us find joy in our sacred roles as women and men and achieve the fulness of joy that the Father has promised His faithful children.

NOTES

1. See *Webster's Ninth New Collegiate Dictionary* (Springfield, Mass.: Merriam–Webster, 1987), s.v. "joy."

2. "The Family: A Proclamation to the World," *Ensign*, November 1995, 102.

HER CALLING—HER BLESSING

—◆—

Donna Smith Packer

> Do you know who you are, little child of mine,
> So precious and dear to me?
> Do you know you're a part of a great design
> That is vast as eternity?
> Can you think for a moment how much depends
> On your holding the "Iron Rod"?
> Your life is forever—worlds without end.
> Do you know you're a child of God?
>
> Do you know where you've been, little child of mine?
> It is hard to recall, I know.
> Do you ever remember that home divine
> With the [Parents who loved] you so?[1]

These lyrics from the song "To a Child," by Ora Pate Stewart, always bring the Lord's Spirit to me.

My husband and I had been married for nine years when we heard these words from the doctor: "You are not going to keep this one."

Donna Smith Packer is married to President Boyd K. Packer, Acting President of the Quorum of the Twelve Apostles of The Church of Jesus Christ of Latter-day Saints. They are the parents of ten children. Sister Packer is actively involved with her family, church, and community. She is the author of On Footings of the Past: The Packers of England.

As parents we looked at the wee baby who so recently had left his heavenly home. We did the only thing we could do. He was named and given a father's blessing. We prayed, had faith, and said aloud, "Thy will be done." Hours passed, and then days, in our very small community hospital. Doctors and nurses continued to work with our son. At last, we heard the words from the doctor, "I believe you will keep this one." During this experience, we as parents grew in understanding and strength and drew closer to the Lord.

In a much larger hospital thirteen years later, this exact experience was repeated with our tenth child. He was named and given a father's blessing. We prayed, had faith, and once again said aloud, "Thy will be done." Hours crept slowly by. Once again we were greatly blessed. He would live. The lessons learned years before had been repeated. Soon President Packer, then an Assistant to the Twelve, was able to catch a flight for a delayed assignment in Europe.

This second time our children were older. We reinforced our teaching of the Father's plan, the Atonement, and the Godhead. In teaching our children we also learned the basic principles of the gospel ourselves. Teaching and growth never end with children or parents.

Sometimes I get a telephone call from one of our children. They need help or they express concern about an overwhelming new Church calling. Other times they just call to report in. The boys "call home" to their father to get advice on practical and spiritual matters. "Calling home" is an important part of our family. "Calling home" through prayer to our Heavenly Father is a necessity. We need His help and comfort and blessing.

Sister Freda Johanna Jensen Lee, wife of President Harold B. Lee, would say, "My first good morning is to the Lord, and my last goodnight is to the Lord." I know she was right to do this.

We can't go too far astray if we, on bended knee, place a call to our Heavenly Father's home twice a day. We will receive the expected help, assurance, and peace of mind.

Some years ago two of our little boys were wrestling on the rug before the fireplace. They had reached the pitch where laughter turns to tears and play becomes a struggle. My husband worked his foot gently between them and lifted the older, four-year-old boy to a sitting position on the rug, saying, "Hey there, you monkey! You had better settle down."

The little child folded his arms and looked at his father with surprising seriousness. His little-boy feelings were hurt, and he protested, "I not a monkey, Daddy; I a *person!*" And indeed he was a person, a child of God loaned to us for a short time, and then he would be on his own.[2]

"The Family: A Proclamation to the World" is akin to scripture. Today I will quote only two paragraphs:

"All human beings—male and female—are created in the image of God. Each is a beloved spirit son or daughter of heavenly parents, and, as such, each has a divine nature and destiny. Gender is an essential characteristic of individual premortal, mortal, and eternal identity and purpose.

"In the premortal realm, spirit sons and daughters knew and worshiped God as their Eternal Father and accepted His plan by which His children could obtain a physical body and gain earthly experience to progress toward perfection and ultimately realize his or her divine destiny as an heir of eternal life. The divine plan of happiness enables family relationships to be perpetuated beyond the grave. Sacred ordinances and covenants available in holy temples make it possible for individuals to return to the presence of God and for families to be united eternally."[3]

In an address at a general Relief Society conference, President J. Reuben Clark Jr. said:

"Eve came to build, to organize, through the power of the Father, the bodies of mortal men, . . . so that God's design and the Great Plan might meet fruition.

"This was her calling; this was her blessing, bestowed by the Priesthood. This is the place of our wives and of our mothers in the Eternal Plan. . . .

" . . . Mother guides, incites, entreats, instructs, directs . . . the soul for which she built the earthly home, in its march onward to exaltation. God gives the soul its destiny, but mother leads it along the way."[4]

The vision of what is expected in earth life can be obtained through scripture study, words of the prophets, and pondering "The Family: A

Proclamation to the World." With the inspiration of the Holy Ghost, we can understand these things. We can understand the past, focus on the present, and see into the future. Work and service are requirements throughout our lifetime.

The gospel of Jesus Christ gives answers to questions that all mankind ponders. These concepts are taught nowhere else in the world. Elder Packer has said:

"There are so many unanswered questions. Why the inequities in life?

"Some are so rich.

"Some so wretchedly poor.

"Some so beautifully formed, and others with pitiful handicaps.

"Some are gifted and others retarded.

"Why the injustice, the untimely death? Why the neglect, the sorrow, the pain? . . .

"The doctrine is simply this: life did not begin with mortal birth. We lived in spirit form before we entered mortality. We are spiritually the children of God. . . .

"The scriptures teach this doctrine, the doctrine of premortal life. For His own reasons, the Lord provides answers to some questions [scattered throughout] the scriptures. We are to find them; [but] we are to *earn* them. In that way sacred things are hidden from the insincere. . . .

" . . . When one knows the doctrine, parenthood becomes a sacred obligation, the begetting of life a sacred privilege."[5]

I have a personal witness that what he said is true. Having a testimony of the gospel of Jesus Christ gives us confidence and courage in life. We can yield our agency to the Lord and let Him manage our lives. I know it requires faith to do this, but our divine nature gives us that strength, and we find joy in our commitment and our duty.

Sometimes, because of another person's agency, we cannot follow through on all our mortal commitments. The Lord loves us, understands us, and will bless us for our desires and efforts.

Our present-day servants of the Lord have made it very plain that marriage and children will not eternally be denied righteous women. The Lord is a just God.

I became acquainted with the book *Gospel Doctrine* by Joseph F. Smith in my early married years. The chapters on priesthood and home and family have been most helpful to me. One section is called "The Truest Greatness." This prophet states:

"To do well those things which God ordained to be the common lot of all man-kind, is the truest greatness. To be a successful father or a successful mother is greater than to be a successful general or a successful statesman. . . .

"We should never be discouraged in those daily tasks which God has ordained to the common lot of man. . . .

"Let us not be trying to substitute an artificial life for the true one."[6]

When our ten children were at home, I sometimes would wonder if our teachings were being transferred to them. One day I noticed a drawing by one of the children. It was of the young boy Joseph Smith and the First Vision. Joseph had been drawn looking up at two Heavenly Beings. I saw individual fingers and toes on the Heavenly Visitors. At that moment it was confirmed in my heart that our gospel teachings were being received by our children.

Another time I had a great learning experience. It was a very busy day when all of our ten children were living at home. Somehow my day had gotten away from me. The dinner hour was near, and I recalled some sound advice my mother had given me: "You plan ahead, and you get your simple nutritious meals going early in the day. You know the children will be hungry before the dinner hour. Use some common sense. Sometimes you may have to feed them early." This advice had been overlooked that day.

I hastily moved into action. The assigned children on meal preparation came to my aid, and soon dinner was underway. I heard the hum of a busy household and then an unusual sound in another room. I found two of the younger children having a difference of opinion. I suggested that each could sit on a chair and think things over. The younger one looked at me in defiance and said, "You not in charge of me!" I was a bit taken aback, but I just quietly drew him aside and calmly explained that Heavenly Father had temporarily assigned me to love and to care for him. It took only a few more sentences, and he climbed up on the chair to think.

Soon the dinner bell rang, and we all sat up to the table. I learned the value of prompt meals. I had been part of the problem that day. Yes, the crisis was over but the learning was not. As I recall, our next family home evening lesson was on obedience.

As parents we worked together in our home. The children soon learned that we were united. The answers from father and mother were always the same. We taught the children that there would come a time when they would leave home. It was time for more schooling, a mission, and marriage. Even with the world going downhill, we had confidence they could face troubled times. We wanted them to have the fulness of life. We would always be available, but we were willing to let them go with our love, faith, and blessings. Even though we as parents knew the adversary had great power in the world, we also knew that worthy sons and daughters of God have power over Satan. Our children had the divine nature, and they could succeed on their own.

My Grandmother Jordan was a great example of one who knew her divine nature. In 1909, as a recent convert to the Church, she had to make difficult decisions and take firm action, unlike her typically quiet, timid self. She told me she received prayerful direction, and she was empowered with vision and strength beyond her own. Because she did what had to be done, I had the blessing of being born in the covenant and having a rich heritage. I have many ancestors who have faced life with courage. Their actions have given me great advantages and responsibilities.

For the past forty-three years my husband has been away most weekends on Church service. This has been a productive family history time. Becoming acquainted with previous generations has given me great joy and happiness. Our family has enjoyed researching, writing, and illustrating life stories and having the temple experiences together. Knowing our ancestors and serving them has brought a richness into our lives. Our ancestors are vitally interested in our successes here on earth. I know on many occasions I have received help from the other side.

I am in harmony with the thoughts of Elder Melvin J. Ballard:

"I believe . . . that the hearts not only of the children are turned to their fathers, but the hearts of the fathers in the Spirit World are turned to their children on earth. . . .

" . . . There are evidences that the dead are interested. If you will go forward with the research work the way will be opened on the right and on the left. You will be astonished to find avenues open. . . .

"When you have done all you can do and have reached the limit, what will happen? . . . *Then will come God's opportunity.*"[7]

Cleo, an auntie of mine, was in a nursing home. After traveling some distance, we made a final visit. Cleo and her husband, Cliff, were content and at peace. At one point during our visit, Cleo spoke forcefully: "I can't just lay around here. I must get on with life." She did not mean this earthly life. The Lord granted her desire. I am certain she was welcomed by loving earthly parents and a multitude of family members for whom she had been instrumental in finding their names and seeing to their temple work.

Because of the divine nature of women, we seem to be very sensitive to the whisperings of the Holy Ghost. In the home, mothers need to act as the receiving station for the communications from a loving Father in Heaven. It is vital that you remain worthy and alert. You must avoid getting too stressed or busy for the quiet promptings of the Spirit.

While raising our seven sons and three daughters, I had a few down days. The budget was very tight, physical demands were high, and I felt the expectations of others were even higher. Even though I recognized my divine nature, knew about the plan of happiness, and knew my husband was a worthy priesthood holder, I still had a few discouraging days as we raised our large family.

I learned that if I felt physically well I was more optimistic and better able to cope with life. I studied and practiced the Lord's law of health. I was responsible to give my children a healthy start in life. Sleep was an essential, so we retired early. We combined this with regular attendance at Church meetings. Renewing our covenants with the Lord and the association with people with similar goals helped us to stay on course. Temple attendance helped me to clarify my vision and gave me a deep feeling of gratitude for all my blessings and my opportunities for growth.

There was consistent help from our extended family—a box of outgrown clothing, a basket of fruit, an hour of babysitting at just the right time. The Relief Society gave thrifty and practical homemaking ideas. I always felt their love and support.

Music had the power to comfort, edify, and bring joy into my everyday living.

Posting uplifting statements around the home as gentle reminders of what life is all about has helped me. I'll give you a few of my favorite statements:

President David O. McKay liked to say, " 'Whate'er thou art, act well thy part.' "[8]

I once heard Sister McKay say, "It is the artful duty for the woman to adjust."

I enjoy the scripture "Be thou humble; and the Lord thy God shall lead thee by the hand, and give thee answer to thy prayers" (D&C 112:10).

The Prophet Joseph Smith said, "There must be decision of character, aside from sympathy."[9]

A 1950s *Children's Friend* magazine had a poem that I posted inside a kitchen cupboard door. The paper was yellow with age before our children were raised. On difficult days this poem quickly brought back my focus:

Plastic little [children],
Made from heaven's clay.
Oh, Father, give us vision,
To mould them right today.
Potential gods in miniature;
We must have help from Thee;
For how they're fashioned here today,
Will endure through eternity.[10]

There are rewards for completion of commitments and promises to the Lord. President J. Reuben Clark Jr. told the Relief Society sisters:

"The Priesthood will wish to proclaim their debt to these their help-meets without whom the Priesthood could not have worked out their destiny. . . .

" . . . Your offspring, saved and exalted in the presence of God, will never forget you, will ever bless you, and will sing hymns of eternal gratitude for the bodies you gave them and taught them to make the Temples of the Spirit of God."[11]

My husband and I have seen some rewards of our teaching as we have watched our children, grandchildren, and, now, great-grandchildren. Children are always desired and welcomed in our family. Sometimes faith is tested, but we have found if we keep our covenants, the Lord will bless us. Our grandchildren's world is more challenging than our world was, but their parents are doing a much better job than we did.

We are grateful other families teach their children the basic principles of the gospel, obedience to all commandments, and of their divine nature. They have raised special children, allowing our children and grandchildren to be married in the temple to worthy partners. We have the assurance that the younger generation is equally yoked, having the same desires and eternal goals. They "shall stand in holy places, and shall not be moved" (D&C 45:32).

In the year 2002 we celebrated our fifty-fifth wedding anniversary with our family of nearly a hundred. We pondered a theme for the evening, "A Legacy of Covenant Choices." This was spelled out in framed needlework and is an important part of our home:

> *Faith in daily living and in the future.*
> *Courage in times of trial.*
> *Power in family unity.*
> *Service to God and Mankind.*
> *Vision of eternities together.*
> *We are covenant keepers.*

"Behold, God is my salvation; I will trust, and not be afraid: for the Lord Jehovah is my strength and my song; he also is become my salvation. Therefore with joy shall ye draw water out of the wells of salvation" (Isaiah 12:2–3).

NOTES

1. Ora Pate Stewart, "To a Child" (Provo, Utah: Fernwood, 1964).
2. See Boyd K. Packer, *The Shield of Faith* (Salt Lake City: Bookcraft, 1998), 27; emphasis in original.
3. "The Family: A Proclamation to the World," *Ensign*, November 1995, 102.
4. J. Reuben Clark Jr., "Our Wives and Our Mothers in the Eternal Plan," *Relief Society Magazine*, December 1946, 800–801, 803.
5. Boyd K. Packer, "The Mystery of Life," *Ensign*, November 1983, 16–18; emphasis in original.
6. Joseph F. Smith, *Gospel Doctrine* (Salt Lake City: Deseret Book, 1939), 285–86.
7. Melvin J. Ballard, "The Joy of Sacred Service," in *Saviors on Mount Zion*, comp. Archibald F. Bennett (Salt Lake City: Deseret Sunday School Union Board, 1950), 200–202; emphasis in original.
8. David O. McKay, *Cherished Experiences from the Writings of President David O. McKay*, comp. Clare Middlemiss (Salt Lake City: Deseret Book, 1955), 174.
9. Joseph Smith, *History of The Church of Jesus Christ of Latter-day Saints*, ed. B. H. Roberts, 2d ed. rev., 7 vols. (Salt Lake City: The Church of Jesus Christ of Latter-day Saints, 1932–51), 4:570.
10. Lucy G. Bloomfield, "Primary Teacher's Prayer," *The Children's Friend*, February 1954, 74.
11. Clark, "Our Wives and Our Mothers in the Eternal Plan," 804.

STRENGTHENING MARRIAGES, FAMILIES, AND HOMES

———◆———

Nancy Murphy

I begin with a firm testimony that our Father in Heaven lives; that His greatest desire—His work and His glory—is that we will return to Him . . . as families!

I know of nothing in mortality or in the eternities that can give us more joy than can our families. President Ezra Taft Benson said: "We must recognize that the family is the cornerstone of civilization and that no nation will rise above the caliber of its homes. The family is the rock foundation of the Church."[1] Is the family important? Sounds pretty important to me.

A few months ago I sat at a fiftieth wedding anniversary celebration for my parents. I kind of like the idea that after fifty years you get a party. If my husband can put up with me for fifty years, that man deserves a party! All of my siblings and most of their children were there. The love and devotion felt in that room that night was tangible. As I thought about the occasion that brought us together and contemplated these two lives filled with goodness and righteousness, I reflected on the question: How? How did they do it? What did my parents do to create these

---

Nancy Murphy is a graduate of Brigham Young University. She married her husband, Dale, on October 29, 1979. They are the parents of eight children—seven sons and one daughter. She served with her husband as he presided over the Massachusetts Boston Mission from 1997 to 2000. The family currently lives in Alpine, Utah.

eternal bonds between daughters and sons, parents and children, brothers and sisters—bonds that will be felt for many generations to come?

As we talk about that question today—How?—my greatest desire is that none of us goes home overwhelmed or discouraged. It is so easy to be too hard on ourselves. We must remember that life—and perfection—is a process. Poet Maya Angelou says that whenever anyone tells her they are a Christian, she always replies, "Already?" Discouragement is truly one of Satan's favorite tools. But discouragement is not an option today! There is much to be done and we cannot waste time being discouraged. As children of God and disciples of Christ, we know who we are, where we came from, where we are going, and how we are getting there. Optimism and hope should fill our souls with peace. Whenever I feel overwhelmed, discouraged, or inadequate, I take great comfort in the continuing admonition of our dear prophet to just do the very best we can.

I think of another prophet, Nephi, and the overwhelmed feeling he must have had when the Lord commanded him to build a ship. My husband and my fourteen-year-old son built a canoe one summer—actually it was more like one year! Dale was bishop at the time and our neighbors, seeing this boat in process, used to say, "Do you know something we don't?"

Anyway, back to Nephi. After all Nephi had so obediently done, I often wonder: At the moment the ship was first mentioned, did the thought cross his mind, "Something *more* to do?" Well, knowing Nephi as we do, we can be absolutely certain that he did not complain or question and that the look on his face was not one of exasperation, but one of determination, obedience, and faith.

We—imperfect mortals struggling to learn the lessons Nephi had mastered—have we ever in frustration asked how we can do it all? Does it always feel like there is something more to do? Nephi's response inspires us. He said, "I will," and he simply asked, "How?"

Knowing full well that we are each doing our very best and with great love and respect for you, the women of the Church, let me offer a few ideas that reflect lessons the Lord has taught me personally in my own life.

As we think of families—our families—there are a few things that I am absolutely sure of:

I am absolutely sure that love is deepened and unity established when we take the time as families to simply *be together*. There is no substitute for it, no shortcuts!

I remember a day, several weeks into our mission, Dale and I were talking about how little we had seen of each other since our arrival in Boston. I told him I was counting on what someone had told us in the MTC—that this calling was so wonderful because it was a calling in which we could serve together. I looked at him and said, "Now when do you think the *together* part starts?"

In our families, as we make the "together" part a priority, we will find those moments together. It need not be an expensive vacation; a trip to get ice cream can be fun, too. It need not be difficult to arrange; an impromptu talk together on the edge of a child's bed can fill an unspoken need. I loved the insight given me on this subject by a friend whose expertise lies in counseling families. He told me that, in his experience, time spent together is vital—even critical—to healthy relationships. He told me that it almost doesn't even matter *what* you do.

During the first year of our mission, we learned this for ourselves. Spring break was approaching. Our children were coming home telling of the plans of friends and fun trips they would be taking: California, New York, Hawaii, even Europe. They kept asking us where we would be going for our vacation. Knowing our mission boundaries well (and quite certain we would not be running into any of their friends on our spring break trip!), we fully expected the reaction we got when we told them our plans. We would be at a hotel in western Massachusetts just one hour from the mission home. Needless to say, the news did not go over well.

We laugh about that now and remember those few days of spring break as one of our very favorite vacations. Not because of where we were or what we did, but because of the simple fact that we were all together.

One study sought to answer the question, "What is your favorite memory from your childhood of time spent with your family?" Number one on the list? Camping. Not some elegant hotel on the beach in Hawaii. Camping! And the really interesting part of that answer was that camping was actually the most memorable because of the things that went wrong. The stories became funnier and time together more precious as the years went by, creating strong and binding memories.

A few months ago, my husband and I were struggling with ideas of how to get our children to spend time together—voluntarily—on their own. We devised a plan for family home evening, and what we learned was an eye-opener. We planned a "buddy night" where each of our younger children would draw the name of one of the older children—or their dad or me—out of a hat. These buddy pairs would get into separate cars, go eat together—just the two of them—and we'd all meet afterwards for ice cream. Thinking that some of them might look at an hour with a sibling as some newly created form of torture, we were prepared for the complaints as the directions were explained. But the complaints never came! They were actually *excited* to spend time together. So excited, in fact, that our youngest child and only daughter, ten-year-old Madison, looked really sad after the names were drawn. Thinking she must have ended up with the name of a brother she didn't want to go to dinner with, we asked her what was wrong. "Did you get the name of a brother you didn't really want?" "No," she said. "I got DAD!" After some trading around, we left the house in five different cars—Madison with an older brother (smiling ear to ear). The two names no one wanted—Mom and Dad—ended up in a car together—alone—just the two of us! Actually, we couldn't have planned it more perfectly.

You know, I think our children *do* want to spend time together. The pull of activities and friends and lives of their own has caused a certain isolation within the family. We must have a steady, sustained force pulling back, bringing our children back into our families where they belong. We can facilitate time together as we make it a priority, spend a little time planning, and then do it!

There's another thing I'm absolutely sure of: Many, many good things call out to us for our time. As women, we passed through a day when we thought we could—and tried—to do it all. The Superwoman

Syndrome was born. Do you remember that? I certainly do. But we are wiser now. Reality, and time, have taught us that we really can't do it all. We must choose on what and how to spend our precious hours. The question again is "How?" How do we make that choice? How do we choose what is best? We have the words of modern-day prophets, scriptures to liken unto ourselves, and the Holy Ghost. What more could we need?

I have hanging on my kitchen wall a reminder to me that I'd better choose carefully. It reads, "That which you give your time to, you give your life to." I have thought of that often as I divide and redivide my time, consider and reconsider where those extra minutes should be spent. Sister Sheri Dew tells us: "Anything that takes us closer to exaltation is worth our time and energy. Anything that doesn't is a distraction."[2] Yes, we must choose wisely, for the hours and days and years we give somewhere to someone will be the legacy we leave behind.

In the words of John A. Widtsoe: "In life, all must choose at times. Sometimes, two possibilities are good; neither is evil. Usually, however, one is of greater import than the other. When in doubt, each must choose that which concerns the good of others—the greater law—rather than that which chiefly benefits ourselves—the lesser law. . . . The greater must be chosen whether it be law or thing. That was the choice made in Eden."[3]

I would imagine that Satan knows very well that if he can keep us busy—really busy—so busy that we don't have time even for each other, that he has gained a victory. Robert Matthews warns us: "A thing does not have to be false to be wrong. It just has to divert us from other, more important things." These words from Elder Neal A. Maxwell beautifully illustrate this thought: "Even something as small as a man's thumb, when held very near the eye, can blind him to the very large sun. Yet the sun is still there. Blindness is brought upon the man by himself. When we draw other things too close, placing them first, we obscure our vision of heaven."[4]

Spending time together brings about a blending of hearts, the joining together of minds, and the overlapping of individual purpose, which, in turn, brings true unity to our homes.

Guard those moments together. Plan for them. Sacrifice for them. Make them happen. When asked what we can do to strengthen the family, Mother Teresa answered, "Go home and love your children." I think she had in mind that we ought to spend time—together!

Another thing I am absolutely sure of was taught to us by a friend and former mission president in Atlanta during our early married years. When we asked him the question, "How?" he said, "Do the basics really well." It has been valuable advice in our lives. And what basics did he mean? Family scripture study, family home evening, and family prayer. Not only are they critical in our spiritual growth, but the simple act of doing them causes us to spend more time together!

If your family is anything like ours, you may wonder sometimes how much you are accomplishing at family home evening when no one is listening to the lesson, or when teenagers wrap themselves up in blankets and fall asleep on the floor during family scripture study. I frequently say that I am no expert. But I do consider myself an expert on everything that can go wrong at family home evening!

I'm sure there are times we all feel like we are failing in these areas and, truly, I suspect you are doing better than you might think. Let me assure you, the day will come that your children will bless your name for your efforts. They will remember, if nothing else, that it meant enough to you that you kept trying. As I sat in a small chapel in southern Japan, I was amazed at the words spoken by my soon-to-be-released missionary son who expressed appreciation to parents who always (that was *his* word—ALWAYS—and I was grateful at that moment that his memory was not perfect!) always had family scripture study. He was one of those wrapped up in a blanket, barely coherent enough (I thought!) to know we were actually reading scriptures together. But he did. And he remembered.

Don't give up. One step forward, two back, three forward, one back. That's the drill at the Murphy home. The trick is to just keep going. Just keep trying! Mosiah 4:27 teaches us that it is not speed, but diligence, and Elder Neal A. Maxwell reminds us that "it is direction first, *then* velocity."[5] I truly believe that most of the blessings come in the trying. Sometimes it is not easy, but it is always worth it. Promised blessings will fill our lives as we remain steadfast in our efforts to "do the basics really well." The First Presidency has written, "We promise you through regular prayer and study of the scriptures and doctrines of the gospel you will be prepared to withstand evil influences that would deceive you and harm you."[6]

I am also absolutely sure that we live in a day unlike any other. It is the day prophesied of for hundreds and thousands of years past. Satan is at work, perhaps at this point working overtime, and in order to withstand the day, we must have strong, resilient families.

I imagine sometimes that it is as if we are all floating along in lifeboats, being tossed to and fro on the sea of life. The storms swirl around us as we hold tightly to our precious cargo—our children—for fear that they might fall overboard. Occasionally, the wind is too strong and the waves too high and, fearing that one might be lost, we hold tightly and pray mightily. Should one fall into the deep, we set out with rescue in mind. For there is no feeling so wonderful for a mother as to know her children are all safe from the raging tempest. John understood this when he wrote, "I have no greater joy than to hear that my children walk in truth" (3 John 1:4).

Because of our love for them, we must create for our children homes of safety and peace; homes where strong examples of righteous living prevail. Wholesome music, kind words, gospel conversations, and everyday examples of faith and devotion will bless the lives of our children. There's a saying in the South: "If mama ain't happy, ain't nobody happy." I'm afraid that is truer than we might want to admit. Sisters, we set the tone.

The philosopher Goethe said: "I have come to the frightening conclusion that I am the decisive element. It is my personal approach that creates the climate. It is my daily mood that makes the weather. I possess tremendous power to make a life miserable or joyous. I can be a tool, a torture, or an instrument of inspiration." It is true!

Because our hands are those that rock the cradle, we hold great power and influence, in partnership with God, in the shaping of souls. We can and must establish an environment for our children where their testimonies can flourish. We cannot, of course, keep them out of the world. But we can certainly keep the spiritual dangers of the world out of our homes.

Many of us must find our way without the benefit and righteous example of those who have come before. How exciting that we can be the starting point for all the generations that follow. We can begin—today—to build a righteous heritage for those who come after us.

Our homes must be fortresses against the unholy things of the world, where our children can feel the Spirit of the Lord. We must do all we can to invite the Spirit there. We must teach our children from the scriptures and from our own life experiences how to recognize the Spirit, for it truly is a still, small voice. Our children must feel the Spirit in their own homes so they can know and feel the difference when they find themselves in places where the Spirit does not dwell and they should not be.

We are all hungry for spiritual things and our children are no different. We can give them opportunities to feel the Spirit and to become well acquainted with its whisperings, in something as grand as a Church history trip or as simple as a testimony borne in family home evening.

Inspiration will come as we ask for recognition of those life-changing moments when the Spirit can touch their hearts and teach them more than we ever could. The Spirit will guide us so that we might guide them. I am absolutely sure that every time our children feel the Spirit it is another drop of oil in their lamps.

As our sons leave on missions, we start to fill a box with the things of the world that happen during the two years they are gone—newspapers of important events, good DVDs that are released, books that are published. We call it their "Babylon Box," and we close the lid and store it safely away, adding to it as time goes by until the day they return home. What fun they have exploring their box of things that represent the world they left behind. I have thought about that Babylon Box and decided that, if I were wise, I would find a box of my own and fill it, figuratively speaking, with all the things of the world that keep me from my eternal goals and store it away where I would never open it again.

Robert Millet shares this thought: "We cannot lay hold on eternal life unless we are willing to disengage ourselves from this world's attachments."[7] We must let go, sisters, of anything that takes our time or our hearts and keeps us from our most important, eternal pursuits. We are women of the kingdom of God. We are women of royal heritage. We have great responsibility.

Bruce R. McConkie said, "There is nothing in this world as important as the creation and perfection of family units."[8] Nothing in this world is important enough to take our time from those things that matter most.

In the play *Joan of Lorraine,* Joan of Arc, a martyr for her cause, said, "Every woman gives her life for what she believes. Sometimes people believe in little or nothing; nevertheless, they give up their lives to that little or nothing. One life is all we have . . . we live it . . . and then it's gone."[9]

No matter the storms around us, the glorious message of the gospel is that we have no need to fear. "Sweet is the peace the gospel brings."[10] Of all the promised blessings available to the disciples of Christ, peace is certainly one of the most desirable and precious. So desirable, in fact, that the world around us seeks it desperately yet cannot find it. For peace comes only through consecration to Christ; and the world, sadly, is looking in all the wrong places. Doctrine and Covenants 59:23 reads, "He who doeth the works of righteousness shall receive his reward, even peace in this world, and eternal life in the world to come."

The words of our dear prophet, Gordon B. Hinckley, define our course: "There is a better way than the way of the world," he said. "If it means standing alone, we must do it."[11] The call to leave the world and stand tall, possibly alone, in defense of truth and righteousness is not new to covenant people. The scriptures are filled with accounts of those who answered the call to take their families and leave the world behind: Lehi, Noah, and a footnote from the life of Lot: don't look back.

Great hope lies in the knowledge that we are not alone. As His daughters, we can go to our Father in Heaven for help. "Let us cheerfully do all things that lie in our power; and then may we stand still, with the utmost assurance, to see the salvation of God, and for his arm to be revealed" (D&C 123:17).

Nephi, when given a charge and directed to obey, turned heavenward. He went to the top of the mountain and was taught by the Lord. How to build a ship was only one of many great lessons. We too can find our mountaintop. We too can be taught from on high. The Lord commands us because He loves us, and because He loves us, He will lift us and help us. He will teach us how to accomplish the things He asks. In our righteous efforts, He will direct us, inspire us, and sustain us so that we, too, can go and do. Another lesson from brother Nephi.

Oliver Wendell Holmes, in his later years, was boarding a train when he realized he could not find his ticket. As he was searching through every pocket, the ticket taker recognized the problem and said, "Don't worry, you can just send it to me later." Oliver Wendell Holmes looked at him and explained, "You don't understand. The problem isn't that I can't find my ticket. The problem is that I don't know where I'm going."

How blessed we are to know our destination, to see the route outlined by God Himself. If we will align our will with His, the path will be crystal clear. The gospel is our guide, the Spirit our instructor. If we watch carefully, we will see the Lord's fingerprints in our lives and we can know for ourselves that He is truly in the details. He loves us.

Sisters, there is another thing I am absolutely sure of. We can do it! It takes courage, commitment, covenant-keeping, consecration, and concentrating on those things we cherish most. Prayerfully ask the Lord to inspire you to know how to bring your family together in unity and love and to protect you from the tempests of the world.

Here's one more thing I'm absolutely sure of: He will hear you, and He will answer.

NOTES

1. Ezra Taft Benson, "Counsel to the Saints," *Ensign*, May 1984, 6.
2. Sheri Dew, *No Doubt About It* (Salt Lake City: Bookcraft, 2001), 9.
3. John A. Widtsoe, *Evidences and Reconciliations*, ed. G. Homer Durham (Salt Lake City: Bookcraft, 1960), 194.
4. Neal A. Maxwell, *Of One Heart* (Salt Lake City: Deseret Book, 1975), 19.
5. Neal A. Maxwell, "Notwithstanding My Weakness," *Ensign*, November 1976, 13; emphasis in original.

6. *True to the Faith* (Salt Lake City: The Church of Jesus Christ of Latter-day Saints, 2004), 1.

7. Robert L. Millet, *Alive in Christ: The Miracle of Spiritual Rebirth* (Salt Lake City: Deseret Book, 1997), 29.

8. Bruce R. McConkie, in Conference Report, April 1970, 27.

9. Maxwell Anderson, *Joan of Lorraine: A Play in Two Acts* (Washington, D.C.: Anderson House, 1947), 127.

10. MaryAnn Morton, "Sweet Is the Peace the Gospel Brings," *Hymns of The Church of Jesus Christ of Latter-day Saints* (Salt Lake City: The Church of Jesus Christ of Latter-day Saints, 1985), no. 14.

11. Gordon B. Hinckley, Worldwide Priesthood Leadership broadcast, January 10, 2004.

REJOICE IN THIS DAY

Diane Bills Prince

The psalmist wrote, "This is the day which the Lord hath made; we will rejoice and be glad in it" (Psalm 118:24). Do we feel the sweetness of each day? Or do we feel stressed out, overly busy, and at times overwhelmed?

Many years ago I had an experience that had a profound impact on me. I was serving in a Relief Society presidency where we had the 9:00 to 12:00 block of church. Relief Society was first and began promptly at 9:00 A.M. Our presidency would arrive fifteen minutes early to greet and hug the sisters.

On one particular Sunday morning, *everything* was going wrong for me at our home. I don't remember clearly all of the details, but I do remember that my husband was gone to an early meeting, the children were fussy, the clothes weren't ready, and, as I recall, it was also a bad hair day. Needless to say, it was 9:15 as we walked out our front door to go to church. I put the baby in the car seat, then strapped in my toddler, Whitney.

I got in the car, put the key in the ignition, turned the car on, and

---

Diane Prince is joyfully married to Robert Prince. They have nine children and three grandchildren. Diane has been a professional motivational speaker for twenty years. She has spoken to thousands across America on family and human relations skills. She has appeared on television and is a frequent speaker at BYU Education Week. She is the author of Trust in the Lord, *as well as five talk tapes.*

put it in reverse. I then pushed on the gas pedal with a considerable degree of force. The car bolted backwards and scraped the pole that was holding up the carport. I was feeling totally frustrated, but I didn't get out of the car to see the damage. I just *wanted* to get to Church. At that moment I turned to three-year-old Whitney and said, "Honey, I am having a difficult morning. Will you say a prayer for us? I will continue driving to church, but you fold your arms and close your eyes and say a prayer."

Very obediently she did just as I had asked. Her prayer went something like this. "Dear Heavenly Father, we are SO thankful that we hit the pole this morning. In the name of Jesus Christ, amen." I began to laugh. She had a totally different perspective from mine. Hers was much more positive, innocent, and refreshing. That moment became a powerful learning experience for me. I realized that much in life is our perspective—it's the way we look at each situation.

While we come from varied backgrounds, one thing we do share is who we are and that our purpose is the same. We are all daughters of a loving Father in Heaven and we all desire to return to Him and live our lives here in joy. So how do we have joy? How do we create joy in our lives daily? Is it a matter of just deciding to be joyful? Does having a positive attitude make the difference?

I would like to share with you some ideas that have worked for me and others over the years. The new perspective is that these ideas do not give us the *answers* to having joy in our lives, but rather this new perspective gives us the *questions*—and then Heavenly Father will give us the answers.

Throughout the scriptures we read to *ask, knock, seek,* and it shall be opened unto us. Joseph Smith read in James, "If any of you lack wisdom, let him ask of God" (James 1:5). Joseph later received liberally because he was willing to ask. Joseph declared, "The best way to obtain truth and wisdom is not to ask it from books, but to go to God in prayer, and obtain divine teaching."[1]

Heavenly Father is the one who knows the answers for your life. He knows you personally and completely and *wants* to give to you liberally. He will answer in His way and His time. If these questions are applied, I have found that the answers can bring overwhelming joy into our lives and bring it every day.

So here are the questions. The first one is **Who am I?** Why is that question so important? It is important because how we act and the level of joy we feel each day is dependent on how we are feeling about ourselves.

As a college student, I served on the student council for the LDS institute at a major university. While traveling to a leadership conference for the student leaders, I had a conversation in the car that has stayed with me these nearly thirty years. The president of the student council, Lee Yates, turned to me and said something like this, "Diane, what is it that makes people motivated?" He went on to say, "I have learned one thing that I think makes all of the difference in how a person responds in life. Those who are motivated have this one thing." I thought for a few moments and then gave what I thought were some great responses. I could tell by the look on Lee's face that I had not given him the desired answer. After several more guesses and just not getting it right, I said, "OK, Lee, tell me what it is that makes people motivated." I was anxious to know and encouraged a response from him. He then told me that the one thing that makes the difference is how people feel about themselves. What a profound idea!

Since that day, I have given that conversation much thought. I studied self-worth, I even traveled the country teaching about it. But it was in humble prayer that the overwhelming answers came to me about understanding worth. I was taught by the Spirit that true worth is not a thing of the world. It is not in the titles or the honors of men; it is not in the amount of money earned or talents developed. *True self-worth is intrinsic;* it is the very core of who we are. True worth is given to all, because *all* are sons and daughters of God. Our nature is divine. Our worth is therefore divine.

I often reflect on an experience that had a measured positive effect on me and some of my friends when we were in the ninth grade. We had a seminary teacher at our school who was a stake patriarch. To us, he seemed much older. He was seasoned with life's experiences and with things of the Spirit. We relished any opportunity to be taught by him.

One particular day he was standing on the steps of the church as we entered for seminary. We were laughing and talking as ninth-grade girls do. He greeted us at the door. A few minutes later Brother Asay came into the room. As he turned around to teach us, we could see that he had been weeping. We were immediately silenced. Then Brother Asay began to speak. He said something like this, "My dear friends, today I have had one of the most spiritual experiences of my life." Now keep in mind that we knew he was a patriarch and had experiences all the time, but he had just said one of the most spiritual of his life. He continued, "As you were coming up the steps and into the building, the Lord lifted the veil from my eyes and allowed me to see who you really are." Then came the line that pierced our hearts. This man, our spiritual giant, said to us, "I felt as though I wanted to bow down before you."

Who are you? Have you ever truly pondered that question? One young woman going through a difficulty in her life received a hand-written note from a friend with these words reportedly from Wilford Woodruff: "The Lord has chosen a small number of his choice sons and daughters out of all the creations of God who are to inherit the earth. This choice company of Spirits have been saved in the Spirit world for 6000 years to come forth in the last days, to stand in the flesh in this last dispensation of the earth, to build it up and defend it and to receive the eternal and everlasting Priesthood. . . . All the angels in Heaven are looking at this little handful of people and are praying that they will succeed."

At times, and on days in our lives when we are struggling, perhaps one of the sweetest things we can do is to humbly go to a secluded spot and pray to our Father in Heaven to build us up. At that moment of need, He can help us remember who we are and feel in our hearts the perfect love He has for us. He is the one who can give us feelings of strength and worth.

So many before us have done just that. Recall with me the experience of Nephi when his brothers bound him with cords on the ship. Things were not going well, but he understood who he was. In 1 Nephi 18:16 we read, "Nevertheless, I did look unto my God, and I did praise him all the day long." Think of the Prophet Joseph Smith, who had

many associates put him down. He did not have the wealth of the world, and at times he struggled with apostates. Through it all, Joseph's strength was always in the Lord.

Look to the most important example of all, our Lord and Savior, Jesus Christ, who had the Sanhedrin against him; others spit upon him; one of his closest associates turned on him; another dear friend denied Him; and yet his strength was not in men. He knew that true strength comes from God. He knew perfectly who He was.

And so it is with us: true strength, true worth comes from God. The image of the world doesn't matter, but as Alma wrote, "Have ye received his image in your countenances?" (Alma 5:14).

The second question is **What is my purpose?** Or better expressed, Dear Father, what is Thy purpose for me today?

God will use us to bless the lives of others. President Spencer W. Kimball stated: "God does notice us, and he watches over us. But it is usually through another mortal that he meets our needs. Therefore, it is vital that we serve each other in the kingdom."[2]

I will never forget a day that I was pregnant and very ill with morning sickness. All of my family except for myself and our two-year-old daughter had gone to the BYU football game against the University of Utah. I just couldn't pull myself out of bed. After everyone was gone my two-year-old stood by my bedside. "Mommy, get out of bed, . . . Mommy, I'm hungry. . . . Mommy, Mommy, Mommy . . ." I slowly got up and went into the kitchen to get her something to eat. My stomach was so sick that I doubled over and knew in my mind that I would not make it through the day without help. My mind raced through the names of those I could call to help. My mom's name came into my mind first, but I remembered that she was helping a sister-in-law that day with her pregnancy. I then thought of all the other family members who were either BYU fans or U of U fans and knew that they would be at the game. I started to think of friends and neighbors—how could I possibly pull someone away from their family on a busy Saturday? I went back into the bedroom and fell upon my knees. My humble prayer went something like this, "Heavenly Father, I am so sick I can hardly move." And then I said this, "I know that Thou hast never been pregnant before—but I

know in Thine infinite understanding that Thou dost have a compre-
hension of how I feel." I believe He wanted me to know that He did,
because before I could say much more, my phone began to ring. I knew
in my mind it was help. I said, "Heavenly Father, that was really fast, in
the name of Jesus Christ, amen." I got to the phone just in time. On the
other end of the line was my visiting teacher, Pat. She said my name had
come into her mind profoundly and she knew to call me. A half an hour
later a loud knock came at my front door. As I opened the door, there
standing in front of me was my mom. "Hi, honey," she said. "The Spirit
told me that you needed my help today. I am here to spend the day with
you." The Prophet Joseph Smith taught to follow the *first* impressions as
they come into your mind—which is exactly what both of these dear
women had done. Many times the people we are to serve that day are in
our own family and sometimes they are not.

I had an experience one morning where I fell upon my knees and
asked Heavenly Father whom He would have me serve that day. As I
prayed, a dear friend's name came quietly into my mind. She was going
through a difficulty in her life, and I knew at that moment God would
have me serve her. I telephoned her and told her that she had been on
my mind *and* asked what could I do to help her out. She thanked me for
thinking of her, but expressed that she couldn't think of anything she
needed help with. As I hung up the phone, I thought, Was my inspiration wrong? Should I have asked in a different way? Should I just go over
and start doing things? I then offered another prayer and asked Father
to let me know *how* I could serve this woman whom He had inspired me
to call. Many hours passed; in the evening a phone call came. It was the
dear sister whom I had called earlier that day. A situation had since
come up and yes, she did need some help. She told me how she had
fallen upon her knees in a moment of grave concern and asked
Heavenly Father what to do. The Spirit whispered my name to her
mind. Isn't it wonderful! One sister praying to help another—another
sister praying for help. And through the Spirit the message is conveyed.
We hardly need telephones! My testimony was strengthened again as it
has been so many times before. He will use us, if we will but ask.

A favorite quote whose author is unknown is this, "Every morning

lean thine arms awhile upon the window sill of Heaven and gaze upon thy Lord, then with vision in thy heart, turn strong to meet the day." Overwhelming joy comes each day in serving. As we look at our perfect example of the Savior, that is what He did each day of His ministry.

The final question is **Am I holding back?** This question is so personal. It is truly between you and the Lord. Are you holding back in any way? Are you holding back in your relationships, in prayer, in tithes and offerings, in temple attendance, in missionary work, in your calling, in bringing more children into the world? There is no way that I know to bring *more peace* and *more joy* into one's life than to have our lives in perfect alignment with God's will for us. Many times the stress or discomfort we feel daily may be because we are holding back in some way. Our spirit is not at peace when we are out of alignment. But when we are doing God's will in God's time, then overwhelming joy can come.

A dear friend shared an experience she had one day while she was busily scrubbing the floor in her kitchen. Her teenage son came home from school, seemed quite upset, and immediately went to his room. She continued to scrub, thinking she needed to let him have some cool-down time, when a quiet voice spoke to her mind, "You are spending a lot of time doing nothing." Instantly she knew that God wanted her to go immediately to this son and spend time with him. That is exactly what she did, which resulted in a sweet bonding experience together. God let her know what was most important at that moment.

Our beloved President Hinckley has said: "Why are we such a happy people? It is because of our faith, the quiet assurance that abides in our hearts that our Father in Heaven, overseeing all, will look after His sons and daughters who walk before Him with love and appreciation and obedience. We will ever be a happy people if we will so conduct our lives."[3]

One of my favorite stories is recounted in an essay by the late Carlfred Broderick.[4] Brother Broderick was serving as a stake president in southern California. His profession was as a marriage and family counselor. On one occasion a woman came to him asking for a priesthood blessing. She was a neighbor, as well as part of a family that he home taught. This woman had had a difficult pregnancy in which she nearly lost her life as well as the life of her baby. But miraculously both had survived. Now a period of time had passed and she felt strongly that God wanted her to have another baby. She went to her husband with her desires. He said, "Absolutely no," because of the danger to her health. So she asked President Broderick for a blessing. He consented.

She then told her husband that she had asked President Broderick for a blessing and expressed to him that she felt like whatever the president said in this blessing is what they should do.

Her husband slipped over to the Broderick home to tell the president all the circumstances of the previous pregnancy and please would he bless her to not have any more children. President Broderick said he would be prayerful.

They went to his home and he gave a blessing. In the blessing he told her that there was another spirit waiting to come into their home and that it would be a man child. He then blessed her that all would go well in the pregnancy and that when the baby was delivered that she would have the strength to nurse the baby.

This couple were obedient, and she became pregnant. All during the pregnancy, it went as promised. The day came that she delivered a healthy, vibrant baby boy. It was on the day that she was leaving the hospital that she contracted a serious disease, one that caused large red spots on the body. There was a medication that she could receive to take the spots away, but if she did, then it would dry the mammary glands and the milk would not come in. She refused the medication because she had been promised the ability to nurse the child. She telephoned President Broderick and asked for another blessing.

He was just getting ready to leave for an important meeting in New York City. But before leaving he came to her home and placed his hands upon her head. He promised her in that blessing that the spots would go away and the milk would come in.

Partway through the week in New York, President Broderick received a phone call in his hotel room from this neighbor. She said that the spots had not gone away and that the milk had not come in. She said that she felt perhaps she was not worthy of the blessing he had given to her. To be more worthy, she had spent the night previous to this phone call pleading in prayer for forgiveness. She had then spent part of that day calling anyone she could think of that she had ever offended and asking them for forgiveness. She told the president that the spots were *still* there and the milk had not come in.

President Broderick was humbled. He began to think of his own life and wondered if he had been worthy enough to give her the blessing she had received. He said that he prayed to the Lord, saying, "Lord, this woman's faith hangs on the blessing she received at my hands. I felt your Spirit at the time. If I was wrong, don't penalize her. Cover me."

By Saturday he arrived back in California, only to find a note telling him to call the woman the minute he came in. When he telephoned, she asked him to come over. Most reluctantly, he walked to the home next door.

The woman said that she had lost her faith. She would never come to Church again because the blessing had not come true. President Broderick pleaded with her to not lose her faith over a blessing he had given. She asked if he would give her one more blessing.

President Broderick said that as he laid his hands upon her head the Lord spoke to her through him. He spoke "not of her disease and not of nursing babies, but of His love for her—that she was His daughter, that He cared for her, that He had died for her. He said that He would have died if she had been the only one. He would have suffered at Calvary for her sins, if hers had been the only ones. He didn't say one word about healing her."

The next day she came to Church even though she said she never would again. It was fast and testimony meeting. She bore a powerful witness of the Savior's love for her. Miraculously, that afternoon the spots went away and the milk came in, but not until after the trial of her faith.

In my mind, this story is not a story of spots and milk, but rather a story of the perfect love that the Savior has for each of us. I had never thought of it before in such a personal way. If you or I had been the only one, He would have still suffered in the Garden. He would have still hung on the cross, just for you and just for me. The Savior held back nothing from His Father. None of the inherent blessings of the

Atonement or Resurrection are held back from us as long as we are worthy.

Who am I? What is Thy purpose for me? Am I holding back? *Yes*, I believe we do have a responsibility for creating joy in our lives on a daily basis. That responsibility is to turn to our Father in humble prayer. He *will* guide us. He *will* direct us. The amazing thing is that as we do, our lives *will* become focused. We will let go of the unimportant and focus on that which counts. The personal answers will come and with the answers come days of joy and true satisfaction. *God lives and hears; Jesus is the living Christ.*

NOTES

1. Joseph Smith, *History of The Church of Jesus Christ of Latter-day Saints,* ed. B. H. Roberts, 2d ed. rev., 7 vols. (Salt Lake City: The Church of Jesus Christ of Latter-day Saints, 1932–51), 4:425.
2. Spencer W. Kimball, *The Teachings of Spencer W. Kimball,* ed. Edward L. Kimball (Salt Lake City: Bookcraft, 1982), 252.
3. Gordon B. Hinckley, "What Are People Asking about Us?" *Ensign,* November 1998, 72.
4. Carlfred Broderick, "The Uses of Adversity," in *As Women of Faith: Talks Selected from the BYU Women's Conferences,* ed. Mary E. Stovall and Carol Cornwall Madsen (Salt Lake City: Deseret Book, 1989), 181–85.

THE WORK THAT ONLY YOU CAN DO

Irene H. Ericksen

INTRODUCTION

Young adulthood is a time of many decisions—you stand on the threshold of life, and it's all up to you. It may also seem somewhat out of your control. For active LDS young men, the road is rather clearly marked with signposts: serve a mission, finish college and start a career, marry a wonderful girl, and start a family. For young LDS women, however, there may seem to be more questions than signposts: How much education should I plan for? What if I'm not dating? What can I do about it? Should I plan on a full-time mission? A full-blown career? Do I live with roommates or get a place of my own? Assuming I do marry, how much education should I pursue? Should we have children right away? Can I have a career and be a mother?

I married at age 28—a little late by Mormon standards. And I can still remember during my single years feeling at times like Alice in Wonderland when she meets up with the Cheshire Cat at a fork in the road and asks him which road she should take. He answers, "That depends a good deal on where you want to get to." She tells him she

---

Irene Ericksen has a master's degree in counseling and has worked for the LDS Church's research office, studying women's programs and concerns. She also has served on the Young Women general board. She and her husband, David, are the parents of two sons and live in Salt Lake City, Utah.

doesn't really know, to which he replies, "Then it doesn't matter which way you go."[1]

Well, I'm sure you're all too aware that many of your decisions at this stage of life really do matter, and perhaps knowing this adds to the sense of anxiety you feel when you come to a crossroads. You may wonder, "Is there one option that is better than the others, or are there several equally good alternatives? What if I head down a road that's going to dead-end just around the corner?" I think underneath these kinds of questions and concerns for all of us is a bigger question: *What does Heavenly Father want me to do with my life?* We want our lives to count for something, to make a difference. The steps outlined in Doctrine and Covenants 9:8 can be helpful when considering your future—that is, to study it out in your mind, seek divine counsel, and then feel a confirmation that the direction you are going in is correct.

The Big Picture

To begin with, step back with me and take a look at the "big picture," the context in which you are making decisions about your life. There are two ideas that I believe form a crucial backdrop to these decisions:

The world is rapidly becoming more evil. It appears that the battle lines have been drawn and the adversary is becoming more bold. The Lord's prophet on the earth today has been sounding a clear voice of warning about this recently. President Hinckley said, "We are living in a very difficult season in the history of the world. Standards are dropping everywhere. Nothing seems to be sacred anymore. . . . The family appears to be falling apart. . . . I do not know that things were worse in the times of Sodom and Gomorrah."[2] And in his recent book, *Standing for Something,* he said, "Never before, at least not in our generation, have the forces of evil been so blatant, so brazen, so aggressive as they are at the present time. . . . Filth, sleaze, pornography, and their whole evil brood are sweeping over us as a flood."[3]

You may be thinking, "Sodom and Gomorrah? A flood of evil? Life's going pretty well for me right now; I don't feel any flood." Yet I wonder if it isn't hard to see because we live in it and have grown so accustomed to it. If you start driving up Parley's Canyon from the Salt Lake Valley on what appears to be a clear day, you can usually turn around at the summit and look back to see a blanket of smog covering the valley. That same smog was not very noticeable when you were driving around in it on the valley floor. Similarly, we live in a thick blanket of moral smog that is polluting us spiritually, according to Elder Boyd K. Packer.[4] Another way I have thought about this recently comes from Tolkein's *Lord of the Rings* trilogy. I wonder if some of us are not like the hobbits, blithely passing away our time in the beautiful shire while the dark forces of evil are being gathered together by satanic sorcerers in preparation for a great battle between good and evil. I believe that this battle is going on around us and that it is a battle for the hearts and minds—the *spiritual survival*—of individual souls. Sounds like a great title for a reality TV show: "Spiritual Survival!" Yet this battle is real, and our prophet is sounding a trumpet to wake us up and call us to join the forces of good.

The second point I want to make is that . . .

Women are *essential* to winning this battle. As a young adult woman you have a unique and crucial contribution that the Lord needs *you* to make. Again, the Lord's prophet has been very clear about this quite recently. In the same talk in which he made reference to Sodom and Gomorrah, President Hinckley said: "It is so tremendously important that the women of the Church stand strong and immovable. . . . If they will be united and speak with one voice, their strength will be incalculable. We call upon the women of the Church to stand together for righteousness. . . . We frequently speak of the strength of the priesthood, and properly so. But we must never lose sight of the strength of the women. . . . When you save a girl, you save generations. . . . I see this as the one bright shining hope in a world that is marching toward self-destruction."[5] And a few years ago, President Ezra Taft Benson said something similar to the young women of the Church: "You have been born at this time for a sacred and glorious purpose. It is not by chance that you have been reserved to come to earth in this last dispensation of the fulness of times. . . . You are to be the royal daughters of the Lord in the last days."[6]

Consider with me the story of a young woman long ago who faced some important decisions and found herself with a very crucial role to play. The young woman is Esther in the Old Testament. The king of Persia had made her his queen, unaware that she was an Israelite. Then his advisors convinced him that the Israelites were his enemies and that they should all be exterminated. She found herself in a very dangerous position, but also uniquely positioned to save her people if she dared take the risk. Her guardian uncle advised her at that crucial moment with these words, "And who knoweth whether thou art come to the kingdom for such a time as this?" (Esther 4:14). You know how the story ends—Esther singlehandedly ensures the survival of her people.

Your Personal Mission

I would like to suggest that young LDS women today are uniquely positioned, like Esther long ago, to play a crucial role in the spiritual survival of their people, that is, of Heavenly Father's children. One reason for this is that you have been directly targeted by the adversary in his campaign to destroy society. Many of his efforts are focused on the sexual exploitation of women your age, whether it be through explicit prime-time television content and advertising, the halftime show at the Super Bowl, or online pornography. The father of lies teaches young girls to dress like women of the night and holds up as role models female celebrities who are sleazy and coarse. And his efforts to devalue and undermine motherhood are aimed directly at you. In the words of Sister Patricia Holland, "If I were Satan and wanted to destroy a society, I think I would stage a full-blown blitz on its women."[7] And I would only add, "especially on its young adult women, who are at the point of making crucial decisions about the future."

Yet young adult women are mature enough to see through these lies, and they are less susceptible to provocative stimuli than are young men. Thus, young adult women are positioned to play a pivotal role in resisting and reversing these attacks of the adversary and in preventing their devastating effects from rippling through society.

I'd like to mention two things that young adult women can do as a group to fulfill this pivotal role. One is to cover up their middles and buy looser fitting clothing. Many LDS girls today are walking around tempting the Lord's priesthood bearers—whether knowingly or unknowingly—by the way they dress. When they do this they are part of the problem, not part of the solution. I know I am doing what's called preaching to the choir—but as a mother of teenage boys I am appealing to you to let your influence be heard on this issue in a loving way, with your friends, little sisters, and cousins. The other thing is to turn off television shows like *Friends*. I know these shows are popular, but they are not real—it's a made-up world and a very immoral one. You can be a great example to your friends and family in these ways.

Now I would like to bring this down to an individual level, to talk about you. President Brigham Young said: "There is neither man nor woman in this Church who is not on a mission. That mission will last as long as they live."[8] And the Young Women Values state, "I am of infinite worth with *my own* divine mission which I will strive to fulfill" (emphasis added). In other words, there are some things you have been given to do that only you are in a position to do. And they represent opportunities for growth, service, joy, and adventure that you might never expect.

How do we cultivate a sense of personal mission or direction at each phase of life? We first want to be sure we are not listening to the wrong sources. The world's message to women for three decades has been *You can have it all!* and *Live for your career!* But the gospel calls us to take a different approach. As women who are striving to follow the Savior's example, we can say, "*I want to give my all!*" instead of "*I want to have it all,*" and instead of planning for your *career,* you can plan for your *contribution* to God's work. In fact, I would like to suggest a motto or a guiding principle you can use in your decision-making. It goes like this:

"I want to maximize my contribution to God's work at this time in my life and plan now to be able to do so in the future."

There are two important things you can do now to implement this gospel-based approach. Both have been given as counsel to young women from President Hinckley. The first is to obtain all the education and training you can while you're in a position to do so. The second is to plan now for having and rearing children. If you can be home full-time with your young children, it will be the most important contribution you can make to God's work at that time in your life—it is the work that only you can do. I encourage all young women to start a "mission savings account"—to start saving money when they are young for the mission called motherhood, i.e., to help fund the option of staying home when they have children.

You can also use this gospel-centered approach as you plan for the future. You can begin with some self-evaluation. You can ask, "What have I been given to use in His service?" I suggest that you look in three areas: What are my personal strengths? What are my personal challenges? And what are the needs in my world? If we look back at the story of Esther we can do a similar evaluation:

Her strengths: great beauty, mental quickness, faith, courage, married to a powerful man, good family support from her guardian uncle

Her challenges: an orphan, had to marry outside her faith, a woman in a male-controlled society, a Jewess in a hostile land, she felt fear and doubt

Needs in her world: her people were to be exterminated, she was the only Israelite in a position of power

It was the intersection of those three aspects of Esther's life that created the mission she was needed to perform, the thing that only she was in a position to do. One of the most interesting things to me is that Esther's *challenges* were necessary for her crucial contribution—if she hadn't been forced to marry outside her faith and been an Israelite in the court of a hostile land, she would not have been in a position to save her people.

I would like you to write three headings on a piece of paper: *My Strengths, My Challenges,* and *The Needs in My World.* Make at least five entries under each heading. It is sometimes difficult to identify your own strengths, but they can include qualities you think you have a little bit but want to cultivate more. Also, think of the things your mother says you're good at! On the other hand, we women are better at identifying our challenges, but not used to thinking of them as keys to understanding our personal mission or direction in life. Yet out of some of our greatest challenges our greatest contributions to others will arise. (Remember Ether 12:27—"Then will I make weak things become strong unto them.") And finally, the needs in your world can be on a large or small scale—ranging from the problem of millions of orphans in Africa to a girl in your ward who is a social misfit, or anything in between. That is why the influence of the Spirit is so important.

Spend some time thinking about how these three lists are related to each other. I believe that a sense of personal direction can be found wherever your unique strengths, challenges, and the needs in your world intersect, that these points of intersection for you are unlike anyone else's, and that this *is* the work that only you can do. I think this holds true at any age or phase of life, especially in times of transition. Fundamental to this personal evaluation, of course, is the process of personal revelation. It includes studying the scriptures and your patriarchal blessing, seeking the counsel of those who love you best—your bishop, parents, grandparents—praying, trying to avoid the obstacles of self-doubt and procrastination, and then going forward in faith and doing something wonderful.

CONCLUSION

I believe we are on the brink of perilous times *and* that there has never been a better time to be alive. Like President Hinckley, I see young LDS women as a bright shining hope in the world today. I believe that this generation of young adult women has a significant, even world-saving role to play in these latter days. And I know that as individuals you each have a unique and needed contribution to make to the Lord's work. It is my prayer that you will feel divine direction and support as you struggle with important decisions and that you will experience the joy that comes from using the gifts the Lord has given you—your strengths *and* your challenges—to respond to the needs in your world as only you can do.

NOTES

Portions of this talk have been adapted from Jan U. Pinborough and Irene H. Ericksen, *Where Do I Go from Here? Finding Your Personal Mission as a Young Adult Woman* (Salt Lake City: Deseret Book, 2002).

1. Lewis Carroll, *Alice's Adventures in Wonderland* (New York: Modern Library, 2002).
2. Gordon B. Hinckley, "Standing Strong and Immovable," *Worldwide Leadership Training Meeting,* January 10, 2004 (Salt Lake City: The Church of Jesus Christ of Latter-day Saints, 2004), 20.
3. Gordon B. Hinckley, *Standing for Something* (New York: Times Books, 2000), 170–71.
4. See Boyd K. Packer, "Our Moral Environment," *Ensign*, May 1992, 66–69.
5. Hinckley, "Standing Strong and Immovable," 20–21.
6. Ezra Taft Benson, "To the Young Women of the Church," *Ensign*, November 1986, 81.
7. Patricia T. Holland, *A Quiet Heart* (Salt Lake City: Bookcraft, 2000), 43.
8. Brigham Young, in *Journal of Discourses,* 26 vols. (London: Latter-day Saints' Book Depot, 1854–86), 12:19.

My God Is an On-Time God

Jerri A. Harwell

After June 1978 I focused on and worked toward my goal of serving a full-time mission. I graduated from college in August 1979 and immediately submitted my paperwork for a mission call. Then I waited. I waited a long time. Nothing came. Finally I called my bishop and was told that my paperwork had not been sent to Salt Lake City yet because I was not old enough to serve a mission. I had graduated from college six months before I turned twenty-one. My papers could not be submitted more than ninety days before I turned twenty-one. Bummer. I had to wait some more.

While I waited, I started to prepare. Being a new member of the Church, I didn't have any background on how to do this. Regardless, I read everything I could and made sure I had read through all of the standard works at least once. I studied the *Gospel Principles* manual a couple of times and marked every scripture cited in my set of scriptures. I asked people what missionaries should read before and during a mission, and I read and studied those books. Finally, after I had done all I could to

Jerri A. Harwell is the author of Leaning on Prayer. *She works part-time as a free-lance writer/editor as well as adjunct faculty at Salt Lake Community College, where she teaches developmental writing. She is also the founder and managing editor of a newsletter for The Genesis Group, the LDS Church's official auxiliary for black Latter-day Saints. She and her husband, Donald, reside in Cottonwood Heights, Utah; they have six children.*

prepare, I went to the Lord in prayer and asked Him what I should do to prepare for my mission.

His answer came quite clearly, "Complete your four generations."

"What?" I thought. "What does my genealogy have to do with a mission?" Since the answer didn't make any sense, I asked again, "Heavenly Father, what do I need to do to prepare for a mission?"

Again, the answer was just as clear as before, "Complete your four generations."

About this time, President Spencer W. Kimball had asked and encouraged every member to research, complete, and submit four generations of his or her family history, so I knew what the Lord was referring to. Still, I thought to myself, "I could do that anytime or when I get back from a mission." Right now, I wanted to know what I should do to prepare for a proselyting mission, not my life's mission. Being the only member of the Church in my family, I didn't have any knowledge or background about how to prepare for a mission. I had faith that if I did all I could, Heavenly Father would certainly help me know how to get ready. Maybe I wasn't asking the question correctly. I tried rewording my prayer to get Heavenly Father to understand what I was asking. But no matter how I worded my prayer, no matter what I said, He kept giving one and only one response: "Complete your four generations."

"Okay," I thought to myself, "I give up. I'll just copy the four generations onto a family group sheet and family record and be done with it." So I did. My mother and Aunt Terry had given me some genealogy, so I just copied it onto some forms with the Church's copyright symbol on them, because I thought that was what the Lord wanted me to do, and placed it in front of me before I knelt down in prayer.

"Heavenly Father, I've completed the four generations you told me to do. *Now,* what do I need to do to prepare for a mission?"

"Verify it," came His reply.

"Oh, it's correct. My Aunt Terry did this research and gave it to me," I assured Him.

"Verify it," came His reply.

From previous experience, I knew I wouldn't get any other reply until I did what He told me to do. So I went to my mother and told her we should verify all our family history information. We, along with my Aunt Terry, planned a trip to Dresden, Ontario, Canada—just a quick trip from Detroit, across the border, to verify her family's information.

As I packed for our trip, I packed a copy of the missionary discussions to take along with me so I could continue to memorize them. I just knew if I could get the Lord to understand what I was asking, about how to prepare for a mission, He would tell me to memorize the discussions in preparation to enter the Missionary Training Center (MTC). I knew I wasn't expected to learn the discussions before entering the MTC. But I thought if I studied them and memorized them prior to entering the MTC, I could skip the MTC to get right down to business and teach the gospel.

We had some official certificates to verify information, but we were really just filling in the gaps and looking for siblings of our ancestors. While in Dresden we met Arlie C. Robbins, a distant relative, who spent all her spare time doing genealogy. She was hampered with arthritis but was still a wealth of information. We visited with her in her home.

As we were talking, my mother told Arlie that I "was preparing to go on a mission for the Mormon Church."

"The Mormons?" she said with surprise. "Why, did you know there was one of those in our family?"

My ears perked up, "No, I didn't."

"Why, yes, there was a Mormon and when they found out he was black, they took his priesthood from him." Right then and there I *knew* that could only be the LDS Church.

She told us the name, and we learned that this Latter-day Saint ancestor was a brother to my direct ancestor in the Richardson line. Arlie then said, just as seriously, "I guess that bad blood just stayed dormant until you." I just smiled, now knowing I had an ancestor in the LDS Church. What a find!

We continued our research and attempted to find some cemeteries around the area. One store clerk said, "The cemeteries *you* want" are located along such and such a road. His emphasis on the cemeteries we wanted was because back then, blacks and whites were not buried together. We found a cemetery or two, but we could not read the head-stones clearly.

Still, our trip was worth it. We found we had mixed up a generation, thinking two individuals were father and son when they were in fact brothers. It was a good thing we verified the records we had. Had it not been for the Lord telling me to verify the records, I would have left well enough alone.

After we returned home, I continued to wait for a mission call. Finally, it came. I had been called to serve in the Texas Houston Mission. I knelt down to thank the Lord for sending me there—after looking at a map to see where Houston was located. I was excited. Finally, I was really going on a mission. The Lord wanted me to go. I wanted to go. I was ready to go.

I flew out to Salt Lake City alone. I arrived a day before my sched-uled check-in, and so I actually had my first night to myself—no com-panion yet. I asked at the front desk what there was to do nearby that I could walk to. She told me about the BYU campus and gave me direc-tions. I walked over to the campus and found the student center in the Wilkinson building. I sat down to watch *Eight Is Enough* on TV, but I didn't feel comfortable. I left there and walked over to the Harold B. Lee Library. As I looked around, I learned the library had a genealogy floor. I went to the fourth floor just to look up a name or two.

Because I had just spent so much time in Canada copying group and family sheets, I knew some names and dates off the top of my head. I looked up the Richardson name to find the ancestor who was supposed to have been LDS. I found his records immediately. I wrote down the name of the person who submitted the information and noted that he lived in Baytown, Texas. I wondered if that was anywhere near Houston. All the temple work had been done, and I thought to myself it was a good thing I had done that research. Who knows when I would have run across this information?

When I arrived in Houston, I asked my trainer-companion, Sister Joan Oka (now Hesley), where Baytown was located. She said it was right across the bay from where we were in La Porte. It wasn't even a long-distance phone call. I told her about having a distant relative who was LDS, and I called the person who submitted the information to the Church's genealogy library. When I called, I told the man who answered the phone that I thought I was related to the Richardsons.

He said, "These aren't the Richardsons you're looking for. These are black."

"Those are the Richardsons I'm looking for," I assured him. "I'm black, and I'm the first black missionary to come to Houston. I'm a distant relative to the Richardson who joined the Church in the 1800s in Canada." I asked if all the information he had had been submitted to the Church. It had. I thanked him for his time and hung up.

"Boy, it's a good thing I completed my four generations before I left," I thought, "or I wouldn't have found out about this gentleman and had a chance to talk with him." I also thought that was the end of the genealogy connection on my mission—but it wasn't.

While in my next area, I met a member, Brother Perry, who grew up near Dresden, Ontario. I told him about my trip there to research my family history and some of the stumbling blocks we ran into, such as not being able to read headstones. He leaned forward and asked for my family names. I told him some names, and he reached for a piece of paper and began to draw a map. As he drew, he told me that as a boy he used to play in those cemeteries where blacks were buried and, for whatever reason, he still had the headstones memorized. He handed me a map of the cemeteries, detailing headstone locations where some of my ancestors were buried.

"Wow," I thought, "it's a good thing I knew about the relatives up in Canada and had attempted to locate the cemeteries."

From my last area, I called my distant relative in Baytown, Texas, to say good-bye before leaving the state. I spoke with his daughter, who told me he had died a few months ago. I expressed my sympathy and hung up. Timing is everything, I thought.

In Isaiah 55:8–9, the Lord says, "For my thoughts are not your thoughts, neither are your ways my ways, saith the Lord. For as the heavens are higher than the earth, so are my ways higher than your ways, and my thoughts than your thoughts." As I look back on my prayers about my mission preparation before leaving for Texas, I realize that Heavenly

Father's answer did not make any sense at the time, but I'm glad I followed His instructions. As events unfolded, His wisdom or "His ways" became evident. Had I not listened and completed my four generations before I left on a mission, I would not have known about distant relatives in the Church who were black, nor would I have had the map Brother Perry drew for me.

I am in awe of the Lord's orchestration in preparing the way for these advances in my family history research—and it wasn't even my focus. I'm sure the hardest part for the Lord was getting me to do the four generations *before* I left on a mission. His inspiration and guidance saw to it that I received a mission call to Houston, Texas. Now, who can doubt that the prophet and brethren are inspired of the Lord when mission calls are issued? The Lord's inspiration and guidance saw to it that a young boy would not only play in a remote cemetery in Dresden, Canada, but that the boy would retain those memories and would be able to draw a map decades later that would include the names on the headstones. God is good!

Years later, I realized my family history experience was not the only long drawn-out answer from the Lord played out during my eighteen-month mission. During this time, I couldn't help but notice much of my time was spent with elderly companions. Because I was told our mission had more sister missionaries than any other mission in the world, I thought it unfair that I was with older sisters so much. Surely, there were some young sisters I could be paired with. I talked with my mission president about my concerns and on the next transfer, I was again paired with an elderly companion. Each month at transfer I was disappointed and became depressed. I would go into my closet, literally, and pour my heart and soul out to the Lord.

"Why am I still with an older sister?" I'd ask.

Those prayers went unanswered for four years, until one afternoon in 1985. Four years after I returned from my mission, I was sitting in a hospital room with my mother when I once again heard the Lord's voice.

"Do you remember asking me why you were with older companions so much during your mission?" I heard.

Startled, I looked all around to see who was talking. I looked in the empty bed on the other side of my mother's room. I was sitting with my back to my mother, and I turned and looked at her. She was still unconscious and motionless. I leaned forward in my chair and looked out in the hallway to see if I could see anyone. I saw no one.

Not knowing where else to look, I looked up and said, "What?"

"Do you remember asking me why you were with older companions so much during your mission?" I heard once again.

"Yes."

"It was so that when you reached this point in your life, you would have the patience and know-how to take care of your mother when she reached this point in her life."

My eyes filled with tears because I knew exactly what He was talking about.

The Lord finally answered the prayer I had uttered *years* before. Again, I am in awe of the Lord's care in preparing the way for me to take care of my mother at her time of need. My mission president, Kay Clifford, followed the inspiration of the Lord as he oversaw each transfer in the mission field that involved me. Surely He saw to it that each companion I needed to learn from was sent to the same mission to give me certain experiences. The Lord knew the future and prepared me for what was to come.

Although it took five years to receive an answer to my prayers, I literally heard an answer, and that answer came right on time. This experience brings to my mind the words of a black gospel song: "He's an on-time God, yes He is. He may not come when you want Him to, but He'll be there right on time. He's an on-time God, yes He is."

Not too long ago I was thinking about my patriarchal blessing while working as a librarian in my ward and also the ward newsletter editor. It felt good to be useful. Still, I sat and pondered my role of being "influential in the church and community" as a ward librarian. While sitting in on a ward correlation meeting one Sunday so I could get dates for the ward newsletter, I heard someone in the bishopric say it was time to reorganize the Relief Society. Then I heard a voice say, "And you will be in the presidency."

"You mean I'm going to be Relief Society president?" I asked in my mind.

"No, but you're going to be in the presidency," the voice said again. I put the thought out of my mind because I didn't like Relief Society.

I didn't think about it again until I was called into Bishop Paul Nance's office just a few short months later and asked to be a counselor in the ward's Relief Society presidency. I looked right at the bishop and, without hesitation, said, "Look, I don't ever want to be considered a hypocrite. I don't like Relief Society and I never have. I can't be in the presidency, so no. I'm not going to stand up in meetings talking about how much I love Relief Society. I don't, and I won't put on airs and pretend I do."

The bishop and his counselor questioned me about why I didn't like it. Maybe *I* could be the one to affect change, they reasoned, but I still said no. They tried their best to get me to accept the calling, but I was not interested. After I left the office, I walked toward the cultural hall to get my kids. Suddenly my chest felt as if someone had stopped me by hitting me with a fist.

"Go back in there and undo that," I heard.

I knew who it was and I knew what He was talking about, but I didn't want to serve in that position, so I looked back down the hall and said, "The door is closed, and they're meeting with someone else now."

"That's okay, they have to come out to go home, and you can talk to them then."

I then asked why I had to be in Relief Society.

He replied, "Because there will be people who will walk into that room in the next two years that you need to be there for." I ignored the voice, got my kids, and went home.

As I pulled in front of my house, I was consciously talking to the Lord and telling Him that I wasn't going back because I didn't want that calling.

He then said, "It's not always about what *you* want." I felt so badly that I immediately called Darius Gray, then president of The Genesis Group, from my cell phone and told him what happened. He told me I needed to accept the calling. I told him I knew that, but I really didn't want to accept it. Next, I called my husband. I told him what had happened, and he said, "I think you need to accept the calling. Go back and tell them you'll accept it."

I went into my house, but I literally could not sit down. I told my kids I had to go back over to the church building and I left. I sat outside the bishop's door until it opened. The bishop said good-bye to the person leaving, and I stood up and humbly asked if I could undo my earlier decision. Bishop Nance looked surprised and invited me in. Everyone who had been there an hour earlier was still there. I told them I'd like to accept the calling, and they allowed me to. One counselor, John Hamren, asked what changed my mind. "The Spirit," I answered, and left it at that.

When I spoke with Leigh Gallimore, the newly called Relief Society president, I told her the whole story. I wanted no misunderstandings about how I felt, and she needed to know that I only accepted the calling after much persuasion from the Lord. She laughed and told me about her experience with her calling. She also related that she had received the prompting, some time earlier, that she would "be called to be the Relief Society president and Jerri Harwell will be one of your counselors." Once again, I'm sure the hardest part of the Lord putting all this together was getting *me* to accept the calling.

Once I accepted the calling, I still needed the Lord's help to change my attitude. I learned that sometimes it means more to just be there for people than to lead and direct. For example, one evening I was having a hard time making myself go to enrichment night. I asked the Lord if it was worth it for me to go. "I'm tired. I'm not interested. I just don't want to go. You said there were people I had to be there for, and I haven't met anyone." I left for enrichment, arrived late, and ate dinner. As I left the cultural hall to go to a class, I turned around and looked back into the room just as a sister was coming out. As I looked at her, I heard the Lord's voice: "And here comes one of them now." She introduced herself to me and said maybe her daughter would have come had the daughter (who was black) known I, being a black member of the Church, would be there. Humbly, I make sure I'm at every meeting I'm supposed to be to now, *especially* when I don't feel like it.

Remember to listen to the voice of the Lord, especially when it doesn't make sense. Remember that in the Lord's plan it isn't always about you. Often it is about the Lord's thoughts, the Lord's way, the Lord's plan.

"ARISE AND SHINE FORTH"

———◆———

Elaine S. Dalton

When we speak of modesty, I am reminded of what Tevya, a character in the musical *Fiddler on the Roof,* said when he spoke of his beloved village of Anatevka. He said, "In Anatevka everyone knows who he is and what God expects him to do."[1] For me, that is the bottom line of any discussion on modesty.

Modesty is often talked of in terms of dress and appearance, but modesty encompasses much more than the outward appearance. It is a condition of the heart. It is an outward manifestation of an inner knowledge and commitment. It is an expression that we understand our identity as daughters of God. It is an expression that we know what He expects us to do. It is a declaration of our covenant keeping. A question in the *For the Strength of Youth* booklet really is the question each of us must consider: "'Am I living the way the Lord wants me to live?'"[2]

Like the people of Anatevka, do we know who we are? Do our daughters and young women know who they are? In speaking to members of the Church, Peter said, "But ye are a chosen generation, a royal priesthood, an holy nation, a peculiar people; that ye should shew forth the praises of him who hath called you out of darkness into his

Elaine Dalton was born and raised in Ogden, Utah. She received her bachelor's degree in English from Brigham Young University. She currently serves as the second counselor in the Young Women general presidency. She and her husband, Stephen E. Dalton, are the parents of five sons and one daughter.

marvellous light" (1 Peter 2:9). He clearly defined our identity. And his use of the word _peculiar_ did not mean "odd." It meant "special."

In the Book of Mormon, the Lord's chosen people are described in this way: "Ye are the children of the prophets; and ye are of the house of Israel; and ye are of the covenant which the Father made with your fathers" (3 Nephi 20:25). Elder Russell M. Nelson of the Twelve said, "Once we know who we are, the royal lineage of which we are a part, our actions and our direction in life will be more appropriate to our inheritance."[3] Even the Young Women Theme reminds us that we are "daughters of our Heavenly Father, who loves us."[4]

When we truly know that we are daughters of God and have an understanding of our divine nature, it will be reflected in our countenance, our appearance, and our actions.

Several years ago, a dear friend married in the Salt Lake Temple. She was a convert to the Church from India, and her entire family came for her wedding. They were not members of the Church, so they waited patiently outside for the wedding to end and the bride to exit the temple. They were dressed in native Indian attire and looked beautiful. When they walked onto the temple grounds, all eyes were upon them. The thing I noticed most was how elegantly they moved and carried themselves and how modest each was. They were not apologetic for their appearance even though it made them stand out in the crowd. They simply knew who they were and were not ashamed. I observed how beautiful they were. The women seemed almost queenly in their attitude and demeanor. In their actions, movements, and conversation, they were dignified and lovely. I thought how much I would like every young woman and woman in the Church to have that same attitude— an attitude of understanding something deeper on the inside that was reflected on the outside.

Our prophet has said, "Of all the creations of the Almighty, there is none more beautiful, none more inspiring than a lovely daughter of God who walks in virtue with an understanding of why she should do so, who honors and respects her body as a thing sacred and divine, who cultivates her mind and constantly enlarges the horizon of her understanding, who nurtures her spirit with everlasting truth."[5]

If our young women know this, they know much more than how to dress—they will know how to live. And they will have the courage they need to avoid the moral decline of the world.

The prophet Brigham Young desired that his daughters reflect their true identity. Visualize this setting with me for a moment. It is 1869, and the prophet Brigham Young became concerned about his daughters and their somewhat worldly interests and actions. He was worried about the general trend toward materialism, commercialism, and sophistication among the younger Church members, and his daughters seemed to reflect that trend. He assembled his children in the Lion House parlor for family prayer. He looked into the faces of his lovely daughters and said:

"All Israel are looking to my family and watching the example set by my . . . children. For this reason I desire to organize my own family first into a society for the promotion of habits of order, thrift, industry, and charity; and, above all things, I desire them to retrench from their extravagance in dress. . . .

" . . . I want you to . . . retrench . . . in your speech, wherein you have been guilty of silly . . . speeches and light-mindedness of thought. Retrench in everything that is bad and worthless, and improve in everything that is good and beautiful."[6]

We don't often hear the word *retrench* in our society. The dictionary defines *retrench* as meaning "to cut down, to reduce or diminish, to curtail, to economize."[7] This definition helps us to understand the last sentence of Brigham Young's declaration. He desired his daughters to curtail and diminish in everything that is bad and worthless and to improve in that which is good and beautiful. He wanted his daughters to be "worthy of imitation."[8]

In the Doctrine and Covenants, we are admonished to "arise and shine forth, that thy light may be a standard for the nations" (D&C 115:5). Perhaps it is again time to retrench.

In our present day President Hinckley has issued a similar call to the women of the Church. He has said:

"It is so tremendously important that the women of the Church stand strong and immovable for that which is correct and proper under the plan of the Lord. . . . If they will be united and speak with one voice, their strength will be incalculable.

"We call upon the women of the Church to stand together for righteousness. They must begin in their own homes. They can teach it in their classes. They can voice it in their communities.

"They must be the teachers and the guardians of their daughters."

Then he said, "I see this as the one bright shining hope in a world that is marching toward self-destruction."[9]

President Hinckley has said to both youth and adults:

"If we are to hold up this Church as an ensign to the nations and a light to the world, we must take on more of the luster of the life of Christ individually and in our own personal circumstances. In standing for the right, we must not be fearful of the consequences. We must never be afraid. Said Paul to Timothy:

"'For God hath not given us the spirit of fear; but of power, and of love, and of a sound mind.

"'Be not thou therefore ashamed of the testimony of our Lord' (2 Timothy 1:7–8)."[10]

Modesty, therefore, is more than the way we dress. It reflects our testimony and the condition of our hearts. It is an outward manifestation of an inward knowledge and commitment. It begins in the little things. It begins with knowing who we are and what God expects us to do. Are we willing to do what is expected of us? Are we willing to do what it takes to dress modestly?

Dressing modestly is a challenge. President James E. Faust said in a general Young Women meeting: "You young ladies may have a hard time buying a modest prom dress. May I suggest that you make your own? You may need some help, but plenty of help is available."[11]

In 2004 at the general Young Women meeting, President Hinckley pleaded again with the young women and their mothers to be modest. In his talk titled "Stay on the High Road," he said:

"You are the strength of the present, the hope of the future. . . .

"You are second to none. You are daughters of God. . . .

"But, my dear friends, we cannot accept that which has become common in the world. Yours, as members of this Church, is a higher standard and more demanding. . . .

"Modesty in dress and manner will assist in protecting against temptation. It may be difficult to find modest clothing, but it can be found with enough effort. I sometimes wish every girl had access to a sewing machine and training in how to use it. She could then make her own attractive clothing. I suppose this is an unrealistic wish. But I do not hesitate to say that you can be attractive without being immodest. You can be refreshing and buoyant and beautiful in your dress and in your behavior. Your appeal to others will come of your personality, which is the sum of your individual characteristics. Be happy. Wear a smile. Have fun. But draw some rigid parameters, a line in the sand, as it were, beyond which you will not go."[12]

The audience laughed when President Hinckley mentioned a sewing machine for every young woman. They thought he was kidding. But I do not think he was. I think he was serious and prophetic. The question that remains for us to answer is, "Therefore what?"—what will each of us do to respond to the call of a prophet of our day to arise and shine forth?

President Spencer W. Kimball suggested we establish a "style of our own."[13] And as wickedness progresses in the world, we may have to do just that. We cannot lead if we are like the world. Instead of spending our energy and our money to look like the world, perhaps we should set a pattern that they may choose to follow. We must have the courage and the gospel understanding to be modest. Modesty will not only set us apart from the world, but it will also protect us.

Are we willing to obey the standard of modesty "at all times and in all things, and in all places"? (Mosiah 18:9).

Modesty is about more than hemlines, necklines, and revealing clothing. It is the appropriate dress for the appropriate setting. It is caring to dress appropriately to show respect for people, places, and settings.

We hear more and more concern from the Brethren about excessive casualness in our dress. "In your attempt to follow the styles and be casual, do not offend good taste. When we go to worship the Lord, we ought to be dressed in our finest, cleanest, and best."[14]

When we understand modesty, we know how to be appropriate in any given situation. We know how to dress to run a marathon as well as how to dress to attend a priesthood ordinance. We understand that having young men wear a white shirt and tie to pass the sacrament is more, much more, than a rule. We invite the companionship of the Spirit by the small things we do that show not only our attitude but our understanding.

Just a month ago the choir for the general Young Woman meeting had a dress rehearsal in the Conference Center on a Saturday morning. Families were invited to attend. As I arrived, I noticed a family of five children reverently waiting in the seats for the practice to begin. Each of the young boys had on a freshly ironed white shirt and tie, and the little girls wore their Sunday dresses. The mother and father were neatly dressed as well. As I shook the oldest boy's hand, I said, "I compliment you on the way you are dressed on this early Saturday morning. I can tell that you understand and have been taught some things that it takes a lot of people all their lives to realize." He flashed his mother a sheepish look, and she gave him that knowing look that says, "I told you so."

The pamphlet *For the Strength of Youth* admonishes: "Never lower your dress standards for any occasion. Doing so sends the message that you are using your body to get attention and approval and that modesty is important only when it is convenient."[15]

Are we as mothers willing to do our part to raise modest daughters?

Mothers play a tremendous role in the modesty of their daughters. President Hinckley has great confidence in us. He said that "we must never lose sight of the strength of the women. It is mothers who set the tone of the home. It is mothers who most directly affect the lives of their children."[16] I might add that it is mothers who can and must influence their daughters to be modest in their dress, attitudes, speech, conduct, and thought.

Mothers teach modesty in the home and model it through their example. Are we as mothers at fault for our daughters' immodest dress and actions? Are we more concerned about popularity than purity? Some say, "My daughter is a good girl. I don't want to make an issue of her tight clothing or skimpy t-shirts." They say, "I won't die on that hill."

It's not about hills, it's about hearts. It's not about confrontation, it's about covenants. These are battles in which we should be engaged because modesty has moral implications. This is a different world. By encouraging our daughters to be cute and trendy, we may unknowingly be putting them at great risk.

Liriel Domiciano is a young woman from Brazil who has an extraordinary voice. Her talent has made her famous in Brazil. She insists on performing in modest attire, always wearing her Young Womanhood Medallion as a symbol of her values. When I asked her what kept her strong, she replied, "My mother is my protector." As mothers, we simply must be our daughter's protector. We must start early. We must set the example as we dress to easily meet temple standards. We can teach these standards to our daughters and help them as they anticipate and prepare for their own temple attendance. We must never compromise those standards in order that our daughters might be popular or accepted by those with not only worldly standards but worldly intentions. We must not only be their example but their protector.

Recently the Church donated $3 million to immunize African children against measles and prevent 1.2 million deaths. In Ethiopia, mothers walked miles from their villages carrying their children so they could be immunized and protected against this epidemic.[17] As mothers, we will go any distance to protect our children physically. It is a "mother bear" instinct. We must be equally anxious to protect their spiritual welfare.

Here is a specific list of things we can do to protect our daughters and young women:

Seek answers in the scriptures. The scriptures contain the answer to every question or problem.

Know the doctrine and teach it. "True doctrine, understood, changes attitudes and behavior."[18] The doctrine is the why—the rules are the how. Our youth must understand both.

Study the For the Strength of Youth *pamphlet.* It describes how to qualify for the companionship of the Holy Ghost. We simply must have this guidance in today's world.

Teach them their eternal identity. My mother always called out when I left the house, "Remember who you are and what we stand for."

Help them gain skills. Teaching skills such as sewing, hemming, and sewing on a button builds bonds between a mother and daughter.

Seek experiences with the Spirit. In your home, pray, read scriptures, and listen to sacred music.

Serve others.

Don't let them base their identity on designer labels. "Pretty is as pretty does."

Teach covenant keeping and obedience above acceptance.

Live what you know—be an example.

Live the standards generously. Don't teeter on the edge of the line.

Modesty is a daily standard, which, if lived, has eternal promise.

Modesty extends to our actions, our speech, our attitudes, our thoughts, even our desires. Our modesty is a reflection of our desire to follow a prophet of God. I repeat, being modest is more than how we dress. Modesty is an outward manifestation of our inward commitment and understanding.

We have a dear friend who worked as a gardener at the Oakland Temple. He shared with us the following insight:

"Our temples are kept beautiful on the outside. I spent many, many hours grooming the temple grounds—weeding, watering, planting flowers, doing all I could to make the exterior reflect the sacred spirit inside the Lord's holy house. Surely the Lord expects us to groom and care for our physical tabernacles also—not as the world does, but in order that the Spirit of the Lord may find a fit sanctuary to dwell with our own spirits."[19]

The outward appearance of the temple and the grounds reflect the inner spirit and beauty of the temple. So it is with us.

Paul said: "Know ye not that your body is the temple of the Holy Ghost which is in you, which ye have of God, and ye are not your own? For ye are bought with a price: therefore glorify God in your body, and in your spirit, which are God's" (1 Corinthians 6:19–20).

He also asked, "Know ye not that ye are the temple of God, and that the Spirit of God dwelleth in you?" (1 Corinthians 3:16).

Our purpose in coming to earth was to gain a body with which to have experience and joy and to exercise our agency. Our body is a precious gift from a loving Heavenly Father. We are made in His image. Our body is the instrument of our agency and the receptacle of our spirit. There is only one to a customer. It is precious. When Adam and Eve had partaken of the fruit in the Garden of Eden and became mortal and subject to temptation, they covered themselves with fig leaves. Later, a loving Heavenly Father, in an act of mercy, placed a covering over their bodies in the form of coats of skins (see Genesis 3:21). He did this not only to protect them from the elements but to protect them from man's fallen nature.[20] Consequently, personal modesty is evidence that we understand that our bodies are sacred.

Our modesty—in fact, all of our standards and our willingness to live them—is a reflection of our covenants as members of the Church. We have made baptismal covenants. We must prepare our daughters and other young women to make and keep sacred temple covenants.

When I was a new Young Women general board member, Elder Robert D. Hales helped me to really understand what my baptismal covenant meant. He said, "When you were baptized, you stepped out of the world and into the kingdom." He said that when we truly understand this, it changes everything. It did for me. Elder Hales's teaching awakened in me a desire to reflect in every way that I am a woman of covenant. Each time I partake of the sacrament, I remember that I promise to "always remember him" (D&C 20:77). I see myself literally stepping across a line out of an ever-darkening world and into the brightness of the kingdom. Again and again I ask myself, "Am I living the way the Lord wants me to live?"

Our covenants provide protection, direction, and focus. They enable us to navigate a very turbulent world guided by His Spirit. When we are keeping our covenants, it is extremely difficult to still keep one foot in the world and the other in the kingdom. Sister Mary C. Hales said, "A temple standard of modesty is an outward expression of an inward commitment—not just looking modest but actually being modest in every aspect of life."[21]

Some young women in Kansas received a lesson on modesty and its relationship to covenants and keeping them. They thought about what they could do. They remembered that the parents of the Ammonite

2,000 stripling warriors had repented of their warlike ways and covenanted with the Lord. They had buried their swords and weapons of war in connection with their covenant. These young women decided that they would go to their closets and take out any immodest clothing. They didn't want to be the cause of anyone else being immodest, so they took their clothes out to the yard and buried them! Their outward actions reflected their inward desires. They desired to be covenant keepers.

When we are modest, we reflect in our outward actions and appearance that we understand what God expects us to do. We reflect that we are women of covenant—that we understand the covenants we have made at baptism to "stand as witnesses of God at all times and in all things, and in all places" (Mosiah 18:9). As we keep our baptismal covenant and "always remember him" (D&C 20:77), our actions and appearance invite the companionship of the Holy Ghost. And we are told in the Book of Mormon that the Holy Ghost will "show unto you all things what ye should do" (2 Nephi 32:5). In the world in which we live, can we risk being without this sure compass and companion? The pressures of the world must not push us into places where the Spirit cannot dwell.

"When you are well groomed and modestly dressed, you invite the companionship of the Spirit and can exercise a good influence on those around you."[22] It is really all about the Spirit. If you go through the entire *For the Strength of Youth* booklet and circle each mention of the Holy Ghost, you will see that it occurs twenty-four times in forty-two pages. This entire book describes, standard by standard, how to qualify for the companionship of the Holy Ghost.

In our day, prophets have again issued the call to young women and women to retrench, to arise, to be worthy of imitation. Our standards are clearly outlined for us, and they carry with them infinitely great rewards. We are promised by prophets of God that if we live the standards, we "will be able to do [our] life's work with greater wisdom and skill and bear trials with greater courage. [We] will have the help of the Holy Ghost. [We] will feel good about oursel[ves] and will be a positive influence in the lives of others. [We] will be worthy to go to the temple to receive holy ordinances."[23]

What more could a mother want for her daughter or for herself?

The people who assembled at the waters of Mormon were converted to the gospel. They were about to be baptized and enter into a covenant that included "stand[ing] as witnesses of God at all times and in all things, and in all places" (Mosiah 18:9). When Alma asked them if they were willing to do this, "they clapped their hands for joy, and exclaimed: This is the desire of our hearts" (Mosiah 18:11). Why was it their hearts' desire? Because, just as it was in Anatevka, they had been taught and understood who they really were and what God expected them to do. They wanted to change. They understood and wanted the promises. And they were willing to do whatever it took to have the blessing of the companionship of the Holy Ghost.

As daughters of God and women of covenant, we have stepped out of the world and into the kingdom. Now is the time to "arise and shine forth, that thy light may be a standard for the nations" (D&C 115:5).

NOTES

1. Joseph Stein, Jerry Bock, and Sheldon Harnick, *Fiddler on the Roof: Based on Sholom Aleichem's Stories* (New York: Limelight Editions, 2004).

2. *For the Strength of Youth* (Salt Lake City: The Church of Jesus Christ of Latter-day Saints, 2001), 40.

3. Russell M. Nelson, "Thanks for the Covenant," in *Brigham Young University 1988–89 Devotional and Fireside Speeches* (Provo, Utah: Brigham Young University, 1989), 59.

4. *Personal Progress* (Salt Lake City: The Church of Jesus Christ of Latter-day Saints, 2001), 5.

5. Gordon B. Hinckley, "Our Responsibility to Our Young Women," *Ensign*, September 1988, 11.

6. Susa Young Gates, *History of the Young Ladies' Mutual Improvement Association of the Church of Jesus Christ of Latter-day Saints* (Salt Lake City: Deseret News, 1911), 8–10.

7. *Webster's New World Dictionary of the American Language*, 1st college ed., s.v. "retrench."

8. Delbert L. Stapley, "A Salute to Youth," *Liahona*, November 2001, 27.

9. Gordon B. Hinckley, "Standing Strong and Immovable," *Worldwide Leadership Training Meeting*, January 10, 2004 (Salt Lake City: The Church of Jesus Christ of Latter-day Saints, 2004), 20.

10. Gordon B. Hinckley, "An Ensign to the Nations, a Light to the World," *Ensign*, November 2003, 84.

11. James E. Faust, "Womanhood: The Highest Place of Honor," *Ensign*, May 2000, 97.

12. Gordon B. Hinckley, "Stay on the High Road," *Ensign*, May 2004, 112, 114.

13. Spencer W. Kimball, "On My Honor," *Ensign*, April 1979, 3.

14. A. Theodore Tuttle, "Your Mission Preparation," *Ensign*, November 1974, 71.

15. *For the Strength of Youth*, 15.

16. Hinckley, "Standing Strong and Immovable," 21.

17. See Sarah Jane Weaver, "Church gives $3 million to fight measles in Africa," *Church News*, September 27, 2003, 7–9.

18. Boyd K. Packer, "Little Children," *Ensign*, November 1986, 17.

19. John S. Tanner, "To Clothe a Temple," *Ensign*, August 1992, 47.

20. See Tanner, "To Clothe a Temple," 44.

21. Mary C. Hales, "An Outward Expression of an Inward Commitment," in *The Power of His Redemption: Talks from the 2003 BYU Women's Conference* (Salt Lake City: Deseret Book, 2004), 178.

22. *For the Strength of Youth*, 15.

23. *For the Strength of Youth*, 2–3.

GIVING GIRLS THE PROTECTIVE, ENABLING GIFT OF MODESTY

Jan Pinborough

As I watched Michelle Kwan skating on TV recently, I was literally moved to tears. She skated with such a sense of grace and beauty, with such focus and discipline, and with such a feeling of joy and freedom. It was easy to forget that all the while she was performing a feat of breathtaking courage—turning, spinning, and leaping across slick, hard ice on two thin blades of steel.

She reminded me of the incredible young women of this generation who are now taking their own beautiful turns on the ice. They are lively and intelligent, with great gifts and ambitions. We watch them as they develop their talents, work hard to do well at school, and volunteer in their communities. Sometimes it's easy to forget that they, too, are performing feats of breathtaking courage as they strive to be strong and pure and virtuous in a world that's anything but.

As women, we share many experiences that give us a common bond—not the least of which is girls' camp. For good or for ill, most of us probably have at least one vivid memory of girls' camp. Our daughter

---

Jan Pinborough has been an editor for the Ensign *and* Liahona *magazines, has written many articles and songs for Church publication, and coauthored* Where Do I Go from Here? Finding Your Personal Mission as a Young Adult Woman. *She has served on the Church's General Music Committee and currently serves on a Church curriculum writing committee and in a stake Primary presidency. She and her husband, Tom, are the parents of two teenaged daughters.*

Elizabeth's favorite girls' camp adventure was the night of the midnight hike. As she told us about it, I could just picture Sister Mortensen's flashlight cutting through the darkness of the thick Tennessee woods as the girls followed close behind her in their sweats and PJs. They had to navigate around rocks, logs, and ravines in the darkness, amidst a rather large population of raccoons, skunks, bats, and insects. But Sister Mortensen knew the way, her flashlight was strong, and the girls held onto one another's shirttails. When they reached a clearing by the lake, they stopped to rest under the starry sky before heading back to their tents. So many things could have tripped them up, but the hike was a brilliant success.

"One Bright Shining Hope"

The young women we love so much are having their own hikes through life at a pretty dark time in the world's history. It just takes a flip of the TV switch, a glance at the magazine stand, a minute in the halls of their schools, or a shopping excursion to the mall to know that. There is so much to trip them up. But they are not alone. We are on the path just ahead, and we have a powerful light to share with them.

In fact, just after comparing the moral darkness of our day to that of those infamous twin cities, Sodom and Gomorrah, President Hinckley made this remarkable statement:

"It is so tremendously important that the women of the Church stand strong and immovable for that which is correct and proper under the plan of the Lord. . . .

"We call upon the women of the Church to stand together for righteousness. They must begin in their own homes. They can teach it in their classes. They can voice it in their communities.

"They must be the teachers and the guardians of their daughters. . . . When you save a girl, you save generations. . . .

"I see this as the one bright shining hope in a world that is marching toward self-destruction."[1]

Did you catch that? Our prophet sees us as the one bright shining hope in this whole dark situation.

And we have one especially powerful light to share with our young women. It is a light that will pierce the darkness of our day. It will help them avoid dangers on their paths. It is the empowering and protective virtue of modesty.

Modesty is much more than having the right number of inches between the skirt and the knee. It is an attitude that says, "I know *who* I am, and I know *whose* I am. I know what I am about and the role my body plays in that." It says, "I listen to and follow a prophet. I am a disciple of Christ."

Who wouldn't want to share such a gift? But how can we best share it?

AWAKE AND ARISE

Speaking to the Church in 1838, the Lord said, "Arise and shine forth, that thy light may be a standard for the nations" (D&C 115:5).

As we consider how to help our girls appreciate and practice modesty, this verse has much to teach us.

First, arise. I would like to suggest that, even before we arise, we must be awake. We must be awake to the temptations and dangers our young women are facing every day.

Among the greatest of these is our popular culture's constant attack on their dignity and their sense of who they are and what they should be about.

This message comes through loud and clear in songs, videos, ads, and reality shows. I think when you boil it down to a few short sentences, the message goes something like this: "Your body is the most important thing about you, and it is primarily a lure. So starve it, straighten it, make it up and make it over, and dress it in trendy clothes. Then you can be happy and successful—just like celebrities!" This ridiculous-sounding message plays a serious role in such problems as eating disorders, low self-esteem, and depression, as well as immorality with all its attendant ills. So we need to stay awake to the effects of the media in our girls' lives.

We must not be lulled into thinking that modesty is something we can just let slide. It is not peripheral. It is central to the well-being of the young women we love.

Arising also implies that we may need to stretch ourselves. Recently a young woman made the insightful observation that just as the young men of our Church have been challenged to raise the bar as they prepare to be effective missionaries, young women need to raise the bar in the area of modesty. And, I think, implicit in those two challenges is a third challenge for their parents and leaders.

In our families and Young Women presidencies, it will take focusing our best creativity and inspiration to know how to best teach and support our girls in this vital principle.

Arising also reminds me that the Lord tells us to arise early. A girl's earliest years are the best time to lay the foundations for modesty in her later years. From the very beginning, a girl needs to learn that her body is the sacred temple of her spirit and that dressing modestly will make her strong and help her accomplish her important mission on earth as a daughter of God. She will also need a healthy sense of self so that she will not need to get her sense of self from dressing immodestly.

Next, shine forth. We must shine forth ourselves in the principle of modesty, valuing and honoring the covenants we ourselves have made in this regard.

As Elder Russell M. Nelson explained:

"Keeping a . . . covenant is not constraining but enabling. It elevates us beyond limits of our own perspective and power. It is like the difference between plodding through a muddy field and soaring through the skies in a supersonic jet. Keeping a covenant with God is both protective and enabling."[2]

The young women in our lives watch us with unblinking eyes, calibrating their own navigational instruments by ours, using us as true north. When they see that we consider our own covenants with the Lord to be enabling and protective, they are more likely to see their own commitments in that same light.

Last, be a standard for the nations. The word *standard* has two relevant meanings. The first kind of standard is a banner carried atop a pole to mark a rallying point in battle. The reality is that we are not the only ones concerned about modesty. Many others are ready to join us as we champion modesty. The second kind of standard is a gauge, a rule for measure, a means of determining what a thing should be. It's a fixed point, not a sliding rule that we adjust to stay just above the popular fashions of the day.

THE BENEFITS OF MODESTY

In order to give our girls the gift of modesty, we need to recognize and explicitly teach them its many protective and enabling benefits. Here are just a few:

1. *First and most important, modesty gives girls spiritual protection.* It's like putting on "the whole armor of God." I think our girls' junior high and high schools are not unlike the fiery furnace of Shadrach, Meshach, and Abed-nego. Because those young men stood by the Lord's standards, opposing the cultural practices of their day, the Lord stood by them, enabling them to withstand the fire with His very presence. Our daughters, too, need great spiritual protection as they face their own kind of fire. As they honor the Lord by dressing modestly, He stands by them to protect them from evils in their world.

Modesty also protects girls in a very literal way. I recently walked into a mall behind a pretty young woman wearing a very short dress. I watched sadly as a much older man looked her up and down and then turned around to watch her as she passed. In our day, pornography and media exploitation of girls have reached scourge proportions. How I wish that girl in the mall had had the protective gift of modesty.

Before girls can appreciate this benefit, though, they must understand the fundamental difference in the way women and men respond to visual stimuli. Otherwise they will assume that just because seeing a boy dressed immodestly creates no problem for them, the same holds true for men and boys. Without this crucial information, they will never be able to understand what all the fuss is about when their shirt doesn't meet the top of their jeans or when their t-shirt fits too tightly.

2. *Dressing modestly is like taking a multivitamin. It has many, many benefits.* Besides being the mother virtue of chastity, modesty helps

others see past the body to the mind and heart of a girl. It helps people focus on her inner qualities such as creativity, compassion, and intelligence. It will help others see and treat her as a whole person. As one young woman put it, "Dressing immodestly is like letting the backup singers drown out the lead singer."

Remember the old motto, Dress for Success? Well, dressing modestly is dressing for respect, something every young woman needs and deserves. Modesty will elevate her relationships to a higher plane.

One young man summed up these benefits: "A young woman's dress tells me a lot about how she feels about herself and the Lord. When a young woman dresses modestly, she has a beauty that comes, I believe, from the Spirit.

"When a woman dresses modestly, it makes me want to be worthy of her. When both partners are dressed appropriately, there is less temptation, and, more importantly, the Spirit can be present in their relationship."

Truly, modesty is a girl's best friend.

3. *Dressing modestly helps girls light the path for others.* No one has expressed the effect righteous women (and I believe this includes young women) will have on the world better than President Spencer W. Kimball:

"Much of the major growth that is coming to the Church in the last days will come because many of the good women of the world (in whom there is often such an inner sense of spirituality) will be drawn to the Church in large numbers. This will happen to the degree that the women of the Church reflect righteousness and articulateness in their lives and to the degree that the women of the Church are seen as distinct and different—in happy ways—from the women of the world. . . .

"Thus it will be that female exemplars of the Church will be a significant force in both the numerical and the spiritual growth of the Church in the last days."[3]

Can the way a young woman dresses actually have such a powerful effect? Just ask Florence Chukwurah. Florence was born into a life of extreme poverty in Nigeria. But at age fifteen, Florence determined that she would be a nurse. Why? Because she had seen nurses, and she admired their clean, white uniforms. She wanted to look like that. She wanted to do what they did.

At the age of sixteen, Florence traveled six hours away from her home to begin her training as a nurse. The year Florence graduated from her training at Queen Elizabeth Hospital, she received the Florence Nightingale Award for best nurse of the year. She continued her education, finishing her training as a midwife five years later.

Florence met and married an educated man, was baptized with him, and has served with him while he was president of the Ghana Accra Mission. She has also served as a member of the Relief Society general board.

I wonder if all that would have happened if those nurses Florence saw when she was just a girl had not kept their uniforms clean or had worn them in a sloppy and disheveled way or only worn parts of their uniforms. Those nurses had a definite *look*. Missionaries have a look. You can spot them at a glance. I love the title of Sheri Dew's book: *No Doubt About It*. Isn't it wonderful when our girls are so clearly and unambiguously modest that you can spot them at a glance? They look wholesome, no doubt about it. They have a *look*.

For a young woman, buttoning that top button may be something like pinning on a missionary's badge. It's the final touch that completes the look. It's closing the last chink in the armor. Imagine a whole army of such girls as living examples to other girls who desperately need the protecting and enabling powers of modesty.

4. *Dressing modestly leads to the temple.* Several weeks ago, my daughter Christiana and I left the Tabernacle after a fireside late one evening. As we walked beside the Salt Lake Temple, we looked upward and caught our breath. It was so unbelievably and radiantly beautiful. We could even seen light glowing out through some of the windows.

"I want to go to the temple right now," Christiana said. I believe most of our young women feel this same way. We can help them understand that dressing modestly is something they can do right now to be worthy now of entering the temple later. If they dress appropriately throughout their young years, they will have no need to buy a whole new wardrobe, or adopt a whole new attitude toward clothing, when it is time to go to the temple.

"We Seek after These Things"—Together

But for our girls, the choice of what to wear is often more an emotional than rational one. They want to be accepted. They want to fit in with their peers. So, just as they sometimes need our guidance in choosing an apple over a candy bar, they need our day-to-day guidance in making wise clothing choices. How can we find modest school clothes for our daughters? And what do we do when a girl keeps coming to activities inappropriately dressed? Of course, I can't answer these questions, and you don't expect me to. I have thought about them, though, and I have a few tips and tools to offer:

On shopping:

Shopping Tip 1: Know before you go.

Long before we hit the mall with our daughters, we must be completely clear in our own minds about what is acceptable and what isn't. We can begin by reading the section on dress from the pamphlet *For the Strength of Youth*—together. Don't wait until you get in the dressing room and find out that the cutest outfit in the store doesn't quite meet in the middle. If we waffle and slide, we will find our daughters being carried steadily downstream to lower and lower standards.

Remember that most of all we are trying to help our daughters maintain a wholesome, modest look. After all, it is the overall look, attitude, and demeanor that convey modesty. A crude logo can make even a sweatshirt immodest. The word *modest* means moderate, unpretentious, chaste, and humble.

And the word *modesty* means freedom from conceit or vanity; propriety in dress, speech, or conduct. An immodest attitude flaunts the body or uses it to get attention. A modest attitude conveys a sense of being humble and having dignity.

Shopping Tip 2: Be prepared for the fact that most trendy clothing right now is immodest.

Styles mostly follow celebrity clothing, and that is mostly designed to be provocative, so it's going to take some searching. But remember, one of our articles of faith clearly states that in order to find anything virtuous, lovely, or of good report or praiseworthy, we will have to seek (see Articles of Faith 1:13).

Shopping Tip 3: Use the mirror.

Pull a chair into the dressing room so that your daughter can make sure the outfit will still be modest when she crosses her legs or bends over to pick up a pencil. Show her how to play "Head, Shoulders, Knees, and Toes" to make sure skin doesn't show when she moves normally.

Shopping Tip 4: Be creative.

Once we are firmly determined, we will do what it takes. We can buy t-shirts and jeans in larger sizes. We can shop in misses departments or through catalogs. Some popular stores are starting to carry t-shirts and jeans with more modest cuts and lengths. Patronize those stores, and write letters to say thank you! Write letters to other stores to ask them to carry more modest styles. If your daughter has to take a pass on some trendy styles, help her use the season's popular colors, shoes, or accessories to update her look without lowering her standards.

Shopping Tip 5: Be willing to have your daughter look a little different than the popular style.

Help your daughter create her own sense of style, one that reflects who she is—a strong, independent-minded person on her way to someplace important. Other girls may follow her. Help her find a look that will help take her where she wants to go—to fulfill her dreams of temple worthiness, education, a mission, and being a righteous mother who will pass these values on to daughters of her own.

Now just two ideas on being a leader:

First: Love is the most important thing. We can only lead a girl along a path if she wants to be close to us. And we must always remember that a girl who dresses or even acts immodestly is in all probability just following a popular style in dress or behavior. Almost all immodestly dressed girls are like sheep in wolves' clothing. Behind the improper style is a girl with a good heart and righteous desires.

And second: Remember the magic of clear, firm expectations. When young women know exactly what is expected, they will rise to meet the expectations. In fact, they will thrive on meeting them. "Marshmallow love" doesn't give the security and safety young women need. Firm expectations are an expression of great love.

"If God Be for Us, Who Can Be against Us?"

Our task may seem great, at times even overwhelming. We may feel that we are trying to hold back a cultural tidal wave all by ourselves. Or we may just feel that we are being pecked to death by a duck—or maybe a whole flock of ducks. And we will probably always wish there were greater consensus on such important matters.

Well, look around your ward. Many people share your love for girls and your desire to help them dress modestly. We need to have conversations with each other, share our best ideas, and find creative solutions.

We are not alone. Many people of other faiths share our ideals too, and we need to support each other.

When our family lived in Kentucky, I had two close friends of other faiths. One day my Christian friend Lauren asked me what I thought of the spaghetti-strap T-shirts that were just getting popular. She didn't like them, and she wondered if she should let her daughter wear them. I told her that I shared her feeling and explained that our Church's dress standards backed up both our opinions. That fact was supportive to her.

About the same time, I was complaining to my Jewish friend, Margaret, about how stores were marketing adult-looking clothing to younger and younger girls. She in turn lamented the way some of the girls were dressing in her synagogue. Then she explained that the Yiddish word *frum* described the modest sensibility we shared about dress. Now it was my turn to feel supported. She not only felt the same way I did, she gave me a word for it!

But ultimately we must never lose heart because, as the Apostle Paul asked, "If God be for us, who can be against us?" (Romans 8:31).

Every now and then we hear news stories of women who perform amazing deeds of strength and courage. You know: the hundred-and-thirty-pound woman who lifts an automobile to free a child; or, closer to home, the woman who speaks up for children at the city council or the school board.

Which brings me back around to girls' camp and one of my favorite girls' camp facts of nature: While it's a bad thing to encounter a male grizzly bear on a hiking trail, it's a far worse thing to run into a mother grizzly protecting her cub.

Women have the determination, the courage, and the strength to guard and protect young women, even against enormous odds.

Let me quote President Hinckley one more time:

"It is so tremendously important that the women of the Church stand strong and immovable for that which is correct and proper under the plan of the Lord. . . .

"We call upon the women of the Church to stand together for righteousness. They must begin in their own homes. They can teach it in their classes. They can voice it in their communities.

"They must be the teachers and the guardians of their daughters. . . . When you save a girl, you save generations. . . .

"I see *this* as [our] one bright shining hope."[4]

May we all find the courage, inspiration, and ingenuity to fulfill this hope.

NOTES

1. Gordon B. Hinckley, "Standing Strong and Immovable," *Worldwide Leadership Training Meeting,* January 10, 2004 (Salt Lake City: The Church of Jesus Christ of Latter-day Saints, 2004), 20.
2. Russell M. Nelson, "Prepare for Blessings of the Temple," *Ensign,* March 2002, 21.
3. Spencer W. Kimball, "The Role of Righteous Women," *Ensign,* November 1979, 103–4.
4. Hinckley, "Standing Strong and Immovable," 20; emphasis added.

"Rejoice in His Labour; This Is the Gift of God"

Kathleen Bahr

The work of caring for our homes and families is a godly activity, and the necessity of doing this work day in and day out is a "gift of God" (Ecclesiastes 5:19). This labor can be a source of great joy.

The truth of this may not be obvious. In fact, these ideas may strike many in our modern world as falsehood. Many today have little sense of how the ordinary, daily work required to sustain and nurture life in our families can be "a gift of God" or a source of joy because for the last forty or more years we have been bombarded with messages that say just the opposite.

I want to explain the why, what, and how of family work: *Why* it is important that our children help do family work, *what* kinds of work we should expect them to do, and *how* we can encourage our children to help do this work.

First, *why?* We all know it usually requires a lot of work to get children to work. They would rather play. And it is especially difficult to get them to do housework. So why bother? Isn't it enough just to play together and hold family home evening together?

Several years ago, White and Brinkerhoff[1] asked parents in 790

Kathleen Slaugh Bahr is an associate professor in Home and Family Living at Brigham Young University. Her teaching and research interests grow out of a life-long study of the importance of family work. She and her husband, Howard, have five sons, four of whom are adopted. She is a Sunbeam teacher in her ward.

homes whether they expected their children to help do housework, and why. The reasons were grouped into four categories. The most common response on "why" was that it helps children develop character and learn responsibility. Other reasons given were (2) it is their duty to help; put bluntly, "they live here, don't they?"; (3) need—parents needed the help of their children; and (4) task learning—parents wanted their children to learn work skills. The interesting part of this research came when they compared the number of hours children spent doing housework each week with the reasons parents gave for having them work. Which children do you suppose did the most work? (The ones where parents needed their help.) Which did the least? (The ones who gave developmental reasons.)

White and Brinkerhoff concluded that "most parents adhere to the conventional wisdom that chores are good for kids," but their understanding of why it is good is sufficiently vague that it doesn't compel the parents to require much work from their children. Unless the parents really need their children's help, it is much easier just to expect a minimum amount of taking care of one's self, one's own room, own snacks, own laundry, own shopping; very little actual "family work" is required.

What this research tells me is that parents need a clearer vision of why this work matters. To understand why it matters, we need to look more closely at the *what*—what kind of work are we talking about? It is the work commonly referred to as housework, yard work, child care. But it is so much more than this; it is family work; it helps build our sense of being a family (if there were more time, I would tell how this work has helped our two adopted Russian boys feel they truly are part of our family—how it has created the sense of being family for them).

This work is also the Lord's work; it is the work of nurturing life. This is the work given to Adam and Eve in the beginning, and they were promised that doing this work would be a blessing to them. You remember Adam was told he must do the hard labor of caring for the fields, but he was promised, "cursed shall be the ground for thy sake" (Moses 4:23). And Eve was to do the hard work of bringing forth children, but promised she would be "saved in childbearing"—it would be the means to her salvation (see 1 Timothy 2:15). A close examination of these scriptures tells us there are spiritual blessings promised for doing this temporal work. While the world thinks of caring for the earth and caring for children as ordinary work, it is anything but ordinary. This is the work of life. In mortality, life does not sustain itself. So the work of feeding, clothing, and caring for each other is the work required to sustain and nurture life on a daily basis.

From the scriptures and modern prophets we learn that the spiritual and temporal are inseparable. There isn't time to consider this idea in depth. Let me just give a few references, and you can read them later. First, in Matthew 25:31–40, we learn that the criteria for determining who will be on the Savior's right hand in the kingdom of his Father is whether or not we fed, clothed, and cared for "the least of these." From King Benjamin, in Mosiah 4:26, we learn that feeding, clothing, and caring for one another is essential to retaining a remission of our sins.

President Spencer W. Kimball frequently taught that it is as we do the ordinary daily work of caring for our homes and for each other, growing gardens, beautifying our yards, that we will "bring again Zion," and it is also by doing this work together that we learn to put the gospel in action in our lives. Similarly, President Hinckley teaches, "Children need to work with their parents, to wash dishes with them, to mop floors with them, to mow lawns, to prune trees and shrubbery, to paint and fix up, to clean up, and to do a hundred other things"[2] just like this because through this work our children will learn to be moral people who care about others.

Another reason why it is important to teach our children to do family work is because it is a good antidote for idleness. The Book of Mormon provides an interesting history of the dangers of idleness contrasted with the blessings of happiness that come from laboring with one's own hands. In the Doctrine and Covenants (especially D&C 68:31) we are also warned against idleness.

There is probably a need to distinguish between the idleness the Lord warns against and some of the "not-work" activities our children may spend time doing. To me, the difference is in whether or not the activity nourishes their souls. I was delighted, as I'm sure you were, with the story told by Sister Hinckley, and retold at her funeral, of a time when one of her sons wandered off on a very busy day. There was much work to be done, and she was upset that he wasn't doing his part of the work. She said she prepared a speech to give him when he returned. But when he returned and she learned where he had been, she decided not to give him her speech. He had been down to "the hollow," a place that inspired musing about the meaning of life and daydreaming about life's possibilities. These are activities that feed the soul. They require creativity and effortful leaps of imagination. Children need that kind of time.

But there is another kind of idleness where growth is blocked, where lethargy replaces effort, where entitlement replaces gratitude. Here is a description of that kind of idleness, from a novel set among the Eskimo. The Inuit storyteller recalls her days in a boarding school.

"I've always enjoyed cleaning. Even though they tried to teach us laziness in school.

"In school we had all our meals served to us. We had a hot bath every day and clean clothes every other. In the village we had bathed once a week, much less often when hunting or traveling. Every day, from the glacier above the cliffs, I had collected big blocks of freshwater ice, and carried them home in sacks and melted them over the stove. At the boarding school you turned on a faucet. When summer vacation arrived, all the students and teachers went out to Herbert Island and visited the hunters, and for the first time in a long while we had boiled seal meat and tea. That's when I noticed the paralysis. Not just in me but in everybody. We could not pull ourselves together anymore; it was no longer a natural thing to reach out for some water and brown soap and the package of Neogene and start rinsing the skins. We weren't used to washing clothes, we couldn't pull ourselves together to cook. At every break we would slip into a daydreaming state of waiting. Hoping someone would take over, would relieve us, free us from our duties, and do what we ourselves ought to have done."[3]

What is so distressing about the lethargy described here? It is that we see so much of it around us, children who complain they are bored, waiting around for someone to wait on them, to make their lives exciting for them. I see young people wandering the streets seemingly without the energy it takes to smile. They do not seem happy. They do not seem grateful for their many blessings. They are looking for easy excitement, for pleasure. Little do they know of the joy that can come through working with their own hands to help feed, clothe, and care for others.

Now, the question of *how?* Given the many distractions (like TV, computers, electronic games), what can we do to motivate our children and help them stay on task?

To help answer this question, I would like to recommend a wonderful book, *Mitten Strings for God: Reflections for Mothers in a Hurry,* by Katrina Kenison. This book would make a wonderful Mother's Day present for yourself or for someone you love. It is a calming book, with lots of wisdom and good ideas on slowing down the pace of life to make time for the truly important things. One of Kenison's first good insights is that we need to begin on a small scale to make changes in the way we think about our lives and move ahead slowly to make needed changes; make small changes at first, and then move on to others. Kenison says:

"I've learned that even a small shift in my own thinking usually has a more powerful effect on my day-to-day life than any full-scale attempt at self-improvement. The same is true when it comes to raising children. Holding a vision of their best, true selves in my mind, I suddenly find that the picture has become a reality. We create our lives within our own imaginations well before we ever realize them here on earth. So I imagine what is possible and try to live my days mindfully, and with a sense of humor. This book, then, is not about changing your life. It is about paying more attention to the life you already have, about taking your own life back as you protect your children from the pull of a world that is spinning too fast."[4]

"Holding a vision of their best, true selves . . ." What a perfect place to begin. These children we are raising are also children of God, with glorious potential. We must recognize we are not doing our children a favor when we allow them to waste away their days with idle distractions. They are capable of so much more.

So how do we encourage our children's participation in daily family work? I have found a distinction used by Dorothy Lee very useful here. Lee distinguishes between motivation and invitation, and she suggests invitation is a more compelling alternative.[5] Most of the methods we hear of, the ones recommended by most "experts" out there, fall under the heading of motivation.

Motivation is an appeal to self-interest. We assume from the start that children are mostly interested in themselves and that they won't do anything unless we provide them with some individual reward. Thus, to motivate them, we must make the work into a game, or prod them on with promised punishments or rewards, with money, candy, a trip to the park. I have nothing against a trip to the park, but when we consistently motivate them by holding out some "carrot," some individual reward, we may be hindering their development of a higher sense of satisfaction that comes from doing work for and with others.

More serious than promising a trip to the park as an incentive to get their jobs done is promising money. Probably every one of us has, at one time or another, resorted to using money as an incentive: "You can't get your money until your work is done." We use money because it works, at least until they get a little older and find other places to earn their money. And we use money because we want our children to learn to manage money, and we have been taught that learning to manage money requires that they have their own money. You need to know there is no research that supports this idea. For the most part, poor money management is more often the result of greed, of never learning to be satisfied with what one has, with always wanting more, than it is of not knowing how to make a budget. It is good for children to learn how to save and how to spend wisely, but we need to think carefully about how we teach these principles. For the moment, I would like to suggest some of the risks we take when we use money as an incentive to get children to do work:

First, money tends to drive out other good reasons for doing the work; if one is paid for the work, that becomes the overriding reason for doing it. If I ask my child to make his bed, and you come along and ask him why he made his bed, he may answer, "Because mother asked me to," or because it needed to be made, or because he wanted to do it. But if I have told him, "Jonathan, if you make your bed I will give you a dollar," and you come along and ask him why he made his bed, almost certainly his answer will be, "So I could get the dollar." There is now an abundant body of research that shows how this works. I was interested and delighted to read an article in a recent *Church News* on the Primary Faith in God award. The article says the Primary presidency want parents to understand "that the Faith in God award program does not include jewelry, pins or other such memorabilia. . . . Studies have shown, Sister Reynolds explained, that if behavior is determined by 'little rewards,' then the good behavior usually doesn't last."

Sister Menlove wants parents and leaders to ask, "Can this be meaningful and help these children develop faith and develop into righteous young men or young women?"[6] It is a good question for us to ask ourselves as we consider ways to involve children in family work.

A second reason to be hesitant about using money as a motivator is that money isolates the recipient, in the sense that what was work to be shared now becomes someone's job, and others have no reason to share it unless they, too, are paid. It delights me when my boys offer to help one another do Saturday chores. If they were paid, would they be as likely to make these offers to help each other? In a research study we are doing, parents who pay their children to do housework report their children are reluctant to help one another when there is a need unless they know they will also get paid. "Why should I help him? It's his job; he's the one who is getting paid to do it," is a common response.

A third reason to be cautious about using money is that paying for family work may actually be reinforcing its low status. When you pay children, you may be sending the message this is work that no one would do unless they did it for money. Its intrinsic importance, its higher spiritual worth, may be lost to the market orientation.

Grace Weinstein and Natalia Ginzburg are two women who advise parents to leave money out of transactions with their children, especially when they are young. For one thing, it is easy for children to confuse money and love and to feel when you withhold money that you are really withholding love. Also, you run the risk of teaching your children to love money and to spend their days thinking about how they can get more money, rather than learning to love the work and learning to devote their thoughts to how they might better love and serve one another.[7]

Using money is a tempting motivator because it is concrete. You can see it, and you can see the need to learn to manage it. But Ginzberg says learning to manage money is a little virtue, and it is more important to teach children the big virtues, like love, service, generosity, sacrifice, and that they don't need money in order to be happy.[8] Yet we tend to leave the development of those virtues to chance, simply assuming they will pick them up somewhere along the way, while we focus our energies on teaching them to manage money.

In this regard, parents need to seriously consider what they are raising their children to become. There is a superb article, available on the Internet, titled "On Rekindling a Spirit of 'Home Training': A Mother's Notes from the Front," by Enola G. Aird.[9]

Aird tells of meeting a group of young exchange students, cultural ambassadors, teenagers from Mexico City. One of them said:

"'In Mexico, children are raised to . . .' He finished the thought by listing a series of striking personal virtues. Among them were 'to be respectful of their elders, to take care of younger children, and to be family-oriented.' . . .

"I was deeply moved by the young man and his companions because of their clear sense of the purposes for which they were being raised and their strong feelings of pride in knowing and claiming those purposes.

"I wondered about the children of the United States. . . . What would they say to complete the sentence, 'In the United States, children are raised to . . .'? . . .

"When I asked my teen-aged daughter, 'What are we raising young people in the United States to be?' she answered without hesitation that we are raising them 'to compete, to go to school, to get good grades, and to get a good job to make lots of money to buy lots of things so they can have children and raise them to compete, to go to school, to get good grades, to get a good job to make lots of money to buy lots of things.'"

Aird cites research showing that "the most powerful and consistent message that our culture sends to young people is that the purpose of life is material success."

Aird warns, "The values of the marketplace—a focus on material things, profit maximization, competition, instant gratification—reign above and threaten to destroy such virtues as sacrifice, commitment, dedication, duty, and responsibility."

Another article, available online in *Meridian Magazine*, "On Grocery Shopping with Children: Nurturing Spiritual Self-Reliance," by Elder L. Whitney Clayton and Kathy Clayton,[10] provides a similar warning: "Be careful with external rewards." The Claytons went on to say:

"We agreed that any method of discipline that depends on imposing external punishment, or even granting rewards, risks becoming manipulative and delays or minimizes a child's privilege of tasting the sweet, personal sensation of the affirming approval of heaven for the right choices. Children who become satisfied to fold their arms and sit quietly in Church services solely because they crave the gold star their parents will put on their foreheads at the end of the exercise may neglect to recognize the sweet sense of worship and connection to heaven they are entitled to for their reverent behavior."

What are the alternatives to using money or other tangible rewards as an incentive to get children to complete their work? Back to the ideas of Dorothy Lee, who contrasts motivation with the idea of invitation. What does she mean by invitation? She doesn't mean that doing the work should be optional. What she is talking about is learning to notice need, to see opportunity. It is need that invites; opportunity invites: the opportunity of working with others invites.

How does need invite? The baby cries. That cry invites you (or it demands) that you respond, that you do something to help satisfy that need. The garbage can is full to overflowing. Seeing it provides an invitation to do something about it, to empty the garbage can. Isn't that the dream of every mother's heart, that children will learn to see need and respond appropriately? Odds are children won't learn this lesson well until they are parents themselves or until they are truly responsible. But we can begin to teach them.

A few years ago, one of my graduate students interviewed Pueblo Indian grandmothers, asking them how they learned to do family work when they were children. She began to notice a consistent theme in the grandmothers' responses: their parents invited them to do work by phrasing the invitation in terms of need: "Go see if your grandmother needs water." "See if there is enough wood in the woodpile; does more need to be chopped?"

In one of my classes we talked about ways to help children learn to see and recognize need, and one student, a mother of a sixteen-year-old, decided to approach her son using this language. When she went home, she asked him to help do some family task by saying, "Son, I really need your help." She says he looked at her with some surprise, "Need! That is a pretty strong word." And he smiled and did what she asked.

I tried this one time with my then-ten-year-old son, Alden. We had just added on to our kitchen and installed a new hardwood floor. The room was empty; no cabinets, no sink or range or refrigerator. Just a big room with a hardwood floor. And it needed sweeping. I asked Alden to look at the floor and see if something needed to be done. He did, and reported the floor needed lines painted on it to make it into a basketball court. Of course, that wasn't exactly what I had in mind.

I find it a challenge to teach my children how to recognize and respond to need. One problem I face is that I still want to maintain some control over what they do; in fact, I need to maintain some control. To illustrate, one day our neighbor rented a stump remover to dig out stumps in their yard and ours. Anton watched with interest. The next day he announced he had begun to dig out a large stump in our backyard, one the neighbor had missed. I winced. I loved that stump; I used it like a low table, to put things on. I looked in the backyard; there was my stump table hacked to pieces. And I looked at Anton, who was smiling broadly because he had done something to help without being asked. I will tell you what I wish I had said to him. I wish I had said, "Thank you, Anton. Next time, please check with me or Daddy before you begin a project." What I said instead may not be appropriate to repeat here.

Kenison, in her book *Mitten Strings for God*, suggests several ways to invite children's activity into the family circle and to make family work more inviting. One is to lower the amount and level of commercial noise: the television, video games, music. She says that in her home they even decided to get rid of the alarm clocks and learned to awake to their own inner clocks. She reports the benefit of this is they learned to talk— and listen—to each other more. She became more attentive to her children and their needs and sensed they were learning to be more attentive and thoughtful in return.

Recently, our stake leaders invited the youth in our stake to participate in a media fast. For one week, there would be no CDs, no videotapes, no radio, no television, no video games. I was told that at least some of the youth found this assignment too difficult. But some did it, and one of these, Deborah Benson, reported on her experience at stake conference. With her permission I will quote from her talk. First, she said it was hard to do. "It is just a habit to walk into the room and turn on the radio or a CD or a movie or something. Like in the mornings on the way to school my brother and sister and I listen to the radio and sing along with it." At first it was quiet in the car, but then "we talked. And, well, I feel like I got to know them a little better and my love for them grew just that much more. About the middle of the week I was fighting temptation after temptation to turn on the radio. So it resulted in me singing out loud to myself and to everyone around me." She told of the fun she had making up new songs. She said she became a more careful driver. She felt more in tune with the Spirit. She felt greater love for her family. On the weekend, rather than watch a movie together, her family played games. When the media fast ended and she returned to her old routine, she said the music gave her a headache.

Kenison, in *Mitten Strings for God,* writes: "I am convinced that the simplest, most effective way to enrich family life is to return quiet to our homes. . . . This is not to say we live in complete silence—far from it. Our home is filled with music and laughter and, yes, noise. But it is noise of our own making, or noise of our own choosing—and we are very choosy!"[11]

Many of my students write that they enjoying listening to music as they do family work, and they present images of dancing around the floor with a mop in hand and music blaring. They say the music makes the work more inviting. My mother recalls her childhood, working with her sisters and singing all the songs they could think of while they worked. Both kinds of experiences may be inviting, but as I think about it, and perhaps I am just old-fashioned, there is something particularly inviting about singing together as we work, blending our voices in musical harmony as we learn to work together in harmony.

And this brings me to the last and most important kind of invitation, that of working together. Working together requires collaboration and, more than any other way I know, helps children feel they are part of the family. The consistent message of our Church leaders, at least from Brigham Young to Gordon B. Hinckley, is that parents and children should work together. This is, in fact, the real key to helping children stay on task.

Here are just a few examples of the teachings of our modern prophets on the importance of working together with our children:

President David O. McKay: "Home is the best place for the child to learn self-control, to learn that he must submerge himself for the good of another. . . . Stay close to your children. Pray, play, work, and worship together."[12]

President Spencer W. Kimball: "We must [learn to] cooperate completely and work in harmony one with the other."[13]

President Gordon B. Hinckley: "(1) Teach and learn goodness together, (2) work together, (3) read good books together, and (4) pray together."[14]

You may not have time to work with your children all the time, but as much as possible, make time to work with them at least occasionally. You will find it sufficiently rewarding to want to do it more often. My friend Karen Rogers said that last weekend she and two of her daughters were each going to clean a room, then decided to work together to clean the three rooms. The results were deeply satisfying as they talked and sang as they worked.

When you are thinking of ways to make family work more inviting, think of the work we do in temples and the ways we do that work. A wonderful essay by Kristine Manwaring, "My Home as a Temple,"[15] will get your thinking going on this. Don't get hung up on the different standard of cleanliness in your home compared to the temple. After all, there are no children in the temple, and they have a professional cleaning staff. But think of the way we do our work there: together. Think of the pace of the work: everything is done at the pace of the slowest member of the group. We all wait patiently while the sweet sister in the wheelchair is assisted to put on her special clothing or while the brother who can't figure out the bow tries to get his tied. Also consider, would it change the meaning of temple work if you were paid to do it? Whatever else you might say about paying children to do family work, one thing is for sure, it changes the meaning of the work.

As with temple work, this work we do to sustain and nurture life in our homes can be a source of great joy. I would like to conclude with a scriptural image that may help stimulate our thinking about the joy to be found in this work. It is Lehi's vision of the tree of life, the tree that represents the love of God. Pay attention to that word, *life*. And think about how the love of God is spread around. Could it be the tree of *life* represents the work required to sustain *life*—the humble work required to nurture life in our families? Isn't that, in truth, the way the love of God is spread—in doing this work of feeding, clothing, and otherwise nurturing life in our homes, neighborhoods, communities?

Think again of Matthew 25, and Mosiah 4, and the teachings of our modern prophets. What makes the daily work of nurturing life in our homes so important from their perspective? Do some in our modern world mock those who do the humble work of feeding, clothing, and caring for the earth (the farmers?) and caring for children (particularly full-time mothers)? What esteem does the world give to those who give priority to doing this work?

And yet this work is the means for nurturing the life of His children; and it is "joyous to the soul" (1 Nephi 11:23). No wonder Lehi desired that his family should partake.

Should you feel discouraged as you try to help your family partake of the blessings of this work, remember the promise in 1 Nephi 13:37: "And blessed are they who shall seek to bring forth my Zion at that day, for they shall have the gift and the power of the Holy Ghost."

NOTES

1. See Lynn K. White and David B. Brinkerhoff, "Children's Work in the Family: Its Significance and Meaning," *Journal of Marriage and the Family*, November 1981, 789–98.

2. Gordon B. Hinckley, "Four Simple Things to Help Our Families and Our Nations," *Ensign*, September 1996, 7.

3. Peter Hoeg, *Smilla's Sense of Snow,* translated by Tina Nunnally (New York: Dell Publishing, 1994), 292–93.

4. Katrina Kenison, *Mitten Strings for God: Reflections for Mothers in a Hurry* (New York: Warner Books, 2000), 5.

5. See Dorothy Lee, *Valuing the Self: What We Can Learn from Other Cultures* (Prospect Heights, Ill.: Waveland Press, 1986).

6. Julie Dockstader Heaps, "Primary Faith in God award helps children develop talents," *Church News*, March 27, 2004, 11.

7. See Grace W. Weinstein, *Children and Money: A Guide for Parents* (New York: Charterhouse, 1975).

8. See Natalia Ginzberg, *The Little Virtues*, translated by Dick Davis (New York: Arcade Publishing, 1989).

9. www.watchoutforchildren.org/html/home_front.html

10. www.lds.mag.com/parentsjournal/040311shopping.html

11. Kenison, *Mitten Strings for God,* 29.

12. David O. McKay, "Making God the Center of Our Lives," *Improvement Era,* June 1967, 110.

13. Spencer W. Kimball, "Becoming Pure in Heart," *Ensign*, May 1978, 81.

14. Hinckley, "Four Simple Things to Help Our Families and Our Nations," 7.

15. www.meridianmagazine.com/voices/000815hometemple.html

"SERVE THE LORD WITH GLADNESS"

Nora K. Nyland

I had been on my mission in Taiwan only a few months when Sister Newton was preparing to return home. Several sisters were visiting with her on the eve of her departure, and someone asked, "What's the most important thing you've learned on your mission?" After a moment's reflection, Sister Newton replied, "I've learned about the joy of serving the Lord. If I'm called to be the light-bulb changer when I go home, I'm going to do it to the very best of my ability!"

I don't know which comes first—serving the Lord with gladness or knowing there is joy in service—but I think they're very closely tied. Psalm 100 speaks of joy and service:

"Make a joyful noise unto the Lord, all ye lands.

"Serve the Lord with gladness: come before his presence with singing.

"Know ye that the Lord he is God: it is he that hath made us, and not we ourselves; we are his people, and the sheep of his pasture.

"Enter into his gates with thanksgiving, and into his courts with praise: be thankful unto him, and bless his name.

Nora K. Nyland is the director of the dietetics program at Brigham Young University and an associate professor in the department of Nutrition, Dietetics, and Food Science. She serves as a Relief Society teacher and enjoys gardening, sewing, and kaleidoscopes.

"For the Lord is good; his mercy is everlasting; and his truth endureth to all generations."

Clearly joy, service, knowledge of the Lord's greatness, and thanksgiving are intertwined. Unfortunately for those of us who are "musically challenged," singing is blended into the mix as well.

When I was a freshman at BYU, I was so looking forward to receiving a call and beginning to serve in my campus ward. During our first week in the ward, we filled out surveys indicating our talents, interests, and experience. About a week later I had an appointment with the bishop. After the introductory exchange he said, "Sister Nyland, we'd like you to serve as the Relief Society chorister." I nearly fell off the chair. I said, "But Bishop, I don't know anything about music." He was quite surprised at that and said, "Well, let's look at the cards." All of the data from our surveys had been entered onto punch cards (something many of you are too young to remember), and he stuck a skinny little knitting needle into the hole for music ability. Mine was the only card that came out of the stack as having no musical skill. He thought that was interesting, as did I, but he asked me if I'd like to try anyway. Well, I'd been raised to accept callings, so I told him that I would accept this call and ask my roommate to help me. Susan and I went to the basement of our dorm, and she sat at the piano, plunking out the melody with one hand and showing me how to lead it with the other. We practiced and practiced each Saturday. I did learn the pattern for 4/4 and 3/4 time, but I never could quite get the pattern to match the beat of the music. Mercifully, after about a month I was released, and my roommate was called to lead the music!

I have since learned that there are many ways to make a joyful noise in the Lord's service—whether or not you can keep the beat.

In thinking about this talk, I've reflected on the unique nature of callings in The Church of Jesus Christ of Latter-day Saints. I have friends of many faiths, some of whom give tremendous service in their respective churches. But the comprehensive nature of the service given in this church is truly remarkable. Why do we do what we do? Why are we willing to put time, effort, and emotion into things that no one could pay us enough to do? I found an interesting entry in the *Encyclopedia of*

Mormonism under "Lay Participation and Leadership," and I'd like to quote from it. Remember that this encyclopedia was written for a non-LDS audience:

"Lay participation and leadership have several implications for the Church and its members. Part of the mission of the Church is to perfect the Saints (Eph. 4:12), to sponsor growth in individual members. Utilizing volunteer members at all levels of the organization may not ensure peak efficiency, but it does provide the experiences and interactions that will help members progress."[1]

It goes on to say that members must balance Church callings with other family and employment responsibilities:

"This provides the opportunity for learning to sacrifice and to balance commitments. In general, members who serve maintain a high level of commitment to the Church, in part because of their awareness that they are responsible for making a contribution and because they take satisfaction from doing so. . . .

"The gospel teaches that this life is a preparatory state for the life to come and that all people are on a course of eternal progression. Lay participation plays an important role in that progression by providing opportunities for service and learning. Church callings offer many opportunities to develop practical skills and spiritual qualities that contribute to continued service and fulfillment throughout life."[2]

The next section describes the fact that people often receive callings of increasing complexity or scope, but that these are not considered promotions. It then makes this wonderful statement:

"The progression that is important, to the individual and to the Lord, is not evidenced by the different callings held by a person, but by the increase in Christlike characteristics developed through years of prayerful and thoughtful service. The potential for personal growth and righteous influence is as great for a nursery leader as for a stake president."[3]

I want to quote one last snippet from the *Encyclopedia of Mormonism,* this time from the entry for "Magnifying One's Calling":

"Magnifying one's calling means taking callings seriously, following through responsibly, and realizing the importance of one's efforts. . . .

" . . . To magnify a calling means to make it honorable and glorious, even to glorify God through service. . . .

"Those who seek to respond to the Lord's admonition to magnify their callings take even the simplest calling seriously as an opportunity to glorify God and serve his children."[4]

From those entries, we are reminded about several important aspects of service:

1. Service is designed to perfect the Saints and contribute to progression.
2. Service teaches us about sacrifice and balancing commitments.
3. Service is related to increased commitment to the Church.
4. Service allows us to make a contribution and brings satisfaction.
5. Service develops practical skills and spiritual qualities.
6. Thoughtful and prayerful service develops Christlike characteristics.
7. The potential for growth is the same regardless of the calling.
8. To magnify a call is to glorify God and serve His children.

What a system! We are sent to earth to be tried and proven and to learn to be like God. As members of the Church, we are then given callings to help us develop the very attributes that will allow us to return to our Father's presence. I think that the working out of our salvation rests in large part, very literally, on the work we do and service we render in fulfilling our various Church callings.

Elder Dallin H. Oaks said: "We need to remember the purpose of our service to one another. If it were only to accomplish some part of His work, God could dispatch 'legions of angels,' as Jesus taught on another occasion (see Matthew 26:53). But that would not achieve the purpose of the service He has prescribed. We serve God and our fellowmen in order to become the kind of children who can return to live with our heavenly parents."[5]

Now that's all well and good when you get the call you've always dreamed of, when you have all the time necessary to do it just the way you'd like, when you have all the skills necessary to fulfill your call to

perfection, and when the people in your stewardship are loving, cooperative, and appreciative. But what about the other 99 percent of the time?

What about the times when you receive the call that has always scared you spitless; when your time demands at work, home, or the community have just escalated; when you feel like you don't have a tenth of the skills needed to carry out the call; and, to top it off, when you're called to work with the teenagers (or toddlers or Cub Scouts or adults—fill in the blank with whatever group scares you)?

There is no magic wand to easily transform those frightening or disheartening situations into treasured ones, but there are several keys that can help.

First, remember whom you serve. In Mosiah 2:17 we are reminded that "when ye are in the service of your fellow beings ye are only in the service of your God." Service to our fellowmen shows our love, devotion, and gratitude to our Heavenly Father. It reflects the depth of our understanding of His purposes for us and our willingness to put Him first in our lives. Elder Henry B. Eyring, in the April 2004 general conference, stated simply, "The Lord's Church has been restored, and so any call to serve in it is a call to serve Him."[6]

In the October 2002 general conference, Elder Eyring said: "You are called to represent the Savior. Your voice to testify becomes the same as His voice, your hands to lift the same as His hands. His work is to bless His Father's spirit children with the opportunity to choose eternal life. So, your calling is to bless lives. That will be true even in the most ordinary tasks you are assigned."[7]

Elder Dallin H. Oaks gave this gentle reminder in the October 2002 general conference:

"There is room for improvement in the commitment of some. . . . Some are not committed and faithful. It has always been so. But this is not without consequence. . . .

" . . . If you are delinquent in commitment, please consider who it is you are refusing or neglecting to serve when you decline a calling or when you accept, promise, and fail to fulfill."[8]

Remembering whom it is we serve is a two-part issue. To put a different spin on King Benjamin's words, when you seek to be in the service of your God, you can do it only by being of service to your fellow beings. Our brothers and sisters, our fellow beings, are the key to our being of service to God.

Do we truly recognize the importance of the people we serve? It is so easy to be put off by mannerisms, attitudes, or behaviors that mask true potential. I think C. S. Lewis captured some of what God sees when looking at His children when he said:

"It is a serious thing to live in a society of possible gods and goddesses, to remember that the dullest and most uninteresting person you can talk to may one day be a creature which, if you saw it now, you would be strongly tempted to worship. . . . There are no *ordinary* people. You have never talked to a mere mortal."[9]

We're not just serving people, we're serving people who have the potential to become gods and goddesses. We're serving people who are precious to their Heavenly Father. Sometimes that knowledge is very helpful to me when I'm worried about a lesson or talk I'm preparing. When I realize that Heavenly Father wants His children to learn and grow and progress, I realize that He will help me prepare something that will help them do that.

I was recently released from an eight-and-one-half-year stint as the institute teacher for my stake and a neighboring stake. I learned so many things while doing that, but one of the most important was the incredible awareness of how much the Lord wants His children to learn and understand the gospel. The many times I received inspiration and insight beyond my own capacity and knowledge about how to teach or illustrate something testified to me of God's concern for each of us.

And that brings me to the second key: Seek the Lord early and often. His ability to change hearts and minds, including our own, is amazing.

Shortly after I began attending a ward, the counselor in the bishopric asked to visit with me after Sunday School. He said, "Sister Nyland, we'd like to call you to serve in the nursery." I began to laugh, assuming he was kidding, and said, "Really, what would you like me to do?" He was a little taken aback by my laughter, but said, "Really, we'd like you to serve in the nursery." I immediately sobered and said I'd be happy to do that. Now, to tell you the truth, I wasn't happy to do that. I liked children in the abstract, but the reality of twenty-five toddlers was a bit much. I was quite comfortable teaching college students, because they were quiet, they hung on my every word (in case it showed up on an exam), and they never chased each other around the room or crawled under their desks. The best words to describe my first day in the nursery were *shell shock*. I have never felt more unprepared, unskilled, and ill-suited for a calling in my life.

I was smart enough to know that the nature of two-year-olds wasn't going to change much, so if I was going to survive this calling, I was the one who would need to change. I made that call a matter of prayer night and day, and each Sunday for six weeks the nursery was, frankly, a nightmare. Then on the seventh Sunday, when I walked into the nursery, it was like a switch had been flipped. I absolutely loved it! I loved the children; I had fun playing with and teaching them; I didn't even mind sitting on the floor. From that day until I was released, the nursery was one of the favorite callings I'd ever had. I was so grateful for that change of heart.

Paul says in Galatians 5:13, "By love serve one another." The Lord can help us feel the love that both leads to and comes from service.

Another reason to seek the Lord often has to do with increasing our abilities. Sometimes we already have the skills a particular calling requires, but sometimes we don't. When we don't, the task can seem impossibly large. Elder Eyring addressed that concern in the October 2002 general conference when he said:

"Just as God called you and will guide you, He will magnify you. You will need that magnification. . . .

"There will be times when you will feel overwhelmed. One of the ways you will be attacked is with the feeling that you are inadequate. Well, you are inadequate to answer a call to represent God with only your own powers. But you have access to more than your natural capacities, and you do not work alone."[10]

Faith that the calling is inspired leads us to faith that the Lord can strengthen our deficiencies and enlarge our capacity. Remember—He wants His children to benefit from whatever you are called to do, and

He wants to bless you as well. Very early in my mission experience I came across this statement by Elder Neal A. Maxwell: "God does not begin by asking us about our ability, but only about our availability, and if we then prove our dependability, he will increase our capability!"[11] I found that enormously comforting as I was trying to perform my labors, all in Chinese.

Our feelings of inadequacy are probably calculated to turn us toward Heavenly Father. If we choose to turn toward Him through pondering and prayer, our reward is comfort, peace, and increased strength. As we experience those feelings and see our skills develop, it becomes even easier to serve the Lord gladly and with gratitude.

And the next key is gratitude. Doctrine and Covenants 59:21 says, "In nothing doth man offend God, or against none is his wrath kindled, save those who confess not his hand in all things, and obey not his commandments." To confess His hand in all things is another way to express gratitude for all that the Lord has provided.

Have you ever tried the exercise of listing ten things for which you are grateful at the end of the day? It is really quite amazing how detailed the list becomes after a week or so. Realizing the source of all those blessings is at once humbling and awe inspiring. King Benjamin taught his people:

"I say unto you, my brethren, that if you should render all the thanks and praise which your whole soul has power to possess, to that God who has created you, and has kept and preserved you, and has caused that ye should rejoice, and has granted that ye should live in peace one with another—

"I say unto you that if ye should serve him who has created you from the beginning, and is preserving you from day to day, by lending you breath, that ye may live and move and do according to your own will, and even supporting you from one moment to another—I say, if ye should serve him with all your whole souls yet ye would be unprofitable servants" (Mosiah 2:20–21).

I know that when I have an attitude of gratitude, I have a strong desire to serve the Lord; to show Him that I appreciate all that He has given me. We can never get the Lord in our debt, but we can demonstrate our gratitude through cheerful, glad service and by using our gifts to glorify Him.

The final key for serving with gladness is having both a firm testimony of the truthfulness of the gospel and a desire to build the kingdom of God. A firm testimony—built through prayer, scripture study, pondering, and keeping the commandments (you know, the usual things)—creates a desire to be of use in the kingdom.

The hymn "More Holiness Give Me" includes these lines:

> *More fit for the kingdom,*
> *More used would I be,*
> *More blessed and holy—*
> *More, Savior, like thee.*[12]

I really like the image those lines portray. When our deepest desire is to be more fit for the kingdom and to be of more use in it, we're able to swallow, smile, and serve when asked to do something we'd really rather not do. A recognition of the intricate pattern the Lord is weaving in the lives of each of His children gives us a sense of responsibility to be sure the thread we offer is acceptable.

Let me illustrate. When I was a Primary president, a counselor and I were visiting the home of a less-active child. In our very enjoyable conversation with the mother, we learned that she didn't know who her visiting teachers were, didn't know who her home teachers were, and didn't know who her child's Primary teacher was. Later that evening, I began thinking about how amazing it would be if every person in the Church truly fulfilled, to say nothing of magnified, his or her calling. Think of the web of love and support that would be woven around each member if every home teacher, visiting teacher, and Sunday School or Primary teacher really understood and carried out his or her call. Think of what it would mean if every Scout leader, every Young Women leader, and every Relief Society teacher and home, family, and personal enrichment committee member attended to their responsibilities. Think of the strength of the web woven by so many strands of dedicated service.

The analogy of the body in 1 Corinthians 12:12 is so fitting as we think about serving in our callings: "For as the body is one, and hath many members, and all the members of that one body, being many, are one body: so also is Christ." Then Paul says, "If the foot shall say, Because I am not the hand, I am not of the body; is it therefore not of the body?" (1 Corinthians 12:15). He is emphasizing that each member needs to realize that it is important to the functioning of the whole body precisely because it is different from the other members. Paul brings it back to the Church in verse 25: "That there should be no schism in the body; but that the members should have the same care one for another."

Our testimonies let us trust that we are part of a very important pattern in building the kingdom of God, even if we can't see it in its entirety. Every skill, talent, and ability we have, whether inborn or developed in callings or other areas of our lives, helps us to be more serviceable in the kingdom. Every skill, talent, or ability lets us "make a joyful noise . . . [and] serve the Lord with gladness" (Psalm 100:1–2).

NOTES

1. Daniel H. Ludlow, ed., *Encyclopedia of Mormonism*, 5 vols. (New York: Macmillan Publishing Company, 1992), 2:815.
2. *Encyclopedia of Mormonism*, 2:815.
3. *Encyclopedia of Mormonism*, 2:815.
4. *Encyclopedia of Mormonism*, 2:850.
5. Dallin H. Oaks, "I'll Go Where You Want Me to Go," *Ensign*, November 2002, 70.
6. Henry B. Eyring, "In the Strength of the Lord," *Ensign*, May 2004, 19.
7. Henry B. Eyring, "Rise to Your Call," *Ensign*, November 2002, 76.
8. Oaks, "I'll Go Where You Want Me to Go," 69.
9. C. S. Lewis, *The Weight of Glory and Other Addresses*, ed. Walter Hooper (New York: MacMillan Publishing, 1980), 18–19; emphasis in original.
10. Eyring, "Rise to Your Call," 76.
11. Neal A. Maxwell, "It's Service, Not Status, That Counts," *Ensign*, July 1975, 7.
12. Philip Paul Bliss, "More Holiness Give Me," *Hymns of The Church of Jesus Christ of Latter-day Saints* (Salt Lake City: The Church of Jesus Christ of Latter-day Saints, 1985), no. 131.

INDEX